Amitav Ghosh

ER

Press

CONTEMPORARY WORLD WRITERS

SERIES EDITOR   JOHN THIEME

ALREADY PUBLISHED IN THE SERIES

Peter Carey   BRUCE WOODCOCK

Maxine Hong Kingston   HELENA GRICE

Kazuo Ishiguro   BARRY LEWIS

Hanif Kureishi   BART MOORE-GILBERT

David Malouf   DON RANDALL

Rohinton Mistry   PETER MOREY

Timothy Mo   ELAINE YEE LIN HO

Toni Morrison   JILL MATUS

Alice Munro   CORAL ANN HOWELLS

Les Murray   STEVEN MATTHEWS

Caryl Phillips   BÉNÉDICTE LEDENT

Amy Tan   BELLA ADAMS

Ngugi wa Thiong'o   PATRICK WILLIAMS

Derek Walcott   JOHN THIEME

Amitav Ghosh

ANSHUMAN A. MONDAL

Manchester University Press

Manchester and New York

distributed exclusively in the USA by Palgrave

The right of Anshuman A. Mondal to be identified as the author of this work
has been asserted by him in accordance with the Copyright, Designs and
Patents Act 1988.

Published by Manchester University Press
Oxford Road, Manchester M13 9NR, UK
and Room 400, 175 Fifth Avenue, New York, NY 10010, USA
www.manchesteruniversitypress.co.uk

Distributed exclusively in the USA by
Palgrave, 175 Fifth Avenue, New York, NY 10010, USA

Distributed exclusively in Canada by
UBC Press, University of British Columbia, 2029 West Mall,
Vancouver, BC, Canada V6T 1Z2

British Library Cataloguing-in-Publication Data
A catalogue record for this book is available from the British Library

Library of Congress Cataloging-in-Publication Data applied for

ISBN 978 0 7190 7004 4 *hardback*
ISBN 978 0 7190 7005 1 *paperback*

First published 2007

16 15 14 13 12 11 10 09 08 07   10 9 8 7 6 5 4 3 2 1

Typeset in Aldus
by Koinonia, Manchester
Printed in Great Britain
by CPI, Bath

for Joanna, with love

Contents

SERIES EDITOR'S FOREWORD   ix

PREFACE   xi

ACKNOWLEDGEMENTS   xiii

LIST OF ABBREVIATIONS   xv

CHRONOLOGY   xvii

1 Contexts and intertexts   1

2 The 'metaphysic' of modernity   41

3 Looking-glass borders   85

4 Tiny threads, gigantic tapestries   130

5 Critical overview and conclusion   163

NOTES   180

BIBLIOGRAPHY   197

INDEX   207

Contents

Series editor's foreword

Contemporary World Writers is an innovative series of authoritative introductions to a range of culturally diverse contemporary writers from outside Britain and the United States or from 'minority' backgrounds within Britain or the United States. In addition to providing comprehensive general introductions, books in the series also argue stimulating original theses, often but not always related to contemporary debates in post-colonial studies.

The series locates individual writers within their specific cultural contexts, while recognising that such contexts are themselves invariably a complex mixture of hybridised influences. It aims to counter tendencies to appropriate the writers discussed into the canon of English or American literature or to regard them as 'other'.

Each volume includes a chronology of the writer's life, an introductory section on formative contexts and intertexts, discussion of all the writer's major works, a bibliography of primary and secondary works and an index. Issues of racial, national and cultural identity are explored, as are gender and sexuality. Books in the series also examine writers' use of genre, particularly ways in which Western genres are adapted or subverted and 'traditional' local forms are reworked in a contemporary context.

Contemporary World Writers aims to bring together the theoretical impulse which currently dominates post-colonial studies and closely argued readings of particular authors' works, and by so doing to avoid the danger of appropriating the specifics of particular texts into the hegemony of totalising theories.

Preface

Readers familiar with the Contemporary World Writers series will immediately notice that the organisation of this book does not follow the pattern of previous contributions. Rather than a chronological, novel-by-novel approach, this book offers a more thematic organisation as the best way to approach Ghosh's work. It is up to the reader to evaluate whether this is justified or not. Although all writers hope that all readers will read their books from start to finish, those who are looking for treatment of specific texts can find guidance as to which chapters emphasise which texts in the final section of '1: Contexts and intertexts'. An explanation of the rationale for organisation of this book can also be found there.

Throughout the book, many terms are employed which may be more or less familiar with literature students but which may be unfamiliar to the general reader. It is hoped that these are explained as thoroughly and accessibly as possible, but readers may wish to follow up some of the debates that surround these terms for it is within this wider context of knowledge that the calibre of Ghosh's work can be most fully appreciated. Some of the key texts in the field will be indicated in the notes at the end of the book, along with full citations of Ghosh's published works; the extant criticism can be found in the bibliography.

Acknowledgements

I would like to thank the Arts and Humanities Research Council (AHRC) for supporting the completion of this book by awarding me a Research Leave Grant for the period of October 2005 to February 2006. I would also like to acknowledge the Department of English at the University of Leicester for a period of study leave January–September 2005. Without these two periods of leave from the rigours of teaching and administration, this book would not have been completed when it was. Particular thanks are due to John McLeod, whose kind words of support were instrumental in my securing the AHRC award. Also, for ensuring that the duties and responsibilities of a new job did not interfere with the final few weeks of this leave period, I am indebted to William Watkin and Steve Dixon.

To John Thieme, general editor of the Contemporary World Writers series, I owe my heartfelt thanks for responding to and supporting this project, and indeed for recognising that the time had come for a full-length study of Ghosh's work. As a Ghosh scholar himself, he has offered advice which I have always found welcome and constructive. I owe a debt of gratitude to Rajeswari Sunder Rajan, and her doctoral student Joy Wang, for securing me a copy of her essay along with the other essays published in the OUP India edition of *The Shadow Lines*; a large section of the concluding chapter would not have been possible without their assistance. I would also like to make special mention of Claire Chambers, who sent me a copy of her dissertation and thereby saved me a trip to Leeds. Her generosity was equalled by the usefulness of her excellent dissertation, to which I make reference in Chapter 2 in particular. Emma Parker supplied me with a reference that was overlooked in most of the bibliographies and databases, and I would like to thank her and my other former colleagues at the University of Leicester – Phil Shaw, Mark Rawlinson, Michael Davies, and Martin Halliwell – for their friendship and intellectual input. Special thanks, in this regard, are due to George Lewis whose companionship has always been highly treasured. Clare Anderson, Claire Mercer, Sydney Jeffers, Prashant Kidambi and other fellow-travellers in the Post-Colonial Seminar at Leicester have all accompanied the gestation of this book and have probably been subjected to the usual moans and groans over a convivial drink and curry. Thanks also to my former student Jenny Richardson for taking the trouble to read a draft of this book to ensure that it remained accessible to the intelligent general reader.

My heartfelt love and respect are due to my parents, Ansar Ali and Anjulika Mondal. Finally, to Joanna Herbert I cannot say enough how much her love and support has meant to me. I dedicate this book to her to repay in some small measure that debt which can never be redeemed.

Abbreviations

CR   *The Circle of Reason*
SL   *The Shadow Lines*
IAAL   *In an Antique Land*
CC   *The Calcutta Chromosome*
GP   *The Glass Palace*
HT   *The Hungry Tide*

References to Ghosh's extensive non-fictional works can be found in the notes at the end of the book in the relevant chapter.

Chronology

1956 Born 11 July in Calcutta to Shailendra Chandra Ghosh, a diplomat, and Ansali Ghosh. Spends early years travelling with parents to postings in Bangladesh (then East Pakistan), Sri Lanka, and Iran.

1974–76 Attends St. Stephen's College, Delhi University. Graduates with BA in History.

1978 Begins DPhil at University of Oxford in Social Anthropology.

1979 Learns Arabic in Tunisia.

1980 Travels to Egypt to conduct field research for DPhil. These experiences would later form the basis for *In an Antique Land*.

1982 Awarded DPhil for thesis 'Kinship in Relation to the Economic and Social Organization of an Egyptian Village'.

1983–87 Appointed Research Associate, Department of Sociology, Delhi University. Begins writing *The Circle of Reason*.

1984 Witnesses anti-Sikh riots in Delhi after the assassination of Prime Minister Indira Gandhi by her Sikh bodyguards.

1986 *The Circle of Reason* published.

1988 *The Shadow Lines* published. Returns to Egypt.

1990 Awarded *Prix Medicis Etrangère* in Paris for *The Circle of Reason*; Awarded the annual prize of the Sahitya Akademi (Indian Academy of Literature) for *The Shadow Lines*.

1992   'The Slave of MS H.6' and *In an Antique Land* published.

1994–97   Appointed Visiting Professor, Department of Anthropology, Columbia University, New York.

1995   Begins reporting for *The New Yorker*.

1996   *The Calcutta Chromosome* published. It is awarded the Arthur C. Clarke Award for Science Fiction.

1998   *Dancing in Cambodia, At Large in Burma* published.

1999   Appointed Distinguished Professor, Department of Comparative Literature, Queen's College, City University of New York. *Countdown* published and earns Ghosh a place on the final shortlist for the *American Society of Magazine Editors Award for Reporting*. 'The March of the Novel Through History: The Testimony of My Grandfather's Bookcase' wins *The Pushcart Prize*.

2000   *The Glass Palace* published. Ghosh declines the Commonwealth Writers' Prize.

2001   *The Glass Palace* wins the Grand Prize for Fiction at the Frankfurt eBook Awards.

2002   *The Imam and the Indian: Prose Pieces* is published in India, gathering together many of Ghosh's non-fiction.

2004   *The Hungry Tide* published.

2005   *Incendiary Circumstances: A Chronicle of the Turmoil of our Times* is published in the United States.

Contexts and intertexts

In June 1997 *The New Yorker* magazine published a special issue on English language Indian fiction to commemorate India and Pakistan's fiftieth anniversary of independence from colonial rule. Inside is a photograph of some of the most celebrated English language novelists to have emerged from the subcontinent in recent decades, writers whose presence on the bestseller lists of Western literary markets has been accompanied by the unprecedented density of their citations for major literary prizes – Salman Rushdie, Anita Desai, Arundhati Roy, Rohinton Mistry, Amit Chaudhuri, and Vikram Seth amongst others.[1] At the back, slightly out of focus, is Amitav Ghosh; the perspective of the shot distances him and he appears somewhat marginal to the main group. The photograph is a large one, taking up almost three-quarters of the double-page spread, but on its left-hand margin is some text, a fragment of an article on the 'forgotten army' led by the Indian nationalist leader Subhas Chandra Bose, which had fought the British alongside the Japanese in South East Asia during the Second World War. The article is by Amitav Ghosh.[2] This fortuitous layout perhaps emphasises with appropriate clarity Ghosh's literary concern with margins – marginal peoples, histories, episodes, knowledge systems, and beliefs.

Paradoxically, Ghosh has become one of the central figures to emerge from the English language literary field after the success of Salman Rushdie's *Midnight's Children* opened up the international Anglophone markets to the new writing emerging from the subcontinent in the 1980s. Moreover, he has developed a substantial body of work that resonates with some of the central concerns of what was then also an emergent field of criticism: postcolonialism. In all his major works, and in his essays and journalism, Ghosh meditates upon a core set of issues but each time he does so from a new perspective: the troubled (and troubling) legacy of colonial knowledge and discourse on formerly colonised societies, peoples, and ideas; the ambivalent relationship to modernity of the so-called 'developing' or 'Third' world; the formation and reformation of identities in colonial and post-colonial societies; the question of agency for those previously seen as the objects but not subjects of history; the recovery of lost or suppressed histories; an engagement with cultural multiplicity and difference; and an insistent critique of Eurocentrism in general.

In many of his public pronouncements, Ghosh has disavowed the idea that his work is a representative example of postcolonialism, or that he is a 'post-colonial' writer; indeed, he has claimed that he does not really know what the term means.[3] Nevertheless, he is on friendly terms with many of the critics and theorists who have done much to define the field, and who in turn acknowledge his work as a crucial index of many of the themes, issues, and problematics that constitute the multi-dimensional nature of the post-colonial predicament today. A critical examination of Amitav Ghosh's writing is thus an opportunity not only to ascertain and evaluate his own predilections and concerns but also to explore the limits and possibilities of postcolonialism itself as a critical practice.

Amitav Ghosh was born in Calcutta in July 1956, the son of a diplomat and housewife. Although the family had hailed from eastern Bengal and migrated to Calcutta before the Partition cataclysms of 1947, the figure of the 'refugee' is one that has continued to inform his fiction throughout his career, most prominently in *The Circle of Reason* (1986), *The Shadow Lines* (1988) and *The Glass Palace* (2000). Other less forcibly displaced persons – economic migrants, travellers, students, researchers on field trips – populate his fictional and non-fictional work and constitute his central characters. Perhaps his early childhood accompanying his diplomat parents to their postings in Bangladesh (then East Pakistan), Sri Lanka, and Iran may have attuned his sensibilities to the rewards of travel and its possibilities for a writer who is keen to examine the world from the perspective of the unsettled, or uprooted – possibilities that might offer insights unavailable to others. He has remarked that 'travelling is always in some way connected with my fictional work',[4] and others have noted that Ghosh visualises 'movement' as in some way fundamental to human experience, not necessarily seeing it as involving a physical journey (though it often does) but also as a potentiality that inhabits the consciousness of even those people often regarded as 'settled', such as peasants.[5] Indeed, much of his work challenges the assumption that human history is one of 'settled' populations and 'stable' cultures.

On the other hand, Calcutta, his native city, exerts a powerful influence on Ghosh's imagination. Its presence is marked and mediated by his birth into what is known as the *bhadralok*, the upper and middle sections of Bengali society that emerged in the nineteenth century as a consequence of the reorganisation of the Bengal economy under colonial rule. Roughly translated, the term means 'gentle folk', and the *bhadralok* of Calcutta constitutes Bengal's intellectual, cultural, and political elite, though at its lower reaches the economic position of many *bhadralok* families can often be precarious – a situation that is memorably captured, as Meenakshi Mukherjee observes, in the precise class positioning of the anonymous narrator of *The Shadow Lines* whose family is 'Bengali *bhadralok*, starting at the lower edge of the spectrum and ascending to its higher reaches in one generation, with family connections above as well as below its own station'.[6] She goes on to add that this class location determines in many ways the spatial experience of Calcutta itself, creating an imaginative geography of the city that, as with all cities, associates certain localities with certain classes. In other words, the physical environment of the city comes to represent itself to the mind of its inhabitants in particular ways, as, for example, it does to the narrator when he visits some poor relations in a part of the city that backs onto Calcutta's ever increasing slums. Thus, if travel is a key register of Ghosh's awareness of the importance of space in human experience, it is nevertheless his recognition that space is not an inert physical dimension exterior to human consciousness but is rather intimately shaped by the particular ways in which it is imagined that determines his examination of culturally created spaces, such as nation-states, and the borders – both physical and imagined – that delimit and define them.

But perhaps the most important impact that Calcutta has had on Ghosh's imagination is through its status as an intellectual and cultural centre. Of all its identities, it is this perhaps above all that appeals to the Bengali cultural imagination and that of the *bhadralok* in particular. Established by the British as a trading outpost for their operations in India, Calcutta quickly became the richest city in Asia and British India's capital – the second most important city in the British Empire. Wealth, power and privilege soon helped establish it as a cultural and intellectual hub, along which traffic between Indian and European ideas helped construct a vibrant, 'modern' vernacular culture and rich intellectual heritage that today, since its decline as a political and economic capital, is cherished by Bengalis as a living bridge to its period of greatness. To the *bhadralok*, knowledge and culture still represent access to the world at large, a cosmopolitanism that was brought into being early in the colonial period and which still persists in the arguments and *addas* (informal conversational gatherings), debates and discussions that take place in Calcutta's legendary coffee-houses, its lecture-halls, student hostels, universities, parks, and around its bookstalls and bookshops (the annual book fair is still perhaps the largest of its kind anywhere in the world).

In a prize-winning essay about his grandfather's bookcase, Ghosh has remarked on the catholicity of the books that he found there as well as its significant exclusions:

> Textbooks and schoolbooks were never allowed; nor were books of a professional nature … the great majority … were novels. There were a few works of anthropology and psychology, books that in some way had filtered into the

literary consciousness of the time: *The Golden Bough* ...
The Collected Works of Sigmund Freud, Marx and Engels's
Manifesto, Havelock Ellis and Malinowski.[7]

These books were hardly read, Ghosh notes, because his family
were 'busy [and] practical ... with little time to spend on books',
but the glass-fronted bookcases 'let the visitor know that this
was a house in which books were valued; in other words, that
we were cultivated people. This is always important in Calcutta'
('The March of the Novel', 288).

However, despite its past eminence Calcutta has always been
something of a marginal centre – first within the British Empire,
then within India itself, after the transfer of the capital to New
Delhi in the latter decades of the Raj – a paradox that has always
generated a great deal of ambiguity in the Bengali intellectual
imagination about its relationship to modernity. Ghosh notes, for
example, that of the novels that made up the bulk of his grandfather's books, 'About a quarter ... were in Bengali – a representative selection of the mainstream tradition of Bengali fiction
in the twentieth century', whilst the rest – the vast majority
– 'were in English. But of these only a small proportion ... had
been originally written in English. The others were translations
from a number of other languages, most of them European' ('The
March of the Novel', 290). Displaying as it does the characteristic literary cosmopolitanism of Bengali intellectual culture, the
bookcase also bears testimony to the inequality of the literary
and cultural cosmopolis and the subordinate status of the Bengali
tradition. Furthermore, it is English, the coloniser's language,
that enables access to this international literary scene, reinforcing
the sense of dependency. Calcutta, then, perhaps offers Ghosh
something more than a familiar environment, both social and
physical; its importance lies as a signifier of colonial relations as
mediated through the global hierarchies of culture. Most notably
in *The Calcutta Chromosome* (1996), but also in *The Circle of
Reason*, the city is both a metaphor for the knowledge/power
relations initiated by colonialism, and the stage on which Ghosh
re-enacts what has been called 'the battle for cultural parity' that
the Bengali cultural elite have waged ever since.[8]

Given the reverence for knowledge (mixed with a fair degree of dissident irreverence, to be sure) that pertains amongst the Calcutta *bhadralok*, it is unsurprising that Ghosh's academic achievements and interests have intersected with his literary ambitions throughout his life and career. As a student at St. Stephen's College, Delhi University, a college that has produced several other world-class writers, he graduated with a BA in History, followed by an MA in Sociology. Like many other academically minded and intellectually gifted students, he embarked on what Edward Said has called 'the voyage in' to the colonial metropolis to undertake doctoral research in Social Anthropology at Oxford University.[9] This would prove to be a pivotal period in his development as a writer, giving him the opportunity to travel to Egypt to pursue fieldwork for his doctoral thesis. That experience would eventually germinate into his ground-breaking and perhaps most important work, *In an Antique Land* (1992). He returned to India to work as a Research Associate and then Lecturer in the Department of Sociology at Delhi University, and at this point began to write his first novel, *The Circle of Reason*, which would be published during his tenure there. On leaving Delhi University, he has since held a number of academic posts in America and India, most notably at Columbia University, at City University New York (CUNY), where he is Distinguished Professor in Comparative Literature, and Harvard, where he is currently a Visiting Professor.

This academic biography, which runs in parallel with his career as a novelist, essayist, and journalist, alerts us not only to his personal investment and proximity to institutionalised knowledge, but also to the debates about knowledge itself across a number of disciplines that inform his work. The striking interdisciplinarity of his work and its close relation to academic debates about the nature of knowledge that have taken shape in the latter decades of the twentieth century – in other words, to 'critical theory' – is obvious, notwithstanding his own disaffiliation from it. Despite his denials, such links to current thinking in the academy are an important dimension of his work and one that gives his writing an intellectual rigour and substance that his contemporaries can seldom match. What really sets him apart from much academic discourse is the accessibility of his work, the ways in which his intellectualism is worn lightly on the fabric of his prose.

Amitav Ghosh has published six major works, of which five can be unproblematically classified as novels. His first, *The Circle of Reason*, was published in 1986 to some acclaim, notably by the distinguished novelist and critic Anthony Burgess. It is an episodic, picaresque novel in three parts, linked only by a young boy with a potato-shaped head called Alu, and a half-hearted young intelligence officer, Jyoti Das. In the first section, Alu arrives as an orphan at the house of his uncle, Balaram Bose, a village schoolmaster with an idiosyncratic regard for scientific knowledge who values both 'mainstream' or 'orthodox' science and 'pseudo-sciences' such as phrenology. Although declaring himself to be an admirer of 'Reason', Balaram's behaviour is ironically portrayed as being both rational and irrational, and his increasingly obsessive and erratic behaviour becomes mono-maniacally fixated on a feud with a neighbour, Bhudeb Roy. This neighbourly feud, in turn, is mistaken by the state authorities as potentially political in nature and by the time Alu escapes as the sole survivor of the disastrous denouement to Balaram's conflict with Bhudeb Roy he is a wanted fugitive, having been absurdly identified as a political extremist and threat to the state.

In section two, Alu, along with other illegal Indian migrants, finds himself smuggled into the Gulf emirate of Al-Ghazira where he lives in a boarding house run by an ageing former courtesan, Zindi at-Taffaha, along with a multi-ethnic, multi-lingual, diasporic community of illegal immigrants from India, East Africa, the other Arab states, and Bangladesh. Like the others, Alu works illegally as a labourer, but one day a half-finished shopping mall which he is helping to build collapses on him. Miraculously, he survives and on his rescue he reprises the ghost of his uncle Balaram by embarking on an idealistic project to set up a money-free commune. Once again, this is misinter-preted by the state and, whilst Alu is on a shopping trip, the community is attacked by the authorities and many are killed, or captured and deported. Alu escapes with Zindi, but is followed by Jyoti Das, who has tracked him all the way to al-Ghazira from north-eastern Bengal.

The final section takes place amongst the dunes of Saharan Algeria with Alu, Zindi and their companions still on the run from Jyoti Das who has, by now, given up trying to arrest them and is only going through the motions. They find refuge with an Indian doctor who is part of a small community of Indians working in this remote corner of Algeria. This doctor is actually the daughter of one of Balaram's college friends, and unbeknownst to Alu and Zindi she is also offering hospitality to Jyoti Das. In a burlesque conclusion, Alu and Zindi realise that Das has no intention of arresting them. After the death of one of their companions, Zindi and Alu prepare to return to India and Das himself journeys on towards Europe, leaving behind his job.

A highly ambitious novel, *The Circle of Reason* is both loosely plotted but also knitted tightly together by a series of motifs and recurring images, such that its open-ended episodic linearity is cross-hatched with patterns that draw on its central metaphor of weaving, which is used as a metaphor for the process of storytelling; at the same time, the history of weaving is used as a synecdoche for the nature of Reason, which is both liberating and oppressive; linear and straightforward, and circular and convoluted; reasonable and unreasonable. The novel dramatises the encounter of colonial, pre-colonial and 'para-colonial' knowledges within a colonial and post-colonial milieu, demonstrating how the formation of colonial power/knowledge complexes is both reproduced and ironically subverted by its reception in colonised societies; how 'subaltern' peoples, in the form of illegal immigrants in a fictionalised Gulf emirate, both elude and fall victim to the 'logic' of the modern state; how diasporic connections increasingly traverse and transgress the boundaries imposed by such *raison d'état*; and eventually how 'Reason' is thwarted by its necessary imbrication with the emotional ties of custom, tradition, and human sympathy.

Whilst writing *The Circle of Reason* in Delhi, Ghosh was to witness at first hand the anti-Sikh communal riots that followed in the wake of the assassination of the Indian Prime Minister, Indira Gandhi, by her Sikh bodyguards in 1984. The experience shook him deeply, so much so that he felt unable to write directly about it until more than a decade later, in an essay entitled 'The Ghosts of Mrs. Gandhi'.[10] Nevertheless, as he admits in that essay, it was an episode that was pivotal to his development as a writer because it informed his next novel, *The Shadow Lines*, and in a more oblique way, its successor, *In an Antique Land*.

Dispensing with the marginal but perceptible elements of magic realism and fantasy which indicated that *The Circle of Reason* was in muted thrall to the spell cast by Rushdie's *Midnight's Children*, *The Shadow Lines* also distinguishes itself in terms of its tightly plotted structure and the greater realisation of its individual characters. The technical skill displayed in his first novel, however, is sharpened and put to brilliant effect at the service of a narrative in which time and space is fluid and constantly shifting from one location to another, and from one given moment to another without any forced transitions. Being, in part, a novel about memory its form mimics the ebb and flow of subjectivity, as it struggles to make sense of a difficult trauma that is at once both personal and subjective and yet intersects with larger historical forces and public events.

The shadow lines of the title are accordingly both subjective and objective; experiential and political; they are those invisible borders that mark the transition from youth to maturity, the past from the present, and those intangible but deeply felt markers of identity that mark oneself off from others, one's own 'community' from others', the correlates of which constitute the material borders of political entities such as nation-states which physically mark and limit the spatial and temporal co-ordinates of their citizens' experiences. In its form, however, the novel also enacts the transgression of these shadow lines, moving across space and time with an ease that challenges the categorical permanence that political borders aspire to represent.

An unnamed first-person narrator, through whose consciousness everything that happens in the course of the narrative is mediated, recalls his boyhood admiration of his uncle Tridib, whose death in a communal riot is the pivot around which the narrator's mnemonic peregrinations revolve. The narrator himself, however, was not present at Tridib's death so his attempt to make sense of it is haunted by this absence. Around this absent centre, the narrator's swirl of memories is constructed through the assimilation of other people's recollections of the event: Tridib's younger brother, Robi, and May Price, an Englishwoman with whom Tridib was becoming romantically involved. It is through their narratives that his own is assembled and the novel discloses how an identity is patched up – or woven, to use Ghosh's favourite metaphor – through interconnecting narratives which may or may not add up to something: at the end of the novel, the narrator is still, to all intents and purposes, at a loss to explain what happened to Tridib.

In the process of constructing his own identity, the narrator's self-fashioning intersects with the formation of collective identities. In his effort to find out why his uncle was murdered in a communal riot, the narrator embarks on a historical quest to try and explain another 'absence', this time the silence about that riot in the historical records, the national media, and consequently its absence in the narrator's own memory. In so doing, he realises that just as traumas might be repressed by individuals in order that a coherent sense of individual identity may be maintained, so too do collective identities repress those things which disturb their self-image, those events that might fragment the coherence of the larger narratives of history, nation and state. The novel demonstrates the fraught nature of 'identity' in the subcontinent, and how national identities are always troubled by their intimate yet conflicting relationship with identities that traverse national boundaries and mock the 'security' – physical, political, existential – that borders are supposed to represent. In the subcontinent, these competing non-state or sub-state identities are religious. The 'permanent disturbance' of Partition, that moment which spliced the respective national narratives of

India and Pakistan along religious lines, initiates a trauma in the national imagination that has to be repressed; and yet, precisely because of this, religion reappears surreptitiously as an unsettled excess that 'rustles through the subcontinent's public imagination' as an alternative vocabulary by which to articulate identities 'around which the inevitable disappointments of modern politics can gather'.[11] The result, in Sunil Khilnani's felicitous phrasing, is 'the pornography of borders' in the subcontinent.[12]

This same concern with religious, national and other identities in the modern world is just one of the threads that run through Ghosh's next book, *In an Antique Land*. Despite the best efforts of literary critics, it is an unclassifiable text. Even its non-fictional status is uncertain, as we shall see later in this book, but this remains one of its many strengths. In some ways, it is appropriate that what is perhaps the pivotal book in Ghosh's *oeuvre* thus far eludes classification because it concerns itself with those small fragments of history that have slipped through the categorical grids of knowledge that have shaped modern thought, identity and experience. It brings together in one work many of the themes, issues, ideas and tropes that recur throughout his novels.

In an Antique Land was, in many ways, a breakthrough text for Ghosh, one that put him on the international literary map. On its publication in 1992, it had been in gestation for well over a decade, from the moment in 1978 that Ghosh, then a doctoral student in Oxford, chanced upon a footnote in a book of translations entitled *Letters of Medieval Jewish Traders*. In the Prologue, we are told that this minute and obscure reference to an unknown Indian slave working for a Jewish trader domiciled on the western coast of India in the twelfth-century CE gave Ghosh 'a sense of 'entitlement' to pursue fieldwork in Egypt. From that point, the narrative follows two interleaving trajectories; the first, is an account of his field experiences as a doctoral student in a couple of small villages in Lower Egypt in 1980, whilst the other tracks his efforts to trace the life of the 'Slave of MS. H.6' from the archival documentation that had been preserved by the Jews of Cairo in their synagogue's 'Geniza' or 'storehouse'. In one, the narrator is an anthropologist; in the other, a historian. The narratives are connected by a series of overlapping motifs and metaphors that bring into juxtaposition two disciplines and modes of writing – ethnography and historiography – that are customarily seen as separate, each with their own concerns and modes of operation, each focusing on different 'objects' of knowledge. *In an Antique Land* suggests that such partitioning of knowledge into separate domains is only one of a series of parallel ruptures that have divided the modern world: divisions of 'identity', of geography, of politics, of history. Ghosh's reconstruction of the lives of the Indian slave and his Jewish master, of the polyglot, cosmopolitan, hybrid world in which they lived and worked, offers a reflective contrast to the rigidities of the modern period.

In *In an Antique Land* Ghosh begins explicitly to critique colonialism and its consequences. If in *The Circle of Reason* and *The Shadow Lines*, the effects of colonialism are registered in the lingering relationships between Indians and Britons, or in the haunting presence of Partition, or in the tortuous convolutions of a mind – such as Balaram's – formed within the matrix of the colonial education system, these are nevertheless implicit critiques. In those novels, Ghosh's tactic is perhaps to resist Eurocentrism by diminishing the centrality of colonialism as an explanatory historical phenomenon, focusing instead on the internal dynamics of non-European worlds that colonial (and some post-colonial) narratives subordinate to the margins of Eurocentric historical narratives. In *In an Antique Land*, however, he tackles colonialism head-on, tracing the various intractable political problems of today – between Hindus and Muslims in India/Pakistan; and Jews and Arabs in Israel/Palestine – back to the violent ruptures initiated by colonial intervention on the one hand, and the 'epistemic violence' of the modern forms of knowledge that accompanied and legitimised it on the other. A complex, hybrid, multi-generic text, it performatively critiques the 'categorical' nature of modern knowledge by transgressing its categories, just as it offers an imaginative rejoinder to Eurocentric narratives of history by recovering lost or silenced histories that disturb Eurocentric representations and undermine myths of Progress.

Ghosh continued his direct engagement with colonialism in his next novel, *The Calcutta Chromosome*, which returns to some of the themes first broached by *The Circle of Reason* – Science, Reason, colonial Power/Knowledge – and expanded upon in *In an Antique Land*. This is combined with the technical skills deployed to such good effect in *The Shadow Lines*, in which a tightly plotted narrative cuts back and forth in space and time, often with almost dizzying velocity. Once again, Ghosh refuses to be hemmed in by generic constraints. *The Calcutta Chromosome* blends elements of the thriller, the detective novel, science fiction, ghost stories, gothic melodrama, and historiography to deliver a tongue-in-cheek pot-boiler that engages seriously with the intervention of scientific knowledge – this time in the form of colonial medicine – in a colonial society and its reception by the colonised. What is at stake in the novel is once again those Eurocentric self-representations about the diffusion of modernity, Reason, Progress and the civilising mission enforced by colonialism.

Taking as its cue the discovery, in 1898, that malaria is conveyed between infected persons by the female *anopheles* mosquito by Ronald Ross, a scientist in the Colonial Medical Service, the novel proceeds to unravel the very concept of 'discovery' itself and the empiricist, supposedly universal but nevertheless culturally determined assumptions of modern scientific knowledge that underwrite such a concept. Proceeding from Ross's own self-aggrandising diary of his researches and 'breakthrough', the novel proceeds to weave an ironic counter-narrative in which Ross's heroic self-centredness is displaced, as is the modern scientific epistemology that he represents. Instead, Ross is shown to be the unwitting pawn of a secretive cult of subalterns whose own knowledge of malaria is far in advance of Ross and the Western medical establishment – although it soon becomes clear that Ghosh is drawing into question historicist narratives of 'Progress' that articulate the language of being 'advanced' (or, conversely, 'backward') in the first place. Whilst

the 'race' to find the cure for malaria (another one of those metaphors that indicate linear notions of history, time and progress)
is seen by Ross – and, by implication, his Western competitors
– as the means to fame, fortune and the immortality bestowed
by History, the counter-scientific cult seeks immortality of a
different, more literal kind, allowing Ghosh to entwine subver-
sively the discourse of Science with one of those Indian 'superstitions' that colonialists loved to belittle: reincarnation.

All of this is grafted together from various fragments of
evidence gathered during the course of his research by Murugan,
an erstwhile employee of an enormous non-governmental
Organisation (NGO) called the International Water Council,
which is implicated in 'development' programmes that are
themselves embedded in the historicist narratives that the novel
critiques. As in *In an Antique Land*, *The Calcutta Chromosome* is
a novel in which the central figure is a researcher, which enables
Ghosh to raise some similar questions about knowledge, its
production, and its consequences in a different disciplinary and
environmental milieu (a key echo is with contemporary debates
about genetic engineering and the 'immortality' that might be
manufactured through it). Indeed, Ghosh has remarked that 'I
think the main influence on this book was *In an Antique Land*
… [y]ou remember *The Calcutta Chromosome* begins with
a guy finding in cyberspace a tiny clue and then he goes off
chasing it. So in some ways it's also a kind of private joke on
myself.'[13] The 'tiny clue' is a fragment of Murugan's ID card,
picked up by a super-computer called AVA which processes and
classifies objects. The narrative springs from AVA's inability to
identify and categorise this fragment. The elusiveness of 'fragments' that remain unrecognised or pass between the categories
of modern knowledge connects the tongue-in-cheek *Calcutta
Chromosome* with its more serious predecessor; both texts dwell
upon the problems of representing those fragments – of peoples,
of histories, of knowledge – using protocols of knowledge that
exclude them in the first place.

Ghosh's next novel, *The Glass Palace*, is his most commer-
cially successful to date. It marks a departure from the formal

experimentation of *In an Antique Land* and *The Calcutta Chromosome*. The spatial and temporal displacements of his previous work are replaced by a more straightforward linear narrative, though the epic dimensions of this grand historical romance mean that, geographically speaking, its canvas is as vast as that of *In an Antique Land*. Its diasporic reach stretches out into eastern arc of the Indian Ocean in contrast to Ghosh's previous fascination with the western half. Here, he focuses on the familial, commercial and cultural links that connect the Indian diaspora in South-East Asia, and the novel's centre of gravity lies in Burma. The narrative concerns itself mostly with the fortunes of three families: the deposed King of Burma and his retinue of servants, one of whom marries a wealthy timber merchant called Rajkumar who had once been a destitute Bengali orphan in Mandalay, the King's capital, at the time of his expulsion by the British; and the family of Saya John, a Malay Christian and Rajkumar's mentor. The novel tracks the ties of family and friendship across a continent and over four generations.

Ghosh's earlier explorations of nationhood and diaspora, of relationships between individuals and communities that transgress and transcend the shadow lines of political borders are extended in this most humanist of his novels. The ties bound by circumstance and endeavour, as well as those sealed by blood and kinship, generate communities of their own which intersect with but also move beyond the social boundaries of race, ethnicity, class, religion and nationality. The use of the family as a trope in most of Ghosh's fiction, but particularly in this novel, signals a very specific gesture *away* from the 'national allegory' that some critics have been tempted to see in 'Third World' fiction. He has stated that such misreading frustrates him and that for him, 'the family is the central unit because it's *not* about the nation, you know? Families can actually span nations.'[14] As in *In an Antique Land*, this is a polyglot diaspora, a network of hybrid identities but like that medieval world it is also a fragile community, one which is violently uprooted at the close of the novel as these communities are displaced by war and embark on the long overland march from Burma and South-East Asia to take refuge in India. The recovery of this forgotten episode in the most documented conflict in history testifies to Ghosh's ongoing interest in 'subaltern pasts'.[15]

The world of Rajkumar, Dolly, Saya John and their children is counterpointed by the other main narrative strand in the novel, which traces the increasing existential perplexity of Arjun – the nephew of another major character, Uma Dey – who enlists in the Indian Army under the British but, in the course of his career and during combat in South-East Asia increasingly begins to doubt his loyalty to the cause of maintaining someone else's empire. He thereby begins to question his own formation as a colonial subject. Eventually, he deserts and joins the Indian National Army – another 'forgotten' element of that war, as Ghosh reminds us in his essay in *The New Yorker* – which was led by the exiled nationalist firebrand Subhas Chandra Bose (revered to this day in Bengal as India's greatest nationalist, more so even than Gandhi and Nehru). The depredations and the defeat of the army results in Arjun's suicide, but the narrative enables Ghosh to work through the psychological pain and existential anguish of colonial alienation much as Frantz Fanon's *Black Skins/White Masks* had done some decades before. In this novel, Ghosh continues to engage directly with colonialism and its aftermath. It attempts to represent the human dimension of living through the violent upheavals brought about by the rise and fall of the British Empire, whilst tracing some of Burma's own current political problems back to that period of dislocation and defeat.

In 2004, Ghosh published his latest novel, *The Hungry Tide*. It stands in immediate contrast to the grandeur of *The Glass Palace*. Although it employs many of the narrative techniques of the earlier novels, such as the 'double-helix' pattern of alternate narrative strands, the use of flashback and memory, and the insertion of textual fragments that offer alternative avenues into a forgotten history, its scope is less ambitious than most of Ghosh's previous works. For the most part, the narrative time frame only extends over some thirty to forty years and, in contrast to the diasporic peregrinations of his earlier novels, the action is concentrated in one geographical area. Set amongst the small, impoverished and isolated communities of the Sundarbans, the mangrove swamps that congregate at the mouth of the huge Ganges Delta, it returns to the themes of modernity and development which he had introduced into his writing with *In an Antique Land*. This is braided, moreover, with that strand in Ghosh's work which has concerned itself with the issues of scientific knowledge and its relationship to subaltern ways of thinking and being.

A principal figure in *The Hungry Tide* is another scientist, this time a cetologist called Piyali Roy. Cetology involves the study of marine mammals, and her particular field of expertise concerns the freshwater river dolphins that are to be found in Asia's great waterways – the Indus, the Mekong, the Irawaddy, and, of course, the Ganges. The daughter of an Indian emigrant to the United States, she has had little contact with her ancestral country but she is drawn to her parents' native Bengal in order to conduct a survey of the marine mammals in the Gangetic delta. The novel opens with her meeting one of the other principal characters, an urbane, highly educated representative of modern India called Kanai. Significantly, he is a translator by profession, expert in six languages and proficient in several others, but he is also the nephew of an elderly woman, called Mashima ('great-aunt') by the local people, who has established an extremely successful rural development organisation called the Badabon Trust: an exemplary non-governmental development agency that has built up a rudimentary modern infrastructure including a school, a hospital and other welfare provisions.

Kanai, however, is on his way to the Sundarbans to examine a newly recovered notebook written by his deceased uncle, a poet and scholar whose dreams of socialist revolution are first dashed and then revived by his experience of 'the tide country' as he calls it. The notebook he has left behind allows Ghosh to inlay the narrative with an account of a forgotten incident in the history of post-colonial India, one that allows him to reprise the theme of a coercive post-colonial governmental machinery first broached in *The Circle of Reason*. This is the Morichjhãpi massacre, which took place in 1979, when the state authorities first barricaded, and then unleashed terrible violence on, a group of refugee settlers who had originally been displaced from the tide country on the other side of the border with Bangladesh by the war for its independence in the early 1970s. They had been forcibly resettled in another part of India but had returned illegally to what they saw as their homeland, and had settled on the island of Morichjhãpi, which the government had declared a wildlife conservation area. The incident dramatises the conflict between different ways of thinking and being, between the logic of modernity and development and the ensuing politics of ecology on the one hand, and the ways of life of indigenous peoples and their relationship to the environment. Despite its generally benign profile in the West, the novel demonstrates how environmentalism and conservation nevertheless has its own costs, and it explores the ethical dilemmas that result from this.

These conflicts are explored and echoed in the relationships between the three principal characters: the scientist, Piya; the modern Indian, Kanai; and an illiterate son of the tide country, a fisherman called Fokir. This subaltern figure is at the heart of the novel and the ethical exploration of the text focuses on his place – or lack of place – in the scheme of things as deter-mined by state authorities in Calcutta and New Delhi, or environmentalists in the West, or even in the minds of those steeped in scientific knowledge and modern education. As the novel reaches its climax, it is finally the environment itself, in the form of an unforgiving storm, which comprises the most significant 'character' in the narrative. For it is the 'tide country' – the novel's central metaphor – that constitutes the common point of reference that binds Piya, Kanai and Fokir together. As the novel makes clear, the tide is a scientific phenomenon that needs to be comprehended by people like Piya, is integral to the rhythms of life for people like Fokir, and it is also a 'text' that is read differently by such people. Kanai is the bridge, the one who is able to translate the idioms of one into that of the other. More than any of his previous texts, *The Hungry Tide* is a novel which foregrounds language and textuality, and its relationship to lived experience. What, it asks, is environmentalism in the abstract worth? Is it a particularly Western way of looking at our relationship to the earth? *The Hungry Tide* is a plea as well as a testimony to the many other songs of the earth, sung by the many different peoples who live on it and claim some portion of it as their own; a plea that they do not go unheard, that they are not swamped by the hungry tides of either development or environmentalism.

Throughout Ghosh's career, his fictional writing has been accompanied by non-fictional work of all kinds: academic articles, travelogues, reportage, journalism, and criticism. His discourse is enormously varied and his subjects eclectic but they are bound by the same core themes and issues that animate his fictional writing. Indeed, it is probably not wise to distinguish between his fiction and non-fiction as it is perhaps another of those artificial boundaries that Ghosh insistently interrogates, the overcoming of which constitutes one of the central threads running throughout his work. Many of his works seek to deconstruct, or at least put into question, the value of distinguishing between 'fact' and 'fiction'. For to speak of 'facts' immediately involves some taxing epistemological problems: whose 'facts'? In whose interests are 'facts' deployed? For what purpose? Ghosh does not endorse the view that there are no such things as facts but he does point out that they do not necessarily mean very much by themselves, and certainly they cannot of themselves deliver something called 'truth'. Facts must be interpreted; they must be embedded in discourse; they only speak when placed in narratives. And this is where the pressure of fiction emerges, because who decides which narratives can best deliver the 'truth' of facts? Are the explanatory narratives of, say, historiography or science *necessarily* more truthful than those of fiction? If, as Ghosh has shown throughout his work, some of the most powerful explanatory narratives are those which have served powerful interests and systematically excluded, distorted or degraded the experiences of those without the power to inscribe themselves into such narratives, or whose knowledges and beliefs are not recognised by those regimes of truth, then the 'facts' which supposedly guarantee the 'truth' must be suspect from such perspectives.

It is unsurprising, then, to find considerable traffic between Ghosh's fictional and his non-fictional work. Many of his novels either originate in his non-fictional work or are in intertextual relation to parallel texts that examine several of their episodes using the discourses of 'fact'. Thus, his PhD dissertation, the essay 'The Imam and the Indian', and the historical article, 'The Slave of MS. H.6' each have a different and significant relation to *In an Antique Land*; likewise, *Dancing in Cambodia, At Large in Burma*, and the reportage of 'India's Untold War of Independence' both stand in an oblique yet complementary relation to *The Glass Palace*. The affiliations between them are clear, the boundaries dividing them less so.

To a greater or lesser extent, all of Amitav Ghosh's major works resonate with many of the preoccupations that have been marshalled under the rubric of 'postmodernism', a difficult and contentious term which has nevertheless proved useful as a label for a set of ideas, concepts, and cultural practices that mark it out as a distinct phenomenon. In all his novels, for example, Ghosh exhibits an interest in the nature of language, textuality, and discourse, and the ways in which human perception, comprehension, and experience is invariably shaped and, to varying degrees, determined by them. For him, the question of 'identity' is always implicated in representations of the 'self' and of the world around it; identity does not stand alone nor is it derived from some inborn 'essence' within a given human being; rather, it is made or 'fashioned' by language and representation. As such it is a 'fiction' (a word derived from the Latin 'to make') but it is nevertheless 'real' and deeply felt and our sense of 'identity' clearly has material consequences insofar as it informs our actions and their consequences. Ghosh's texts interrogate the commonly held belief that 'fiction' is equivalent to 'unreal' or untrue, a position that is common within postmodernism. Moreover, Ghosh's texts also represent the correlate view that identity is therefore 'unstable' and fluid, because what is made can be unmade, and often is – over time or in different contexts: again, a central preoccupation of postmodern writers.

The notions that 'fiction' is untrue, or that identity inheres in a fixed and sovereign individual consciousness, are part of the system of knowledge initiated by the intellectual revolutions of early modern Europe, which crystallised in what has come to be known the 'Enlightenment' of the eighteenth century. Enlightenment conceptions of rationality, knowledge and truth (and, by implication, their opposites) intensified in the course of the nineteenth century and became the index of 'modern' civilisation; accordingly, postmodernism is seen as a challenge to the hegemony of Enlightenment ideas. As those ideas were deeply implicated in colonial missions, the unpicking of its intellectual legacy constitutes one of Amitav Ghosh's central concerns, as does his challenge to the protocols of some of the key disciplines established by the Enlightenment, such as History and Anthropology. In the case of history, in particular, Ghosh shares the postmodern disavowal of 'universal' historical narratives that encode ideas about modernity, development and Progress, focusing instead on those 'fragments' of human experience that have been occluded from the historical record, and which find no place in such grand designs.

However, it is in terms of its formal and stylistic experimentation that Ghosh's work can be most closely aligned with postmodernism. The generic multiplicity and indeterminacy of his texts splices together in contrapuntal formation genres which are commonly associated with 'popular culture' such as science fiction, or the detective novel, or the thriller, with those modes of writing often seen as constituting 'high', or institutionalised, culture such as historiography, ethnography, *bildungsroman*, and scientific discourse. It is indicative of what Steven Connor has identified as an inherent interdisciplinarity within postmodernism that is part of its assault upon Enlightenment conceptions of discrete and specialised fields of knowledge.[16] This is accompanied by yet another feature of postmodern cultural practice, a chronic self-consciousness about the fragile and provisional status of its *own* claims that leads to self-reflexive mechanisms such as 'metafiction' whereby the text is constantly aware of its own production *as* a text. In Ghosh's works, a self-reflexive narrator often introduces metafictional meditations on the value and purpose of the narrative. This in turn is attached to one of the key registers in postmodern discourse: irony. As we shall see, irony is one of the most important features in Ghosh's work, though its precise character is somewhat distinct from those kinds that predominate in most postmodern fictions.

The attraction of Amitav Ghosh's work for many post-colonial thinkers is based on the obvious overlap in the objectives of postmodernism and postcolonialism. Such critics find in postmodernism, and particularly that philosophical variant of it known as post-structuralism, some vital intellectual and ideological resources that might help them dismantle the hegemony of European ideas and ideologies that have survived formal political decolonisation, and it is indeed useful to see Ghosh's work as a critical juncture between postmodern and postcolonial perspectives and objectives. Moreover, just as his work helps to map out the potentialities and limits of postcolonialism, so too does it offer a means of evaluating any strategic alliance with postmodernism. In a sense, Ghosh's work displays both the value and the pitfalls of such an alliance.

However, Ghosh himself often seems aware of the risks attendant to such an enterprise. It would be wrong, therefore, to characterise Ghosh unproblematically as a postmodernist; his work *does* show certain affiliations to it but there are other factors that are germane to the context of his work. In fact, to overlook these other factors would misrepresent the emergence and purchase of postmodern ideas in India during the 1980s and 1990s and ironically repeat a familiar Eurocentric narrative that envisages the 'diffusion' of cultural practices from their authoritative centres in the West. The arrival of postmodernism, which has been a feature of English-speaking intellectual and cultural life in India since that time, was not a simple importation or imitation of ideas from elsewhere. Rather, postmodernism emerged as a valuable discourse for some intellectuals and artists because of the conjuncture of intercultural exchange in ideas between Western and Indian intellectuals on the one hand, and, on the other hand, the social and political upheavals of the late 1960s and 1970s that created a crisis in national identity precipitated by a crisis of the post-colonial Indian state. Postmodernism provided a critical vocabulary for working through the implications of this crisis.

The origins and parameters of this crisis are worth examining in some detail as they shed considerable light on some of Ghosh's most important preoccupations. The post-colonial Indian state was subject to the same pressures that had moulded its colonial predecessor in the latter decades of the Raj. The historians Sugata Bose and Ayesha Jalal have pithily described them as 'the overlapping dialectics of centralism and regionalism [and] nationalism and religious assertion'.[17] In other words, from its inception the Indian state was marked by a tension between central government and regional autonomy on the one hand, and by tensions between its constituent religious communities, on the other, that continually picked away at the national fabric. Both of these dimensions were only partially resolved by independence – through the federalism enshrined in the Constitution – and by the self-mutilation of the national body represented by the Partition of 1947 – a deferral which meant that these dialectics continued to develop and inform each other throughout the subsequent decades. Though initially muted during the afterglow of independence, and held in abeyance by the considerable personal charisma of India's first Prime Minister, Jawaharlal Nehru, they periodically surfaced nevertheless (such as during the language riots of the 1950s, or the periodic communal violence that has punctuated India's national narrative) to serve notice that the fundamental dynamics of modern Indian social and political history could not simply be dissolved by formal decolonisation.

Predictably enough, from the latter years of Nehru's premiership onwards these political pressures intensified. First, various military interventions into 'unresolved' territories such as Goa and, more importantly, Kashmir, whetted the political appetite of India's central authorities, and the 'steady pilferage by the Centre of powers that constitutionally belonged to the regions' paradoxically provoked regional assertion.[18] With all effective power being increasingly routed through New Delhi, local grievances and problems were invariably channelled *against* the federal centre whilst, at the same time, the frustrations of having no proper autonomy to speak of also encouraged greater radicalism, resulting in a number of secessionist movements in regions such as Assam, Punjab and Nagaland, as well as Kashmir. The central authorities responded by flexing their political muscles to even greater extent, dispatching the army to these regions and effectively imposing martial law. The increasing authoritarianism this heralded was sealed by the declaration of a state of emergency in 1975 by the Prime Minister, Indira Gandhi. With the dissolving of parliament, the harassment of the judiciary, and stifling of political dissent, the period of emergency between 1975 and 1977 constituted the greatest abrogation of India's democratic political culture since independence and it was to prove a defining moment in the accelerating crisis of the Indian state.

It was at this point that the centre–region dialectic enmeshed most significantly with the dynamics of religious communalism that had always been present on the flip side of the Indian nationalist imagination. After ending the state of emergency in 1977 by calling surprise elections, Indira Gandhi was perhaps equally surprised to find herself at the wrong end of the result. The resulting coalition government, which was based on nothing other than a concerted attempt to stop Mrs. Gandhi from legitimising her authoritarianism by claiming a democratic mandate, was quickly mired in its internal feuds and squabbles and soon fell; meanwhile, Indira Gandhi had begun to salvage some of her popularity by subtly changing the discourse of 'national' identity, altering her rhetoric to appeal to a core 'Hindu' constituency that could act as an electoral bulwark against the increasing appeal of regional secessionists. On returning to power in 1980, Mrs. Gandhi's calculated appeal to Hindu majoritarianism emboldened her to strengthen the grip of the centre over the recalcitrant regions, matters being brought to a head when she ordered the storming of the Golden Temple in Amritsar – Sikhism's holiest shrine – by the Indian army in order to capture the leader of a militant Punjabi separatist movement. The unhappy consequences of this action were momentous; she herself was assassinated by her Sikh bodyguards, which in turn precipitated anti-Sikh riots orchestrated by Hindu gangs with the connivance of leading figures in the central government. The pattern had been set for the communal underbelly of the Indian nationalist imagination to emerge from out of the shadows; an increasingly militant and chauvinistic Hindu nationalism emerged from the political margins to challenge post-colonial India's secular credentials.

The impact of this turbulence on the Indian cultural imagination and its national self-image was profound. Two dimensions of the subsequent re-evaluation of modern Indian identity and history are particularly relevant here. First, and most importantly, the grand narratives of Indian nationalism that had animated the struggle against colonial rule lost their credibility. The slow crisis of the Indian state dissolved the rhetoric of national unity on which Nehru's vision of a secular, democratic India was founded. All three – unity, secularism, and democracy – now seemed little more than empty vessels, signifying nothing. National unity had fragmented into a multiplicity of regional, religious, caste, class, and linguistic identities; secularism had been undermined by the deployment of religious identities in the service of political expediency and the price was being paid by the increasing entrenchment of communalism as a political logic; and democracy itself had been reduced to little more than a periodic performance, a masque that hid beneath its subtle veils the corruptions of a gargantuan bureaucracy. The crisis of the state thus resulted in a corresponding crisis of representation in both its political and discursive senses. The ideational structures that had upheld the ideology of a secular, democratic nation – structures derived from the political legacy of the Enlightenment – had buckled under the pressure, and splintered India's sense of itself. Second, the very notion of the modern,

representative state itself – another of the Enlightenment's legacies – was subject to scrutiny and reappraisal. Once seen as the
handmaiden of Progress and modernity, a harbinger of liberty
and freedom, the machineries of the state had come to be associated with coercion and repression; its apparatuses and protocols
entrenching power in the hands of a select few at the expense of
the majority of people. This dark reappraisal of the post-colonial
state would repeatedly coalesce around the state of emergency,
when the state assumed its most authoritarian mantle, and
amongst many of the most notable works of the 1980s we see
the figure of the sinister state looming over its citizens, inserting
itself into their most intimate spaces or just disposing of them
as and when it needs or must: in Salman Rushdie's evocation
of the Widow and the slum clearances in *Midnight's Children*;
in Shashi Tharoor's *The Great Indian Novel*; and, of course, in
almost all of Amitav Ghosh's works, where the state and its logic
of colonial (and post-colonial) 'governmentality' is represented
variously as a menace, a threat, a distant and peremptory presence, or is ironically mocked as a perversion of 'rationality'.[19]

It is unsurprising, then, that postmodernism begins to emerge
at this time among English-speaking intellectuals and artists as
a cultural vocabulary through which the superseded discourses
of Indian nationalism might be subjected to interrogation, for
its basis is in critiques of the very concept of 'representation'
itself, which in turn is correlated ideologically to a suspicion of
grand narratives and the state. The convergence between a disavowal of Indian nationalism's grand narratives, suspicion of the
state, and postmodern theory has been most forcibly articulated
by a group of radical revisionist historians with whom Amitav
Ghosh has had close personal and professional ties. This group,
known globally within postcolonial studies as the Subaltern
Studies group, was initially composed of a number of Bengali
historians who had themselves been steeped in the discourses
of the Enlightenment through their intellectual affiliation to
Marxism and its grand narratives of a universal history, as well
as their political investment in communist parties, both Marxist
and Maoist.[20] It is perhaps no coincidence that Subaltern Studies

emerged at precisely that moment in Indian history when the crisis of nationhood was at its most intense for their challenge to the dominance of elite or state-centred perspectives on Indian colonial and post-colonial history was one of the most creative responses to, as well as devastating critiques of, the formation of the post-colonial nation-state. Their focus on the histories of 'the people', or subalterns, which had previously escaped the notice of nationalist and colonial historians, was both an affirmation of the role of subalterns in the historic formation of the modern Indian nation – in ways usually at odds with the narratives of elite historians – and a critique of the nation's self-representation, which had systematically silenced or excised their contributions.[21]

Both dimensions of the Subaltern Studies project – its affirmation of the subaltern, and its critique of prevailing conceptions of Indian nationhood – are clearly discernible in most of Ghosh's work, and he has himself acknowledged that they 'came out of a similar moment in the intellectual life of India and that's really been the connection'.[22] But it could also be argued that the intellectual and intertextual connections are stronger and deeper than is suggested by Ghosh here. For one thing, one of the narrative elements of *In an Antique Land* was first published in a volume of *Subaltern Studies* as a more straightforward historical piece of writing, 'The Slave of MS. H.6'.[23] Beyond that is a shared but nevertheless complex relationship to some of the ideas and techniques of postmodernism. In particular, as the Subaltern studies project has developed, their own implication – as professional historians – in the Enlightenment's legacy has been increasingly dissected by some members of the collective which in turn has pushed them towards a highly self-reflexive 'meta-discursive' relationship to their own discourse that is aware of the limits imposed by the protocols of historical representation. This is analogous to Ghosh's more daring self-reflexivity and metafictional experiments. Indeed, it could be argued that Ghosh has the licence to explore areas of the Subaltern Studies project that the historians themselves are prohibited from by virtue of their investment in 'historiography'. Fiction, in this sense, might be seen as the flip side of subaltern historiography: a consideration of the problem of historical representation as a problem of form. For it may well be that one of the most significant implications of Ghosh's work is to draw into question the respective valuation of historiography *over* fiction as a vehicle of historical 'truth'.

And yet, despite the need to critique and revise the discourses of Indian nationalism and national identity; despite the desire to challenge the authoritarianism, violence and coercive reflexes of the post-colonial nation-state; for many Indian intellectuals, of whom Ghosh is one, the Nehruvian vision of a secular, democratic nation-state that accommodates India's 'diversity' into a syncretic unity remains an indispensable bulwark against the forces of religious and ethnic chauvinism, and the further political disintegration or violent ethnic cleansing that might result. This contrary impulse has perhaps strengthened over the years, especially for Ghosh, in response to the political ascendance of Hindu nationalism. One notices, for example, in Ghosh's melancholy and ambivalent meditation in *Dancing in Cambodia, At Large in Burma* that the war of the Karenni tribes against the Burmese state was both heroically appealing but politically disastrous, 'What could nationhood possibly mean for a landlocked, thinly populated tract of forest? What made it worth dying for ... ? I began to be very curious about what 'freedom' meant for the Karenni. Did it mean democracy and the rule of law, or merely the right to establish yet another ethnic enclave?'[24] The shadows of India's own ethnic tensions loom large here in his disquiet about separatism even as the concept of 'nationhood' is radically destabilised. Whilst 'national' freedom could mean 'democracy and the rule of law', it could equally mean little more than ethnic separatism. In such cases, 'freedom' – whether from colonial rule, or an oppressive post-colonial state – could once again amount to nothing more than empty rhetoric.

Indian intellectuals such as Amitav Ghosh who matured during the period of India's protracted and corrosive crisis of identity are therefore caught on the horns of an acute political and ethical dilemma. On the one hand, the critique of prevailing conceptions of nationhood are absolutely necessary in order to realise the larger goal of 'freedom' promised at independence; on the other hand, that very goal may be increasingly jeopardised by the acceleration of India's political disintegration.

The central argument of this book is that Amitav Ghosh's affiliations to postmodernism are in perpetual tension with his continuing investment in ideas and ideologies that are ultimately derived from the Enlightenment but have developed in India along unique and specific historical trajectories. In particular, his ideological attachment to the syncretic nationalism espoused and popularised by Nehru is a major determinant of his work and the underlying political impulse of most of his work is shaped by his attempt to think through the implications of its failure. However, Nehruvian nationalism is itself grounded in more fundamental ideas that also emerged from the Enlightenment such as secularism and humanism. These too have charted their own specific courses in India, as we shall see, and it is Ghosh's sympathetic but critical relationship to their *Indian* forms that gives his work its particular character.

There are many aspects of Ghosh's work that signal this secular and humanist orientation. Whilst one of his principal narrative topics is the drama of cultural difference, there is nevertheless an accompanying emphasis on the underlying similarity of human experience across both space and time. The divisions that fracture humanity – social, cultural, political, religious, sexual and so on – are recuperated through evocations of a transcendence that characterises humanity as a 'whole'. Furthermore, unlike some of his more resolutely postmodern contemporaries, such as Rushdie, Ghosh is relatively sanguine about the concept of the 'individual', one of the cornerstones of Enlightenment humanism. In contrast to Rushdie's preference for two-dimensional 'cartoon' characters who are subordinated to the demands of the narrative, which formally represents the postmodern emphasis on the discursive formation of subjectivity, Ghosh's fictions (and, indeed, his reportage) are populated by 'full', three-dimensional characters who are a complex ensemble of motivations and desires. Extending this, one might also point out that (auto)biography is one of the most recurrent features of Ghosh's work, in both fiction and non-fiction. It indicates his abiding interest in exploring the confusions and conundrums of self-fashioning in the context of colonialism and its aftermath. In *The Shadow Lines, In an Antique Land,* and *The Glass Palace* he draws on his own personal experiences and those of his family to dramatise the difficulties of pinning down a coherent sense of identity for colonised peoples who have, in their differing and multitudinous ways, responded to the violent interventions of colonialism in their physical environment, their social being, their cultural formations and their *mentalité.* Addressing the psychological and affective effects of colonial 'defeat' as much as its political or economic dimensions, this constitutes a more humanist attempt to recuperate some measure of subjectivity and agency as a viable basis for a future decolonisation of the mind and body.

These interests in individuality, experience, self-fashioning and (auto)biography perhaps owe something to V.S. Naipaul, who has been a major literary influence on Ghosh since his childhood.[25] At pivotal moments in his non-fiction, when Ghosh is trying to sift through the conflicting memories and emotions that surround episodes of his own personal experience – such as the emotive passage in 'The Ghosts of Mrs. Gandhi' when he recollects his motivations for joining an anti-communal demonstration – he often turns to Naipaul, even though his political affiliations are usually diametrically opposed to the Trinidadian. However, this in itself demonstrates that urge to transcend differences in order to find a common humanity in the nature of experience. Correspondingly, another aspect of Naipaul's influence is on Ghosh's prose style – a polished and smooth prose that renders experience 'transparently'. This sits alongside Ghosh's awareness that language is itself one of the divisions that separates human beings, and animates the metafictional musings on the relative *inaccessibility* of 'experience'.

And yet, by far the greatest influence on Ghosh's humanism is the modern literary and artistic tradition of Bengal in particular, and India in general. Ghosh's work thus represents a particularly interesting and complex example of the tenacious hold that humanism has had on the Indian – and especially Bengali – cultural imagination since the mid-nineteenth century vernacular 'renaissances', of which the Bengali variant is perhaps the most well-known. The 'Bengal Renaissance', as it is called, constituted the first attempt by colonised Indians to wrestle with the ideological challenges of colonial modernity and it laid the foundations for most conceptualisations of what an *Indian* modernity might look like.

It is important to note that the humanism that emerged from the Bengal Renaissance was not a mere copy of that which had formed in Europe and had arrived in India on the back of commerce and conquest. Like the postmodernism that emerged more than a century and a half later, it is better to think of it as a *translation* that is marked by an intense negotiation of the meaning and value of a concept such as 'humanity' for Indian society – both in relation to India's prevailing social and cultural traditions, but also in the context of colonial subjugation. It could never, for example, be fully at ease with the 'myth of essential and universal Man: essential, because humanity – human-ness – is the inseparable and central essence, the defining quality, of human beings; universal, because that essential humanity is shared by all human beings, of what ever time or place'.[26] Since this abstract universal humanism actually derived from the political discourse of 'rights' established by the Enlightenment philosophers and realised by the French and American revolutions, its reception in a colony denied those rights could not be anything other than problematic.

The humanism that emerged out of the Bengal Renaissance was thus a conflicted and contradictory discourse that shows all the marks of 'the battle for cultural parity' that prefigured the later emergence of nationalism as its political corollary and has inflected Indian political and cultural discourse ever since. Born within the unpalatable crucible of an historic defeat, the giddy optimism of European nineteenth-century humanism was inevitably tempered by deep insecurity and despair. As a result, the cosmopolitanism of Enlightenment humanism, which the Bengali *bhadralok* received through the early Orientalist scholarship of William Jones, Henry Colebrooke and others, was juxtaposed with national particularism, creating a dialectic between the universal and the local that would be present in each discourse that emerged from the initial matrix of Bengali humanism, such as nationalism. The battle for cultural parity meant that for Bengali intellectuals, '[a]ccess to universality becomes a competition for relative cultural greatness,' and each successive cultural milestone – most notably the award of the Nobel Prize for Literature to Tagore – was celebrated as an affirmation of Bengali culture's legitimate place in 'the world's republic of letters'.[27] That mindset survives to this day; in *Countdown*, for example, Ghosh notes that the argument for India's nuclear weapons programme 'is status-driven not threat-driven' – a contemporary echo of the Bengal Renaissance and its anxious need for approval, for some sense of its place in the modern world.[28]

The Bengal Renaissance was a multi-dimensional cultural formation, and from it emerged several correlated ways of thinking that accompanied its humanism. All of them have become entrenched in the mentality of modern India. First, Bengali humanism was grounded in the emergent historical consciousness that was fostered by the rapid development of clock time and print culture, developments which had taken place over a few centuries in Europe but which burst forth over a few years in colonial Bengal. Clock time not only transformed patterns of work and leisure and rearranged social relations, but it also introduced new ways of thinking about time which were secular and linear as opposed to sacred, cyclical and seasonal.[29] Print culture, for its part, stimulated new genres such as the novel, the short story, and biography, all of which memorialised a larger range of everyday experience and this helped to revolutionise notions of identity and subjectivity. The plotting of experience through secular, linear 'empty' time (that is, time that is not invested with sacred significance but is in fact a neutral or natural 'dimension' of 'experience') in the form of historiography was enthusiastically embraced by Bengali intellectuals, who would henceforth see history as a resource in its battle for cultural parity.[30] In addition to historicism and individualism, and in fact triangulating between the two, was a new emphasis on 'rationalism' as defined by the positivist and empiricist epistemologies that had triumphed during the Enlightenment. For the intellectuals of the Bengal Renaissance, the allure of modern scientific rationality was enhanced by the ideology of science that was promoted by the colonial state, whereby science came to be seen as a sign of power, modernity and progress. If the battle for cultural parity were to be won, it would have to be through the language of Reason.

And yet historicism, individualism and rationalism in colonial India would all inevitably be marked by that battle such that none of these could be adopted in unmodified form. In every respect, the discourse of the Bengal Renaissance is shot through with tensions that were determined by the reception of European ideas in the humiliating context of colonial subjection. Thus, the engagement with these ideas was both positive and defensive. Whilst historicism was accepted, there was nevertheless an ambiguous relationship to notions of Progress amongst an intelligentsia who had absorbed the Orientalists' representations of an Indian Golden Age far back in the mists of antiquity. Whilst positivism and empiricism were wholeheartedly endorsed, their secularist implications were nevertheless contained. On the one hand, attempts were made to 'Indianise' scientific rationality itself by identifying antecedents and equivalents in classical Hindu religious and philosophical texts; on the other, those very same philosophical and religious traditions were seen as unique resources available to Indians in order to 'humanise' science.[31] In both strategies, rationalism is mediated by religion. And emergent notions of individual 'identity' in India were always far more fragile than the more robust collective identities that subsumed them. Liberalism, the political logic of humanism, was precariously articulated because in the colonial context the notion of individual 'rights' were not allowed by the British to take hold. As a result, liberty was always seen as 'a nation's collective right to self-determination' but not as an individual right.[32] All of these tensions were codified in a modernised Bengali language that served as a vehicle for the articulation of these ideas and through which the Bengal Renaissance wrought its greatest achievement: the creation of a modern vernacular culture from which Bengal's modern literary tradition has emerged and of which Amitav Ghosh is a part.

Two towering figures from this tradition stand out as major influences not only on Ghosh's work but also on virtually all Bengali cultural production in modern times. One is the poet, novelist, dramatist, songwriter and artist, Rabindranath Tagore (1861–1941) and the other is the filmmaker, artist and writer, Satyajit Ray (1921–92). Tagore's stature amongst the *bhadralok* is pre-eminent, a cultural reference point that is in some ways equivalent to that of Shakespeare in English, and in other ways even more important because his works permeate the everyday lives of most middle-class Bengali households. His songs and poems are often sung or recited during the course of the daily routine, and many of his memorable phrases are habitually quoted in arguments or discussions. All Bengali writers and artists have to engage with his legacy as the epitome of the modern Bengali vernacular artist, and his rich body of work has, throughout the twentieth century, proved to be a valuable resource for later writers. Ghosh has spoken of his debt to Tagore's short story *Kshudito Pashaan* (The Hungry Stones) whilst writing *The Calcutta Chromosome*, but perhaps Tagore's greatest importance as an intertextual reference lies in his own tortured and complex relationship to colonial modernity, which represented with acute sensitivity the dilemmas and internal conflicts of the Bengal Renaissance as a whole. Ghosh's reading of 'The Hungry Stones' – which he has translated into English – as 'an elaborate metaphor of colonialism' identifies Tagore's anxious attempt to repress the knowledge that his formation as a colonial subject resulted in his self-alienation, and by extension the self-alienation of the cultural tradition within which he was writing.[33] This tradition, the urban *bhadralok* tradition based in Calcutta, had fashioned itself under the colonial gaze and, in the course of its 'modernization', had gradually discarded or purged those elements of the rural folk culture that the upper and middle classes had originally shared with the peasants.[34] Late in his life, Tagore would regretfully acknowledge his distance from the rural folk culture of the Bengali peasantry, which he saw as being more 'authentic'.[35]

Tagore's relationship to modernity was an agonised and complicated one for he was not an anti-modern traditionalist who dismissed modernity out of hand, and indeed he found much of it worthy of respect and admiration. But his concerns about it can best be gauged by his antipathy to nationalism, and it is in this respect that Tagore's impact on Ghosh's work can be most profoundly felt. For Tagore's argument against nationalism displays considerable affinity with many of the tropes deployed by Ghosh. Identifying the concept of 'Nation' as 'that aspect which a whole population assumes when organised for a mechanical purpose', Tagore deplores the way such a 'political laboratory' dissolves 'personal humanity' and concludes, 'When [society] allows itself to be turned into a perfect organisation of power then there are few crimes which it is unable to perpetrate.' [36] Invoking the language of science and technology that, as we have seen, were seen as signs of power, Tagore evokes the 'Nation' as a perpetrator of scientised violence. What is really at issue for Tagore here is the concept of the 'State', which embodies the 'mechanical' organisation of the scientific worldview for political purposes and thus oppresses 'society' (which Tagore distinguishes from 'Nation'). Tagore's views on nationalism were crystallised in the context of the Great War of 1914–18, and they were to profoundly influence Nehru who nevertheless disagreed with his evaluation of the role of the state. However, Ghosh, whose own ideological affiliations were moulded by Nehruvian nationalism (and thus indirectly by Tagore) would gravitate towards the poet rather than the politician in his own critique of the nation-state. Thus, Ghosh's critique of Indian nationalism does not just draw on postmodernism but also on a tradition of dissent against colonial modernity (and not just colonialism *per se*) that has encompassed numerous figures such as the mystic Ramakrishna Paramhansa, the Theosophists,

Gandhi and Jayaprakash Narayan, as well as Tagore throughout India's troubled modern history.

If Tagore is the figure that looms over Ghosh's troubled and ambivalent relationship to modernity and humanism, then Ray represents the obverse impulse in Ghosh's work *towards* humanism and the other legacies of the Enlightenment. Born, like Tagore, into one of the most creative and well known of *bhadralok* families, Ray's relationship to modernism is more straightforward. Like Tagore, his presence in the modern middle-class Bengali household is ubiquitous and inspirational. A prolific writer as well as filmmaker, his work is often accessed by Bengali children, not only through the more immediate vehicle of cinema but also through his well-loved short stories, particularly the Felu-da detective stories (his father, Sukumar Ray, was also a much loved humourist and writer of children's literature). Although he was a versatile filmmaker, whose canvas was broad and varied, some of his best films, such as the internationally acclaimed *Pather Panchali* (Song of the Little Road) or *The Adventures of Goopy and Bagha* (based on his own stories about these two comic characters), either addressed children or explored the world through their eyes. This interest in childhood is a register of inno-cence that is often invoked by Ghosh, whose central characters are often represented as child-like, without artifice or conceit, and very often naïve and gullible – one thinks, for example, of Alu in *The Circle of Reason*, the narrator of *The Shadow Lines*, or that of *In an Antique Land*. But the innocence of childhood was for Ray also a kind of metaphor of his vision of humanism. His aesthetic project of 'affirming the human' amounted to an idealistic recuperation of the humanist potential endowed by the Bengal Renaissance, and it is a phrase that Ghosh almost dupli-cates in his essay 'The Ghosts of Mrs. Gandhi' to describe his own ethical preference when confronting the horrors of human violence.[37] Moreover, the influence of Ray's interest in individual characters can also be witnessed in Ghosh's own fascination with vividly realised, highly individuated personalities, as can Ray's 'ability to resolve enormously complex plots and themes into deceptively simple narrative structures'. [38]

In addition to Tagore and Ray, the Bengali literary tradition that emerged out of the Bengal Renaissance has shaped Ghosh's outlook and influenced his writing in other ways, notably through the popular fiction of the 1930s and 1940s that Ghosh has acknowledged as being at the front of his mind during the writing of *The Calcutta Chromosome*. Ghost stories, science fiction (Ray was also influential here), fantastical novels, and detective fiction, as well as the immensely popular social realism of Saratchandra Chatyopadhyay and Bhibutibhushan Bandhyopadhyay, have all left their mark on the Bengali literary field and traces of them can be felt throughout Ghosh's work, which he sees as a 'small link' in 'an unbroken chain of aesthetic and intellectual effort that stretches back to the mid-nineteenth century'.[39]

The legacy of the Bengal Renaissance is therefore an important factor in any critical assessment of Ghosh's work but it should also be remembered that he is not an uncritical admirer of its achievements or merely a reproducer of its ideological and intellectual concerns. His relationship to it is more complex. For one thing, Ghosh's interest in 'popular' culture, and the interesting value that the 'popular' has as a positive motif in his writing – whether it is popular forms of culture, or folk religion – runs against the grain of the Bengal Renaissance's dismissal of popular culture and belief as 'backward' and 'superstitious'; even the literary vernacular signalled the cultural *hauteur* of a modernising *bhadralok* class that spurned the simpler idioms and speech of the lower classes of Bengali society. He therefore has a conflicted relationship to an intellectual heritage that is itself conflicted.

Nevertheless, one can trace many of the dilemmas that Ghosh addresses in his work to the continuing tradition initiated by the domestication of humanism in Bengal, and in India generally. It has left a dual legacy that writers such as Ghosh continue to negotiate. On the one hand, the parallel vernacular renaissances of the nineteenth century bequeathed the cultural resources that successfully inspired the struggle against colonialism; on the other hand, it was always marked by the humiliation of defeat. For Ghosh, who matured during the period of crisis which marked the dissolution of the renaissances' greatest achievement – the construction of a politically viable Indian nationalism – the sense of pessimism is evident in the recurring references to defeat that are scattered throughout his writings. In the course of an interview discussion about *The Glass Palace*, Ghosh remarked that 'this has really been our history for a long, long time: the absolute fact of defeat and the absolute fact of trying to articulate defeat to yourself and trying to build a culture around the centrality of defeat'.[40] This sense of defeat is registered in the elegiac tone of much of his writing; it perhaps lurks behind his ubiquitous sense of irony, an irony he shares with many postmodern writers who similarly envisage a world 'beyond repair';[41] and in the melancholic tone that lies beneath many of his reflections on the contradictions of India's encounter with a colonial and post-colonial modernity.

And yet he continues to find in that encounter resources of hope that may not be able to 'repair' the world but might at least prevent greater disaster. In its more optimistic moments his writing imagines moments of possibility in the interstices of modernity, in those cultural practices and personal encounters that elude and transgress the categorical boundaries established by modern knowledge and its political apparatuses. The ambivalence that results is characteristic not of a moral, political or intellectual failure, not of a chronic inability to face up to political realities but rather an ethical affirmation of the need to explore how best to cope with the post-colonial predicament today. To paraphrase Seamus Heaney, Ghosh's writing constitutes an attempt to find a language adequate to that predicament.

This book is organised somewhat differently to the previous studies in this series. Instead of the customary chronological, novel-by-novel approach, the chapters are organised thematically. This reflects the fact that Ghosh has over the years built up what amounts to a largely coherent and substantial intellectual project that gravitates around a set of core themes and issues. Although his novels are very different from each other, the above outline of his development as a novelist demonstrates how certain strands of thought have woven themselves into the fabric of his discourse, and these threads bind his works into a whole that is more than just the sum of its parts. Each of the chapters could, for instance, have dwelt on every single one if his texts because every novel is relevant to each of the chapters. However, in order to avoid repetitiveness and to aid the reader who is not so familiar with Ghosh's texts, two of the main chapters that follow emphasise particular texts that are more relevant than some of the others. Though there are references to the other texts as and when required, these chapters will thus focus on a core set of texts that, in the view of this author, offer the best avenues for analysis. Chapter 2, for example, focuses on Ghosh's exploration of knowledge, science and rationality with respect to *The Circle of Reason*, *The Calcutta Chromosome*, and *In an Antique Land*. Chapter 3 examines Ghosh's meditation on questions of identity, colonialism, religion, and nationalism in the post-colonial world by concentrating on *The Shadow Lines*, *The Glass Palace*, and *In an Antique Land*. *The Hungry Tide*, which was published quite recently, is explored in each of these chapters whenever it is apposite to do so but on the whole it is, unfortunately, treated less extensively than the other works.

Chapter 4, on the other hand, concerns itself with *all* of Ghosh's major works, including *The Hungry Tide*. This chapter concentrates on Ghosh's engagement with history and historiography, and such is the fundamental importance of this subject to Ghosh's overall body of work that it is necessary to analyse how each of the major works in turn wrestle and come to terms with the theoretical, methodological, political and ethical problems posed by historical knowledge and its various protocols. Once more, however, certain texts are inevitably more visible than others, with *In an Antique Land*, *The Shadow Lines* and *The Glass Palace* attracting the bulk of the chapter's attention.

Finally, Chapter 5 offers an overview of the extant criticism on Ghosh, a body of writing within which this book takes its place, to which it is related, and on which it has drawn for many insights and observations. The argument delivered in the course of this book, however, is an original one and not just a summary of previous critical positions. This final chapter will help orient the reader as to the specific claims made in this book and its relation to other critical perspectives, and it concludes with some reflections on the argument presented here and its contribution not only to the burgeoning critical work on Ghosh himself but also to the wider field of postcolonial studies.

The 'metaphysic' of modernity

During his fieldwork in Lower Egypt in 1980, Ghosh arranged to meet a local Imam reputed to be highly proficient in the practice of folk medicine. Since folk customs and knowledge were a matter of some relevance to his anthropological research, his meeting with the Imam was surrounded by the expectations established by professional anthropology's interest in 'primitive' or non-modern knowledge. In the event, Ghosh's expectations were confounded for the Imam had discarded his traditional medicine in favour of modern medical knowledge. Producing a hypodermic syringe as a talisman of the 'future', he advised Ghosh to forget about those 'discredited' superstitions. Having learnt 'the art of mixing and giving injections', for which there was a 'huge market' in his village, he had nothing but contempt for his inherited learning; Ghosh's interest in him as an embodiment of that knowledge in fact causes him grave offence.[1] When Ghosh met the Imam in the village square on another occasion, the latter taunted him about the Indian custom of cremation, which the Imam regards as 'primitive and backward'; unable to contain himself any longer, Ghosh exploded in fury and became embroiled in an argument about the relative development – and backwardness – of their respective societies.

Ghosh wrote up the episode twice. In the first, a short account entitled 'The Imam and the Indian' (1986), he focused almost entirely on the episode itself, although it is contextualised within the larger frame of his experience as an Indian in an Egyptian village. Ghosh would later incorporate it into the larger text of *In an Antique Land* as a poignant and pivotal moment that would dramatise the conjuncture of several threads in that narrative, some of which will be the focus of this chapter: the problem of 'Development' and 'Progress' in Third World societies; the discourses of the 'humane sciences' such as anthropology, and the ideological assumptions that govern them; the nature of science and technology and their relationship to violence. Although much of the detail of the episode remains intact in the later text, Ghosh makes some telling additions which magnify the significance of the episode the most important of which is the passage that explains his interpretation of the experience as paradigmatic of the wider cultural and intellectual defeat suffered by colonised peoples, 'we had demonstrated the irreversible triumph of the language that had usurped all others in which people had once discussed their differences … the universal, irresistible metaphysic of modern meaning' (IAAL, 236–7). The insertion of the complex word 'metaphysic' here is a bold stroke which confirms that by 'language' Ghosh does not mean a particular linguistic formation – such as English, or Arabic or Hindi – but rather a *rationale*, a general system of ideas and an ensemble of knowledge that enables a particular way of thinking and being which encompasses all aspects of experience. As such, it extends to the ways in which we think about space and time – the co-ordinates of our experience – as well as everything *in* space and time. This universalism enables the 'metaphysic of modern meaning' to become the common reference point for all people despite their differences, but paradoxically it is a universalism that is tied to a particular location – the West – at a particular moment in time, namely the 'modern' period. This is why its triumph is a matter of some regret for Ghosh because its universality is purchased at the cost of other non-Western, non-modern ways of thinking and being that have been lost or erased in the process.

The Imam episode suggests that it is science and technology that are the most visible signifiers of this metaphysic for both Ghosh and the Imam try, on behalf of their respective nations, to 'establish a prior claim to the technology of modern violence' such as 'tanks and guns and bombs' (IAAL, 236). Its 'grammar', however, is constructed out of the particular form of rationality that emerged in seventeenth-century Europe and was eventually organised in the doctrines of empiricism – which argued that all knowledge is derived from 'experience', experiment (the two words are, clearly, related) and the observation of phenomena – and positivism, which was based on empiricism but applied its methods to human activity thereby extending the influence of the 'natural sciences' into human society, culture and behaviour. This scientific 'Reason' saw itself as deriving knowledge from the world 'as it is' and thus science was seen as 'universal', value-neutral and disinterested. But it also saw knowledge as a source of power over the natural world, as a means of technical control. Therefore, scientific knowledge and technological development were from the outset embroiled in discourses of power and these translated easily from the mastery of 'Nature' into the mastery of other people. As the historian Gyan Prakash puts it, 'is it possible to deny the simultaneity of the formation of Western scientific disciplines and modern imperialism? One thinks, for example, of connections between the West's global expansion and the formation of the disciplines of ethnology, political economy, botany, medicine, geology, and meteorology.'[2] Far from being disinterested, science has always been implicated in politics and it has always been accompanied by an 'ideology of science' because it is always pressed into service on behalf of powerful interests. It is through the complex construction of scientific knowledge as a sign of power and authority that its force in the 'metaphysic of modern meaning' can be most acutely felt. For Amitav Ghosh, the Imam episode demonstrates how the evolution of modern knowledge into a metaphysic has had dramatic consequences in the colonial and post-colonial world, reshaping the environment, society, culture and mentality of its peoples.

Whilst the metaphysic of modernity was ideologically encoded within a range of knowledge disciplines that were disseminated by the colonial education system, it was science that was seen as the guarantor of the superiority of Western knowledge. It was the measure against which non-European peoples were judged.[3]

Whilst Macaulay's influence may indeed have inspired a colonial curriculum that gravitated around an education in the humanities, science remained the exemplar of Western Reason in the colonial imagination. In fact, the emphasis on the humanities could be seen as the other side of science's authority, reserving it for the West whilst other disciplines translated the 'metaphysic' of modernity into idioms capable of being recognised and assimilated by colonial subjects. That authority rested on the erasure and debunking of other ways of thinking, other systems of ideas, as being the antithesis of proper knowledge: non-Western epistemologies would henceforth be classified under the rubrics of religion, mysticism, superstition, and myth. Non-Western knowledge was quarantined as 'belief' and identified as irrational which in turn helped establish modern Western rationality as a universal Reason applicable to all times, all places, and all peoples.

But since it was clear that not all peoples possessed this rationality, how then could Reason be universal? This contradiction was resolved by the construction of a historical narrative of progress and development, which displaced the yardstick of scientific reason across time and measured non-Western peoples according to varying degrees of backwardness. The march of Reason through time coincided, therefore, with the march of the West across space – a justification for colonial power that is the subtext of 'diffusionist' histories of scientific achievement.[4] This possessed a distinct ideological advantage: scientific rationality was posited as an aspirational standard that could be attained but only in the future. In the meantime, colonial authority could be displayed – and legitimised – by staging scientific knowledge as a spectacle. This staging of science encompassed the construction of visible motifs of colonial authority such as the railway network, organised scientific exhibitions, and the building of colonial museums.[5] Such an emphasis on the visual was of course consistent with the logical premises of empiricism.

If colonial authority rested on the display of its Reason, its 'civilizing mission' nevertheless depended on the universalism of modernity's metaphysic, which in turn meant that it had to be made available to all. This raised a tricky problem. How are people who are as yet without scientific knowledge supposed to understand and absorb it? Resolving this problem would, in fact, dissolve those boundaries that policed the distinctions between the rational and the irrational, the scientific and the pseudo-scientific, knowledge from superstition. Prakash notes that 'addressing and reforming the eyes of such viewers demanded that science express itself as magic, that it dazzle superstition into understanding'.[6] Mesmerism, for example, emerged in British India as part of an effort to impress upon Indians the value of science but its scientific credentials were precariously perched between this desire to visibly demonstrate science and the scepticism of scientists themselves.[7] Pseudo-science was, therefore, as much part of the discourse of colonial science as other 'proper' sciences and this in turn destabilised the very notion of scientific rationality itself. The claims of colonial science are menaced by this unstable ambivalence about what actually counts as scientific knowledge, and the discourse of colonial science was constantly marked by the ghostly presence of those 'other' knowledges that it sought to marginalise or erase. Whilst, for example, the contribution of Indian scientists could be excised from the record of colonial scientific achievements, the dependence of colonial scientists on indigenous knowledges meant that the pressure these supposedly inferior epistemologies exerted on the dominant discourse could never be eliminated.[8] David Arnold notes that 'it is hard to see how, even at a superficial level, Western science could have functioned in many parts of the world without being able to draw upon "local" knowledge and "native" agency of various kinds … many of the scientific discoveries formerly claimed for the West have been traced back to earlier sources of indigenous knowledge'.[9]

The triumphant self-affirmation of Western scientific rationality as an enlightenment that banished the heathen darkness was therefore undercut throughout by its encounters with other knowledges, encounters it has sought to erase in order to project itself as a universal knowledge. Ghosh, however, seeks to reinscribe those encounters and to draw attention to the formation of scientific knowledge as a contested, collaborative and dialogic process that illuminates the colonial framework within which western scientific knowledge came into being. In *The Circle of Reason*, *The Calcutta Chromosome*, and *In an Antique Land*, Ghosh undertakes a deconstructive enterprise that seeks to reveal the gaps and fissures of modernity's metaphysic and thereby opens up a space for the exposure, if not articulation, of other knowledges, of other ways of thinking and being. It is perhaps unsurprising that, in this respect, he is at his most postmodern in these texts.

As its title suggests, one of the principal themes of *The Circle of Reason* is the concept of Reason on which the metaphysic of modernity rests and from which the authority of modern science derives. The novel's interrogation of Reason is achieved primarily through the characterisation of Balaram, who acts as a prism that refracts and magnifies the ideas that Ghosh wishes to explore. Through him, and despite him, Reason emerges as a far from straightforward concept, one far removed from the definition proposed by empiricism and positivism, which see it as a transcendent, transparent operation of human intelligence simply making sense of the world 'as it is' through sensory perception and logical cogitation. Balaram himself suggests a possible epigraph for the novel when he reflects, somewhat bemusedly, 'How tortuous … is the path of reason' (CR, 83). This is, however, a brief epiphany for a character shown throughout the novel's first section to be the epitome of the convoluted, paradoxical nature of Western, scientific Reason in the colonial and post-colonial milieu.

It is clear that Balaram is quite happy to see himself as the embodiment of Reason, and much of the novel's critique lies in its ironic distance from his self-description. He is an archetypal figure of the colonial subject as envisaged by colonial ideologues, a mimic man schooled in the historic achievements of Western knowledge. It is significant, for example, that the novel dwells on his experiences as a student at Calcutta's prestigious Presidency

College, the pre-eminent college of Calcutta University, which was established as Hindu College prior to the University itself. Built and financed by rich Calcutta *bhadralok*, Hindu College would be a monument to their engagement with Western learning, and the most important conduit for Western ideas in nineteenth-century colonial India. Though its importance began to decline along with Calcutta's in the twentieth century, it nevertheless remained a potent symbol of Bengal's – and India's – assimilation into modernity.

However, Balaram shows this assimilation to have been quite problematic, despite his investment in the 'ideology of science' that was promoted by the colonial educational system. He possesses an ardent belief in the universality of its metaphysic, which blinds him to its cultural origins in Europe and its colonial moorings, 'Science doesn't belong to countries. Reason doesn't belong to any nation. They belong to history – to the world' (CR, 54). His statement reveals the other dimension of modernity's metaphysic, namely a grand historical narrative of Progress. Following the German philosopher Hegel's conceptualisation of History as the universal unfolding of (western) Reason, Balaram subscribes to the linear narrative of scientific Progress that is indicated by such metaphors as 'Man's ascent to Reason' (CR, 39), or 'March of Reason', which he seriously proposes as a name for a department in his 'School of Reason' (CR, 117).

Believing as he does, like all nineteenth-century positivists, that Reason is manifested in the transcendent operation of universal 'laws' – of nature, of society, of history – he sees the history of science as a series of heroic discoveries by individual scientific geniuses such as Pasteur, whose biography, as written up by Vallery-Radot in his hagiographic *Life of Pasteur*, is one of Balaram's most prized possessions and a recurring motif throughout the novel, '[Balaram] began to read him [Alu] the chapter about that turning-point in *the history of the world* – 6 July 1885 – when Louis Pasteur took his *courage* in his hands and at the risk of his reputation … filled a Pravoz syringe and inoculated poor, hopeless ten year-old Joseph Meister, only that day ravaged by a rabid dog, with his still untested vaccine' (CR, 28, my emphases). But this heroic vision of scientific discovery overlooks what his friend Gopal already knows, that '[e]ven Reason discovers itself through events and people' (CR, 38). In other words, Reason is not transcendent at all but rather embodied in particular people and places at particular moments; that is, scientific reason is historically produced within given social *milieus* and not 'natural'. Texts like *Life of Pasteur*, by promoting the idea of the lone scientific genius who works in isolation and sees through the veil of reality to grasp the 'natural' laws of science actually reinforce a particular ideology of science that helps Western science to universalise itself and to write out of its history its contexts of production. Balaram unwittingly testifies to the social production of science when he suggests that Pasteur was first led to science, and to the momentous discovery of 'the Germ … as an answer to the everyday problems of simple people' (CR, 49), but this characterisation of science as an altruistic endeavour for the universal benefit of 'mankind' is nevertheless attached to specific social and economic interests, 'It was because the brewers of France came to him and said: What makes our beer rot? … Who did the silk farmers of Europe go to when disease struck their silkworms?' (CR, 49).

Indeed, one of the social and economic dimensions of Pasteur's science that Balaram overlooks is its implication in colonialism because the discovery of the germ was a key moment in the development of tropical medicine, 'a branch of healthcare which, in the nineteenth-century, was oriented towards maintaining the health of soldiers and administrators'.[10] In fact, Balaram's general emphasis on practical science as opposed to research mimics colonial attitudes to science in the colonies. It is only fair to point out that Balaram sees 'Pure' and 'Practical' Reason as two sides of the same coin, 'like two halves of a wheel: without one the other is incomplete and useless' (CR, 117). But his humiliation at the airport pushes him away from research scientists like Joliot-Curie – 'They were all the same, all the same, those scientists. It was something to do with their science. Nothing mattered to them – people, sentiments, humanity' (CR,

16) – and towards those 'practical' sciences so beloved of colonial administrators such as tropical medicine or phrenology, which he discovers whilst still smarting from his *faux pas*. Even before this episode Balaram had shown a marked inclination towards 'practical science', as is evident in his confrontation with the Rationalists at Presidency College when he first expounds on Pasteur's humanitarianism, of science as 'an answer to the everyday problems of simple people'. Indeed, despite his School of Reason being composed of Faculties of Pure and Practical Reason, the former teaches only practical skills – 'elementary reading, writing and arithmetic' – and disseminates the 'ideology of science' through 'lectures in the history of science and technology' (CR, 107).

In this way Balaram demonstrates his internalisation of the colonial ideology of science which stressed the importance of the colony as an arena for applied science – science made visible, as it were – or, at most, as a site of raw data (field research) which would then be processed back in Europe. In the colonial economy of knowledge, 'pure' or 'theoretical' research is reserved for and exclusively located in the West, and it then circulates around the colonial peripheries as applied science wrapped in Western flags and stamped with Western approval. Balaram assimilates this imagined map of knowledge and even institutionalises it in his School of Reason.[11]

Balaram thus enables Ghosh to open up the dark side of Reason to inspection. For instance, the invocation of phrenology and criminology – a correlate 'science' that Balaram also admires – illustrates how far removed the actual history of science is from its representation in grand narratives of scientific Progress. Far from being a series of discoveries of a transcendent Reason, the history of science is bound up with 'false' knowledges which once possessed the aura of scientific truth but which are now discredited.[12] Phrenology, which examined the shape and formation of the skull and interpreted these as signifiers of personality, and criminology, which identified persons with certain markings or 'stigmata' as being predisposed to criminality, were both hugely popular in the nineteenth century and considered scientifically robust. It is no coincidence that such discourses were particularly popular amongst colonial scientists, amongst others, for they were founded on racial and cultural prejudices that were prevalent amongst colonial administrators. These theories were derived from popular stereotypes of 'primitive', 'backward' and barbaric peoples, and the 'scientific' credibility of phrenology or criminology was established because they reinforced such prejudices by conferring upon them the respectability of 'scientific truth'. Thus, although such pseudo-sciences were applied within Europe with respect to the lower classes and other 'deviants' from the middle-class norm, they also demonstrate the *colonial* context within which modern scientific rationality emerged. Pseudo-sciences hold up a mirror to science in general and show how *all* scientific discourse is context-bound, value-laden and far from 'disinterested'.

Of course, Balaram's faith in these pseudo-sciences is heavily ironised. When Bhudeb Roy, for example, asks for Balaram's 'scientific' second opinion on the life prospects of his new son because the astrologers' predictions were not encouraging, Balaram solemnly declares that his son demonstrates all the signs of a 'Typical Homicidal'. In the event, the baby dies of pneumonia before he has had the chance to kill anybody thus ironically proving the astrologers correct after all (CR, 22–25). Ghosh deploys irony throughout the novel – it is perhaps the novel's single most important register – to deconstruct the idea of Reason itself. In contrast to the straightforward concept of reason put forward by empiricism, which universalises a particular form of logic, Ghosh uses irony to problematise the notion of logic itself. The operation of Reason in this novel is far from logical, to the point where 'logic' becomes so convoluted and twisted in reversals and paradoxes that the very idea of Reason as being founded on (Western) logic is thrown into doubt. To put it another way, Ghosh uses irony to introduce a series of reversals which demonstrate that reason is paradoxical not logical. As such, the Western concept of reason – which finds paradox to be a problem – is deconstructed.

This is the subtext of the theme of purity that runs

throughout the novel. Modern western logic, which is unable to tolerate paradox, delivers a knowledge that is compelled towards classification and categorisation and sees any contamination of its categories as a breach of the rules of Reason. When preparing to examine Alu's skull, for example, Balaram knows that he has to 'eliminate all taint of the haphazard' (CR, 25). Categorical knowledge is manifested throughout the novel, not least in the invocations of phrenology and criminology, which were deeply implicated in the formation of pernicious social classifications that have acquired the status of truth, such as race. Thus, we are told that in 1914, the year of Balaram's birth,

> an American judge in San Francisco, arbitrating on the second ever application by a Hindu for citizenship in the United States, took refuge in prehistory and decided that high-caste Hindus were Aryans and therefore free and white. And equally … the colonial government in Canada rewrote a different prehistory when it turned the eight thousand Indians on board *Kamagatamaru* back from Vancouver, after deciding that the ancient racial purity of Canada could not be endangered by Asiatic immigration. (CR, 39)

We shall examine the ways in which Ghosh tackles the social and political consequences of categorical knowledge later in this chapter. However, it can be noted from this passage that paradox emerges *despite* the categorical logic of modernity. Or, to put it more finely, it *coexists* with that logic because the same logic of racial purity that binds these two examples delivers contrasting – let us say, paradoxical – judgements. Despite its seeming emphasis on rigour, modern Reason is in fact extremely malleable. In the service of political interests, its logic can accommodate any number of convolutions, reversals, and contradictions.

It is therefore not surprising that despite Balaram's insistence that he and Bhudeb Roy are complete opposites, the text represents them as mirror images of one another because of their shared investment in the logic of 'purity'. For Balaram, this logic is played out in his obsession with hygiene, whilst for Bhudeb Roy it involves a talismanic belief in straight lines as signifiers of modernity, progress and civilisation, 'Look at Europe, look at America, look at Tokyo: straight lines, that's the secret' (CR, 99). Ironically, it is Shombhu Debnath, a weaver with no investment in modern reason who identifies their similarity, 'you're but two halves of an apple if you only knew it, one raw, one rotten, but the same fruit' (CR, 141). Despite this, Balaram and Bhudeb Roy become sworn enemies, and each ironically sees the other as his antithesis. Not only is Reason shown to be self-divided but also, in a further ironic twist, it is then shown to double back upon itself as it mutates into paranoia, obsession and madness. Again, it is ironic that it is Debnath, the weaver who exists outside modern Reason, who sees the truth, 'You must stop this: this is madness. There's no reason to go on like this. No reason' (CR, 142). And then, with precise irony he notes, 'You're the best sadhu I've ever known, Balaram-babu, but no mortal man can cope with the fierceness of your gods' (CR, 142).

Debnath touches here on the core of *The Circle of Reason* for throughout the novel it is clear that reason cannot exist without its 'others', that rationality is bound up with irrationality, that 'falsity' is as much part of knowledge as 'truth'. These paradoxes are what constitute Reason itself. It is only an illusion of knowledge to see it as context-free, limitless, and transcendent. Ghosh indicates this by invoking classical Hindu philosophy in the titles of each of his three sections: Satwa (reason), Rajas (passion), and Tamas (death). These three *gunas*, or strands, together make up the human personality. Each is bound to the other, and none can exist without the other.[13] He elaborates the point by offering another metaphor for Reason, which suggests that paradox is not a problem – that reason is, in fact, paradoxical. When Balaram tries to explain why he has apprenticed his nephew Alu to a weaver he excitedly suggests that it was but a natural choice because, 'Man at the loom is the finest example of Mechanical man; a creature who makes his own world as no other can, with his mind' (CR, 55). Balaram's voice is quickly dispensed with, however, and replaced by the omniscient narrator who goes on to suggest that weaving can be seen as a metaphor for an alternative, non-linear, non-categorical form of reason. Weaving, we are told, 'has never permitted the division of reason' (55), unlike modern scientific Reason, which tries to extricate itself from its other elements. The narrator goes on to suggest that the history of weaving is, in many ways, the history of Reason, which in turn is the engine of human history. In contrast to the view of reason as unbound and transcendent, the metaphor of weaving dwells on 'binding', 'it has never permitted the division of the world ... The whole of the ancient world hummed with the cloth trade ... All through those centuries cloth, in its richness and variety, bound the Mediterranean to Asia, India to Africa, the Arab world to Europe ... soon cotton was busy spinning its web around the world.' (55–6) And yet, from the outset of this long and complex passage, the other side of reason is acknowledged, 'The machine is man's curse and his salvation ... The loom recognizes no continents and no countries. It has tied the world together with its bloody ironies from the beginning of human time' (55). The 'hum' of the ancient cloth trade and the 'web' of cotton is balanced by the 'garrotte' of Lancashire mills. The passage ends by emphasising the paradoxical nature of the metaphor, 'It is a gory history in parts; a story of greed and destruction. Every scrap of cloth is stained by a bloody past. But it is the only history we have and history is hope as well as despair ... having once made the world one and blessed it with its diversity, it must do so again ... Weaving *is* Reason, which makes the world mad and makes it human' (57–8).

If reason is paradoxical, then the history produced *by* reason must also therefore be paradoxical. In contrast to the utopian idealism of the Enlightenment which envisaged a 'Pure Reason' advancing with great linear strides towards the future, *The Circle of Reason* offers a muted assessment of knowledge, seeing in it both profit and loss. Both Balaram and Alu initiate utopian projects that fall prey to the contingencies and contradictions of time, of everyday life, of those ironic reversals and unintended consequences that consistently thwart attempts to build a better world. Reason is, therefore, neither emancipatory nor necessarily oppressive. True, both Alu's and Balaram's projects end in disaster but the point is that such projects never could succeed because although they both find a rationale for their projects – hygiene and money (and insofar as Alu sees money as equivalent to the germ, his rationale is the same as Balaram's) – they are unable or unwilling to recognise that they are motivated as much by desire as by reason. The novel therefore argues that Reason will always be bound to its other side: desire, hope, despair, madness, obsession, and all those other elements of life that elude rational analysis. This is why the novel consistently traces the ironic reversals that reason is vulnerable to; why it demonstrates how trivial events such as a neighbourly feud or a shopping trip can be misread as threats to the state; why a naïve orphan can be mistaken for a political extremist. Such ironies demonstrate how larger purposes and meanings can explode out of trivial and seemingly meaningless events because, in fact, knowledge does not describe the world 'as it is' but rather expresses our *desire* to see order, coherence and purpose in the world, even when it is not warranted.

In his fourth novel, *The Calcutta Chromosome*, Ghosh would return to these problematic questions about science, knowledge and colonialism in a more sophisticated and aesthetically successful manner. In this later novel he would move his attention from pseudo-sciences and train his sights on orthodox scientific knowledge itself. Indeed, by focussing on medicine he wrestles with one of the cornerstones of modern scientific achievement, a science which perhaps more than any other was seen as *the* index of the superiority of Western scientific rationality and 'a sign of the progressive intentions and moral legitimacy of colonial rule in India'.[14]

As is the case in *The Circle of Reason*, *The Calcutta Chromosome* engages with the scientific legacy of an iconic figure in the grand narrative of Western scientific discovery and subjects it to post-colonial scrutiny. This figure is Sir Ronald Ross, who discovered that malaria is transmitted between infected persons by the female *anopheles* mosquito in Calcutta in 1897, for which he was awarded the Nobel Prize in 1902. Ross documented his research in his *Memoirs*, published more than twenty years after the achievement for which he is remembered. Unlike *The Life of Pasteur*, which is only used as a *leitmotif* in *The Circle of Reason* and never directly quoted, Ross's *Memoirs* operates as a key intertext and it has a significant presence in the discourse of the novel. Murugan, for instance, quotes sections of it verbatim though not without his tongue firmly in his cheek. Like *The Life of Pasteur*, however, Ross's memoirs project the heroic narrative of scientific discovery but *The Calcutta Chromosome* reads his narrative against the grain in order to deconstruct and displace it.

Scholars of medical history have noted that Ross's text is a highly biased account of the events which led to his breakthrough.[15] During his research Ghosh also noticed that there were several marginal references to Ross's household – in particular to 'Lutchman', his manservant – and that 'most of the connections [Ross made] came from his servants.'[16] Murugan's alternative account of Ross's discovery accordingly reverses the authority of the colonial situation so that whereas Ross had written about how he had performed experiments on unsuspecting Indians, Murugan claims that it was Ross himself that was being used, 'He thinks he's doing experiments on the malaria parasite. And all the time it's him who *is* the experiment on the malaria parasite' (CC, 78). This in turn reverses the direction of scientific knowledge and challenges the 'diffusionist' narrative of scientific discovery whereby knowledge travels out from the Western centre to the non-Western periphery. In so doing, Ghosh actually shows how subalterns and subaltern knowledges trouble the very concept of 'discovery' itself. For it is clear that at the margins of Western histories of science there is a tacit acknowledgment that colonial scientists, for example, drew on prevailing indigenous systems of knowledge, and that scientific knowledge was less a one-way process of scientific discovery than a dialogic process of interaction and interdependence.[17]

The Calcutta Chromosome occupies the margins of that grand narrative of Western scientific heroism and it seeks to displace the usual relationship between the West and its Others, metropolis and colony, centre and margin. It enacts three displacements in particular that are reflected in the structure of the novel, which can be seen as a series of interrelated displacements between narrative levels. The manipulations of time and space by methods which one critic has seen as equivalent to the 'film techniques of the cross-cut, dissolve and montage', enable the narrative to jump from one level to another that is removed in time and space but which nevertheless takes up where the previous level had left off, 'The quests that belong to different times and places and are motivated so differently are juxtaposed from the beginning of the novel: Antar's for Murugan, Murugan's for the truth behind Ross's research, Ross's for the malarial parasite ... Phulboni's for Laakhan, Farley's for Cunningham, and so on.'[18] These displacements create a narrative structure without a centre; there is no central character or event (there is a plurality of them, each with equal status). The effect is to create a 'marginal' or 'subaltern' text – that is, one that embodies the paradoxical idea of a margin *without* a centre.

In terms of the three thematic displacements in the novel, the first is the geographical one that positions Calcutta (and not New York, London, Oxford, Paris, and so on) as the site of scientific discovery. In fact, according to Murugan's counter-narrative, if Ross's research is indeed being directed by the mysterious Mangala-bibi and her cult of subalterns then scientific knowledge – at least in this instance – has its origins not in the West but in India. This geographical displacement reprises *The Circle of Reason* which, although it ironically demonstrates the belatedness of colonial knowledge through Balaram's espousal of discredited and outdated knowledge, nevertheless illustrates through references to J.C. Bose, Satyen Bose and C.V.Raman that Calcutta was by no means a scientific backwater.

The second displacement, which parallels the first, is a social and cultural one. It involves the displacement of scientific authority from the British to the Indian, and from the elite to the subaltern. Ghosh's rewriting of Ross's *Memoirs* is the crucial strategy in this respect. Ross repeatedly notes – with a mixture of anger and exasperation – the bureaucratic and political obstacles put in his path by the colonial state. This was clearly due to the prevailing ideology of science amongst colonial administrators who believed that only 'applied' science was appropriate for a colony, and were therefore not prepared to allocate 'any large outlay' in resources on scientific research, 'which must, however useful in its remote results, be immediately unremunerative'.[19] But whilst the standard narrative of Ross's discovery would emphasise the heroic individualism of the lone genius battling against the odds, *The Calcutta Chromosome* puts forward a different perspective. The function of the recurring trope of 'obstacles' and official hostility in the heroic narrative is to prove the worth and determination of the individual genius in the face of social, official and bureaucratic constraints – and Ross's narrative is no exception. Power and agency lies with the individual himself, who is the origin and centre of the narrative. In Ghosh's subaltern narrative, power is decentred and shifted not towards officialdom but into the hands of a number of subalterns who display an agency outside and beyond that of Ross or the official machinery of the colonial state.

The third displacement is an epistemological one that challenges the initial displacement or erasure of other epistemologies by modern scientific rationality. But Ghosh is not seeking simply to replace modern knowledge with 'other' knowledges. In fact, in *The Circle of Reason* he had parodied nineteenth-century attempts by *bhadralok* intellectuals to achieve parity with Western scientific knowledge by trying to 'Hinduise' science; the Rationalists' attempt to find antecedents to western science in ancient Hindu scriptures is represented as being absurd, and Ghosh also hints that J.C. Bose's attempt to dissolve the distinction between organic and inorganic, animate and inanimate matter was a brave but futile attempt to ground Western scientific rationality in the monistic philosophy of Vedantic Hinduism. Instead, Ghosh recognises the more profound point that the universalism of modern knowledge is founded in its monopoly of claims to 'valid' or legitimate knowledge – all 'other' knowledges cannot be admitted *as* knowledge. This raises a particular problem for any attempt to recover subaltern epistemologies: how is one to articulate these 'other' knowledges if the only language through which knowledge can be articulated *as such* is through modern scientific rationality? If, as had been claimed, modern scientific rationality is haunted by the erased presence of these other epistemologies, how can they be exhumed if the only means available is scientific rationality itself?

Ghosh's strategy is one that possesses considerable affinity with that of the post-structuralist philosopher Jacque Derrida, whose deconstructive philosophy admits that it is impossible to create from first principles an alternative to the prevailing logic of Western philosophy. This logic, he states, is that of the 'metaphysics of presence', a belief that meaning can be grasped in its entirety because it is 'present' in language. Language is therefore seen as a stable and transparent system of representation that unproblematically conveys its meanings when we communicate with each other. The metaphysics of presence underlies scientific empiricism, for instance, which believes that experience can be translated into knowledge by means of a stable and transparent language. Derrida's point is that the 'meaning' and 'truth' of experience can never be fully represented to us because it must be necessarily mediated by language, which is unstable and prone to a multiplicity of meanings. In other words, knowledge can never fully (re-)present the truth, a point that is acknowledged by Murugan, 'to know something is to change it' (CC, 104). Ghosh, then, must disavow any attempt to construct the subaltern epistemology as a 'presence' for that would involve a claim to knowledge and this would change it so that it was no longer subaltern. Murugan thus suggests that subaltern knowledge, 'would in principle have to refuse all direct communication, straight off the bat, because to communicate, to put ideas into language, would be to establish a claim to *know* – which is the first thing that a counter-science would dispute' (CC, 103). Paradoxically, then, the language of counter-science is 'silence'.

This staging of subaltern knowledge as anti-knowledge does at first seem to replicate the colonial monopoly of knowledge that Ghosh is challenging. Therefore, in order not to repeat colonial claims, Ghosh must find a means of representing counter-science as a knowledge that cannot be fully represented. First, this means a recognition that 'knowledge couldn't begin without acknowledging the impossibility of knowledge' (CC, 104). This rather paradoxical point, to which we shall return in due course, is a space-clearing gesture which enables Ghosh to suggest that *The Calcutta Chromosome* has set itself an impossible task, that its effort to represent subalternity is not fully achievable, that there is no means by which to represent 'pure' alternatives to modern knowledge. Indeed, the very notion of a pure knowledge cannot be admitted – whether modern or subaltern. Just as Ross depends, without knowing it, on the counter-scientific cult so too do they depend on Ross's science. The novel goes on to suggest, at its conclusion, that 'pure' knowledge is only possible if there is 'a single perfect moment of discovery when the person who discovers is also that which is discovered' (CC, 306). If this is the case, then the purpose of this counter-science is not the impossible salvage of subaltern knowledge but rather a deconstruction of the myth of scientific rationality, which bases its claim to 'pure' knowledge on the very concept of 'discovery' that is shown to be impossible. In fact, the denouement of *The Calcutta Chromosome* shows that such a claim is not based on scientific rationality at all because the 'single perfect moment of discovery' is a moment of *revelation*.

The discourse of scientific rationality is thus shown to be founded not only on 'Reason' but also on faith – faith in the metaphysics of presence. *The Calcutta Chromosome* executes a strategy whereby subaltern knowledge – all those pre-modern and/or non-Western forms of 'belief', 'superstition', 'myth', and 'religion' that were evacuated and distanced from modern 'knowledge' – is revealed (and not represented) as being secreted within the recesses of Reason itself. This troubles the discourse of modern science by contaminating it with its ghostly doubles. Hence the themes of occultism and Gnosticism that run throughout the novel. Gnosticism is registered in the Manichean dualities of 'matter and antimatter … rooms and anterooms … Christ and Antichrist … science and counter-science' (CC, 103), as well as through references to Valentinian cosmology, 'in which the ultimate deities are the Abyss and Silence, the one being male, the other female, the one representing mind and the other truth' (CC, 214).[20] It is interesting that Silence is associated here with femininity and 'truth' because, of course, whilst 'science' is represented by the male Ross, counter-science is associated with the female Mangala-bibi. That it is counter-science that is associated with the 'truth' alludes to the Gnostic belief in the *gnosis*, the secret knowledge that the flawed universe is created by a lesser God – a demiurge – and that beyond experience, beyond understanding lies the 'true' Creator who is unknowable.[21] By suggesting that truth is beyond knowledge, Ghosh is using a religious register to map the limits of scientific rationalism.

The haunting of scientific knowledge is also displayed through Ghosh's intertextual references to a number of ghost stories. This becomes evident during the story of Phulboni's visit to Renupur, which is one of the key episodes in the novel. There are at least three intertexts which overlap each other here. One is Charles Dickens's 'The Signalman' (1866), which is also set in an isolated location and contains a similar, sinister red lantern, and the motif of being run over by a train. Another is the story 'Smells of a Primeval Night' by the Hindu writer Paneshwarnath Renu (1921–77), who gives Renupur station its name. His story also involves isolation, and the motif of being run over by a train. In the story, it is difficult to distinguish between dream and reality, which is also the case with Phulboni's tale. The third intertext is to Rabindranath Tagore's short story, 'The Hungry Stones,' which Ghosh has translated, and which is well known amongst Bengalis.[22] Ghosh has spoken of this story as having been a key influence whilst he was writing *The Calcutta Chromosome*, and he describes it as 'a sort of elaborate metaphor of colonialism and this man looking for an identity'.[23] Like the main character of 'The Hungry Stones', Phulboni is presented as highly Westernised and they are both colonial representatives. The character in Tagore's story represents its bureaucratic arm as a collector of cotton tax; Phulboni, who works for a prominent British merchant, represents colonialism's economic wing. Like the other two stories, the location of Tagore's narrative – it is narrated to the frame narrator and his companion on a train – juxtaposes scientific rationality, as represented by the railways, with the supernatural subject matter. As such they all dramatise an encounter between scientific rationality and that which exceeds its understanding, between secular knowledge and non-secular beliefs in ghosts and spirits. This encounter can also be read as an allegory of the ethnological encounter between colonisers and colonised peoples and cultures.

If *The Calcutta Chromosome* reveals these 'irrational' forms to be intimately bound up with science then it dissolves the boundary between science and its others. This is clear from Ross's own discourse. His research is shown to be as much about belief as it is about knowledge, as much about faith as about reason. When Ross makes the connection between the mosquito and malaria he thanks 'the Angel of Fate', which earns him a sharp rejoinder from the abrasive Murugan, 'Angel of Fate my ass! With Ronnie it always has to be some Fat Cat way up in the sky' (CC, 77), and indeed Ross 'frequently brings religious imagery and allusions into his descriptions of scientific procedure' throughout his *Memoirs*.[24] Conversely, the truth-claims of discourses conventionally seen as non-scientific may be as valid as those sanctioned by legitimate forms of knowledge. Is a belief in immortality that is promised by genetic engineering any less dependent on faith than one based on a theory of reincarnation? The use of reincarnation in *The Calcutta Chromosome* challenges the colonial devaluation of Hindu 'superstition' but it also calls into question – using the metaphor of the chromosome – some of the wilder fancies of contemporary genetics.

As James Clifford has pointed out: 'Western science has excluded certain expressive modes from its legitimate repertoire: rhetoric (in the name of "plain", transparent signification), fiction (in the name of fact), and subjectivity (in the name of objectivity). The qualities eliminated from science were localised in the category of "literature"', and in this novel Ghosh dwells at length on the function of fiction and its relationship to knowledge.[25] Claire Chambers has suggested that *The Calcutta Chromosome* is 'playing with the notion of "science fiction"', not only by fictionalising the lives of scientists but also, 'with a playful twist ... [it] seems to suggest that many of the claims made for science are fictions'.[26] Indeed, one could take this further and show how the discourse of scientific rationality might be seen as a 'fiction' in the sense of its Latin root, *fingere*, 'to fashion'. For the fashioning of scientific empiricism is, as we have seen, based on the 'fiction' of 'discovery' that the novel deconstructs. Not only does it show that the 'perfect moment of discovery' is impossible, but it also represents one such fictional moment – Antar's 'crossing over' at the end – as the result of a carefully fashioned plot. In other words, it suggests that it is only *in* fiction that the fiction of the perfect moment of discovery can be represented. An ideology of science that is grounded in a concept of discovery but refuses to acknowledge that such a concept is not 'natural' but 'fashioned' – that is, culturally produced – is revealed to be duplicitous and dishonest.

The pun on the word 'plot' – of the novel, on the one hand, and of the 'conspiracy' on the other – is part of the novel's self-reflexive irony, which prevents it from losing its sense of critical distance from Murugan. For Murugan's desire to find proof of that which cannot be proven, and his desire to know that which must remain beyond knowledge, namely his desire to 'discover' the Calcutta chromosome, is lampooned by the text, which is aware that his notion of a counter-science is as metaphysical as the ideology of science. In fact, it is shown to be a mirror image of the science it contests. The text does this through the articulation of a minor chord that runs throughout the narrative focusing on the concept of 'coincidence'. The plot is actually driven by such coincidences, such as Murugan's ID card showing up on Antar's computer; his introduction to Tara by Maria; Murugan's choice of the Robinson Guest House; his encounter with Sonali Das and Urmila Roy at Phulboni's award ceremony; the fish-seller arriving at Urmila's door selling fish wrapped in newspaper Xeroxes that contain vital clues just when she needed fish, and so on. It soon becomes clear, however, that perhaps these are not coincidences but part of an elaborate pattern – a plot, one that encompasses every aspect of the narrative from

Ross's research, and the anomalous malaria attack in Antar's childhood village to the unfolding of events in the novel itself. The plot (as conspiracy) is thus a thematic parallel to the plot (as narrative structure). The careful plotting of the novel so that the conspiracy begins to expand to vanishing point is revealed in a seemingly inconsequential episode when Urmila Roy, seeking shelter from the monsoon with Murugan, begins to reflect on the 'coincidences' that had occurred to her that morning, 'It was so hard now to know what was a part of it and what wasn't: the kitchen window which looked out over the Haldar house, was that a part of it? Her parents? Her brothers … Was it a part of it that she was dressed in this horrible, dirty sari … ?' (CC, 219). Later in the novel there is an 'objective' corroboration of the extent of the conspiracy when it turns out that Mrs. Aratounian, Mangala's present incarnation, had ordered the removal of Murugan's items from her house even though he himself had no idea that he would be in Calcutta on that day, never mind in her house.

The 'plot' is thus a correlate of questions concerning chance (coincidence) and destiny (pattern). Murugan's faith in the all-pervasiveness of the 'Other mind' conspiracy is shown to be a mirror image of Ross's belief in Fate: the conspiracy theorist, like the believer in destiny sees order, pattern and design behind the seeming chaos or randomness of experience – as does the scientist.[27] The logic of the conspiracy theory drives Murugan to believe that the conspiracy can explain everything just as the scientist believes that, ultimately, science can do the same. Indeed, the universality of science rests on this belief. Murugan is used, therefore, to shine a reflective mirror on the metaphysical assumptions that lie behind scientific knowledge, which scientific discourse routinely disavows.

Unlike Murugan, Ghosh does not seriously propose a counter-science as an alternative to modern science. Rather the function of this tall tale is to put into question the 'official story' of Western science, and it is summed up by Murugan himself, 'Someone's trying to get us to make some connections; they're trying to tell us something; something they don't want to put together themselves, so that when we get to the end we'll have a whole new story' (CC, 216). The 'us' in this passage refers to us, the readers, as much as it does to Murugan. The serious purpose of this tightly plotted but tongue-in-cheek novel is to enable us to 'make connections' that may otherwise be obscured by the 'metaphysic of modern meaning'. Fiction is thus a ruse, a means of deconstructing scientific discourse from within so that we are able to see connections between science and 'other' knowledges that have been discarded or devalued in order to shore up the universality of Western science, or so that we might glimpse the hidden relation between 'rationality' and 'irrationality'. For instance, colonial medicine may have actually done more harm than good in many cases because it was often practised according to a set of 'irrational' beliefs and prejudices:

> physicians deployed a range of 'heroic' measures, including copious bloodletting, violent purges and the extensive use of mercurials that owed little, if anything, to indigenous practice but were adopted in the belief that the severity of disease in the tropics and the rapidity with which fatal symptoms developed there demanded a degree of 'boldness' that would 'surprise the practitioner in more temperate countries'. Thus, while decrying the use of 'dangerous' drugs such as arsenic and aconite by Indian physicians, European doctors were themselves engaged in acts of therapeutic violence that did more to swell the death-rate than effect lasting cures.[28]

The Calcutta Chromosome suggests that we re-read the historical record, uncover its subtexts, and rewrite its narratives so as to come up with a 'whole new story' about the meaning and value of science from a properly post-colonial perspective.

The metaphysic of modernity may be founded on scientific rationality but it is most effectively embodied and displayed as technology. The equivalence between science and technology, between scientific progress and technological development, is as much a feature of the popular discourse of science in the West as it is in the so-called developing world. It is, however, more

acutely imagined in the 'Third World' because although technology is presented in Eurocentric narratives and colonial narratives as a benign effect of modernisation – as proof of the benefits
of the 'civilising mission' – colonial societies have always seen
technology for what it is: a sign of power. Moreover, whilst they
may have subscribed to the view that technological development
might represent the universal 'march of Reason' – as the Imam
clearly does in *In an Antique Land* – they also recognised that
'technologies, like trade, came "wrapped in flags" and so politics was the most important factor'.[29] This was because technology in the colonies was a vehicle of *state*, and not social or
economic, development. Thus although technology signifies a
general 'ladder of Development' to such people as the Egyptian
fellaheen, development is itself particularly associated in their
minds with machineries of state violence. In *In an Antique Land*,
the narrator is mocked by the young Jabir for being naïve until
one day his standing improves dramatically because Jabir's rela-
tives purchase a water pump made in India. Later, the narrator
reflects, 'I tried to imagine where I would have stood in Jabir's
eyes if mine had been a country that exported machines that
were even bigger, better and more expensive – cars and trac-
tors perhaps, not to speak of ships and planes and tanks' (IAAL,
74). This logic reaches its apogee during the narrator's argument
with the Imam over which of their countries has 'prior claim
to the technology of modern violence … tanks and guns and
bombs' (IAAL, 236).

Technology thus manifests itself at the nexus of power and
knowledge that Foucault has called 'governmentality'.[30] This is
a neologism coined by Foucault to suggest that the techniques
of modern government are founded on the development of a
particular *rationale* – the 'mentality' of governance. According to
Foucault, governmentality emerged out of new ways of thinking
about the state and its relationship to society in early modern
Europe and so, in Ghosh's terms, one can say that governmentality is part of the metaphysic of modernity. Foucault defines
it as a form of pastoral power, 'To govern a state will therefore
mean to apply economy, to set up an economy at the level of

the entire state, which means exercising towards its inhabitants, and the wealth and behaviour of each and all, a form of surveillance and control as attentive as that of the head of a family over his household and his goods.'[31] The purpose is to deliver 'prosperity and happiness' because this theory of political power recognises that 'the real basis of the state's wealth and power lies in its population, in the strength and productivity of all and each'.[32] But the colonial state was not oriented towards the prosperity, productivity and happiness of 'all and each'. Rather the productivity of one section of colonial society – the subject peoples – was to be the basis for the prosperity and happiness of another, the colonisers. Colonial governmentality was therefore different to and distanced from the European model and it is in this gap that Ghosh sees another fissure in the metaphysic of modernity. Ghosh's critique of modern knowledge is also, therefore, a critique of (post-)colonial governmentality, and vice versa.

Ghosh sees the post-colonial state as an extension of its colonial predecessor, operating according to the same logics of governmentality and it is rarely, if ever, seen in positive terms. One can draw on numerous instances in most of Ghosh's novels where the state is seen as a threatening or obstructive presence, its will to knowledge a corollary of its coercive – as opposed to pastoral – power. In *In an Antique Land*, for example, the 'sly allegory on the intercourse between power and the writing of history' (IAAL, 82), includes an observation that 'a beribboned letter from the Vice-Chancellor of Cambridge University was no mere piece of embossed stationery: it was the backroom equivalent of an imperial edict' (IAAL, 91). In *The Circle of Reason* the entire sub-plot concerning Jyoti Das is an exploration of the post-colonial state's will to knowledge even if that will is subverted and lampooned, as we shall see. His most recent novel, *The Hungry Tide*, represents government servants and government machinery as a corrupt system of power which seeks knowledge only for the purposes of political control and believes other forms of knowledge to constitute a threat.

Foucault's notion of governmentality is based on the

scientific order that emerged following the rearrangement of knowledge in the 'classical' period of the sixteenth to eighteenth centuries in Europe. In *The Order of Things* he argues that this scientific order moved away from the late medieval and early Renaissance emphasis on knowledge as a demonstration of 'resemblances' between things: a knowledge that 'brings like things together and makes adjacent things similar, [for] the world is linked together like a chain'.[33] In the pre-classical – that is, premodern – period knowledge is thus 'coeval with the institution of God,' and discourse is linked to 'nature' by a language which 'is not an arbitrary system' so that 'nature and the word can intertwine with one another to infinity, forming, for those who can read it, one vast single text'.[34] For Foucault, modern knowledge dissolves this 'vast single text' according to 'a universal science of measurement and order' that is the basis of modern 'rationalism', and knowledge is arranged not in terms of 'resemblances' but in terms of systems of identities and differences that can be categorised and represented in the form of 'tables'.[35] Measurement and order – *mathesis* and *taxinomia* – are extended across the entire field of knowledge to encompass the social and the natural sciences, and it is this particular form of *categorical* knowledge that governmentality is based upon. 'Measurement and order' were translated into 'statistics' – i.e., as the name implies, 'the science of the state'[36] – that form the basis of the state's administrative apparatus. Statistics measured and ordered the population – itself a concept produced by statistics – into systems of identities and differences.

It is for this reason that 'identity' becomes increasingly important for modern government. If effective government must be grounded in the correct interpretation and management of statistics – produced by the census, and other social 'surveys' – which are representations of social identities, then effective government involves the management of identity. In that sense, governmentality *produces* identity as an effect of modern social scientific knowledge. The state must construct an identity, as it were, between itself and its population, and its legitimacy rests on that because '[i]n contrast to sovereignty, government has as its purpose not the act of government itself, but the welfare of the population, the improvement of its condition, the increase of its wealth, longevity, health etc.'[37] Colonial governmentality on the other hand was not based on an identity between the state and its population but on a *difference*, and this difference in turn limited the colonial state's interpretation and management of the identities of the population. The logic of the colonial state thus meant it could exercise sovereignty but not government and thus the colonised population could only be managed by coercion. Colonial governmentality therefore enacted a slippage from a state of 'police' – which is perhaps better rendered by the term 'policy' – to a 'police state'. Technological development in the colonies was always therefore oriented towards the maintenance and efficacy of the coercive apparatuses of the state. Foremost among these were those communication technologies which apologists for colonialism always boast about to justify the civilising mission – the railways, in particular, but also the telegraph system and the road network. The principal reason for the development of these was not so much the welfare of the population but for the deployment of the army, the police, and the colonial bureaucracy. It is no wonder, then, that *The Calcutta Chromosome* concentrates on locations that exhume this hidden rationale of colonial governance: Secunderabad, we are told, is a railway hub and a garrison town, and key episodes take place in or around railway stations.

Ghosh's work suggests that tragically the legacy of colonial governmentality continues in the rationale of the post-colonial state. It is therefore no coincidence that his critique of colonial and post-colonial governmentality focuses on elusive identities, or moments when identity becomes a problem for the state. The narrator of *In an Antique Land* discovers that his identity is suspect in the eyes of the Egyptian authorities because it does not conform to their expectations. Visiting the tomb of a Jewish saint in Egypt, but being neither Egyptian, Muslim, Christian, Jewish, nor Israeli, he eludes the categories that define the tomb in the eyes of the state. He is detained until his identity can be established and proven not to be a threat. Alu, in *The Circle of*

Reason, has no identity to speak of since he has no family and no identity documents. Clearly, his subsequent classification as a political extremist parodies the governmentality of the state, but he is classified as a fugitive precisely because he has no identity that the state can recognise. In a sense, he is a fugitive from identity itself. This is what defines the 'subaltern', for a subaltern is not merely dominated but also is not a 'subject' because s/he is not subject to the rationale of governmentality and eludes the categories that determine its policies.

On the boat to al-Ghazira, Karthamma is dimly aware that as a subaltern she has no identity or 'official' status, and she mistakenly invests her hopes for her soon-to-be-born son in the procurement of 'papers' that will confer an identity on her son so that he can be drawn into what she believes are the benign arms of a 'welfare' state, 'Someone's brought her onto the boat by making all kinds of promises – your child will be this, it'll be that, it'll have houses and cars … Sign a few forms and the child will be a Ghaziri' (CR, 177). The episode illustrates the ways in which bureaucratic governmentality produces identities as well as polices them but the situation is rendered ironically in order to emphasise the hopelessness of the subaltern situation because not only does the state misinterpret the subaltern but the subaltern also misinterprets the state. Karthamma invests her hope in the procedural practices of the state without awareness of the juridical aspects of the state which preclude recognition of any child born to 'illegal' immigrants. The subaltern and the state simply have no conceptual language in common. In fact, given what happens after the shopping trip, the episode reveals that, in many instances, elusiveness increases the subaltern's chances of survival.

The subaltern counter-scientific cult in *The Calcutta Chromosome* embodies this elusiveness. Their goal of interpersonal transference literally renders identity unstable and multiple. Mangala and Laakhan inhabit several identities – Lucky, Lutchman, Romen Haldar, Mangala, Mrs. Aratounian, Tara – and this constant switching of identities enables them to remain 'subaltern' even though, for example, their latter identities are rich and powerful and therefore occupy non-subaltern social positions. Romen Haldar, we are told, appeared at Sealdah station as if 'out of nowhere' and after the crossing disappears back into the subaltern void, leaving behind him merely the identity-effect of Romen Haldar that may be lodged somewhere as a ghostly presence in the official statistics. Such mutability delivers two key points. First, it reminds us that in the colonial context, 'identity' has always been problematic. The protagonist of Tagore's 'The Hungry Stones' constantly changes clothes and Ghosh reads this as 'a fable for switched identities' that represents the internal division of the colonial subject who aspires to modernity and Enlightenment universalism and yet is constantly held at bay by colonial racism.[38] Secondly, it challenges the notion of identity altogether. John Thieme argues that immortality through interpersonal transference erodes 'Western conceptions of discrete subjectivity through the dismantling ... of autonomous selfhood'.[39] Such dismantling of identity confounds governmentality.

Both *The Circle of Reason* and *The Calcutta Chromosome* suggest, however, that the very same technologies that enable and serve (post-)colonial governmentality may also offer opportunities for its subversion. The railway was a principal means of control, but it was also the means by which anti-colonial movements organised protests, drew disparate political arenas into a common cause and disseminated their ideologies. In short, the railways were a medium of resistance as well as repression. This is dramatised in *The Calcutta Chromosome* when Grigson, a member of the Linguistic Survey of India (and therefore part of the ensemble of knowledge that constituted colonial governmentality), is almost lured by Laakhan to his death at the rail junction at Secunderabad (CC, 92–3). This is reprised later in the novel when Farley is killed by a train at Renupur station, which symbolically renders this ambiguity in the status of the railways as a site of subaltern agency. Furthermore, the railways intensify the instability of identity. Martin Leer has perceptively pointed out that the railways 'engineered new possibilities for passage, where "Laakhan" may turn into a "Lutchman" by boarding a train to another station, and thus become harder for the (colonial) authorities to pin down'.[40]

In *The Circle of Reason* too the railways constitute an elusive subaltern network that lies beneath the palimpsest of governmental technology. With the help of a weaver caste – again, weaving is a positive and significant figure – Alu eludes the clutches of the police and intelligence services, moving from station to station, 'he passed down a chain of Rajan's Chalia kinsmen, scattered over every factory along the South-Eastern Railway' (CR, 157). Eventually, however, Alu has to leave the railways because although they may facilitate resistance to the state, they are nevertheless part of its infrastructure – he is spotted and a sketch is drawn up of him. Moving deep into territory beyond the infrastructure of the state, Alu is nevertheless constantly menaced by 'informers' and this recurring trope – the narrative is liberally populated by state informers such as Bhudeb Roy, Jeevanbhai Patel, Forid Mian, and Mast Ram – indicates that in every state governmentality is enabled by 'surveillance and control'. In this respect, it is worth remembering that Ghosh is not the first to represent the railways as arenas of contest between authority and resistance to it. Kipling's *Kim*, an imperial fantasy which proves that absolute surveillance is the precondition of colonial power, also locates the railway as the structuring principle of its picaresque, footloose narrative. And yet, as the novel bears out, surveillance and the categorical logic that underlies it are constantly thwarted, not only by that which eludes it but also from within. The logic of (post-)colonial governmentality is rendered absurd by the distance between its knowledge and reality. The surveillance on which it depends also distorts the knowledge that is derived because the state becomes embroiled in the petty politics of its informants. Alu becomes a fugitive because Bhudeb Roy's 'intelligence' is coloured by his feud with Balaram. As such, the state does not disinterestedly stand above the reality it seeks to govern using an 'objective' social science; instead it is ironically portrayed as merely one interest among others. Like Ronald Ross, it is manipulated without knowing it.

Jyoti Das's recognition of this fact, and his subsequent

abandonment of the chase in fact subverts the form of the detective thriller that this subplot gestures towards. Thrillers, spy fiction, detective novels and cognate genres – all of which, according to Yumna Siddiqi, can be drawn under the rubric of 'police fiction'[41] – are expressive modes that channel the metaphysic of modernity into particular narrative forms. Elizabeth Deeds Ermarth points out that 'in the telling and retelling of detective stories or stories with investigative interest we not only pursue particular truths, we also reconfirm a way of approaching questions of truth … one that values empirical procedure, reasoned discovery, problem solution, linear causality and temporal unfolding, individual subjectivity, and so on'.[42] Such narrative forms also thereby narrate the logic of governmentality, and therefore disruption of generic expectations constitutes a challenge to governmentality. In *The Circle of Reason*, not only does the detective give up, but he realises that there is in fact nothing to detect in the first place. The mystery is only a mystery from the point of view of the state, and not that of the reader because the novel gives the reader the ironic distance to recognise that the mystery is based on false premises. Reason and knowledge are not used to restore order but are shown to be somewhat unreliable and two simultaneous endings both thwart the generic conventions of police fiction. On the one hand, linear narrative development is undermined by the circular form of the novel which, in the words of one critic, 'is not a straightforward narrative but one full of resonances harkening back and forth like an unfolding raga circling and repeating notes and sequences of notes, each contextually different'.[43] Symbolically, this circular pattern is verified by Alu's return to India at the end. On the other hand, the traditional 'closure' of the detective novel is disrupted by the novel's open-endedness, with Jyoti Das refusing to return to the order of his home and career and instead journeying on to Europe. The novel therefore ends with a 'beginning' – this being the final word.

   The Calcutta Chromosome is also part-thriller, but whereas *The Circle of Reason* had juxtaposed police fiction to elements of fantasy or magic realism, the latter novel generically splices the thriller with ghost stories and science fiction, each of which also are implicated in the metaphysic of modernity (especially if the ghost story functions as a means of shoring up conventional rationality). Ghosh, however, chooses to use them in ways that offer more radical interpretations. Ghost stories, for instance, can actually disturb conventional rationality by dwelling on the 'uncanny' that remains inexplicable, and the careful plotting of *The Calcutta Chromosome* delivers many such moments, particularly the Renupur episode. Science fiction, too, can open up a radical perspective on current ways of thinking by estranging the reader from their familiar milieu and using an imagined future to stretch the limits of possibility or credibility. Although the World Wide Web now functions in ways that would perhaps not have been imaginable in 1995 when *The Calcutta Chromosome* was published, science fiction enables him to use the web to subvert the conventions of the mystery thriller. Thus science fiction is the means by which police fiction and governmentality is subverted, and his choice of the Web is an apposite one for the Web eludes and exceeds governmentality by rendering space, time and identity virtual.

The Web also operates as a metaphor for the structure of the novel itself which, as we have seen, consists of several narratives that are laterally placed alongside each other between which the narrative shuffles in a non-linear manner that mimics the hypertextuality of the Internet. The paradigm of the 'network' indicates Ghosh's affiliation to a postmodern assault on Enlightenment conceptions of knowledge and rationality. Following George Landow, Claire Chambers has noted that French postmodern and poststructuralist thinkers like Foucault and Derrida show a 'predilection for imagery such as "link (*liaison*), web (*toile*), network (*reseau*) and interwoven (*s'y tissent*)"'. This indicates 'a paradigm shift that has taken place in recent conceptual enquiry', which has sought to 'abandon "conceptual systems founded upon ideas of center, margin, hierarchy, and linearity" and replace them with models based on "multilinearity, nodes, lines, and networks"'.[44] The structure of *The Calcutta Chromosome* thus attempts to represent a new, postmodern framework for posing questions about truth based on these alternative models.

Similarly, *In an Antique Land* is structured as what Ghosh calls a 'double-helix' that moves back and forth in time and space through a 'network of foxholes' (IAAL, 16) and this reminds us that the Web in *The Calcutta Chromosome* is only one manifestation of a metaphor that runs like a thread through Ghosh's oeuvre. Networks are but a variant on the weaving metaphor that Ghosh introduced in his first novel and which reappears in almost all his texts. It stands for a non-coercive, non-linear, non-categorical knowledge that deconstructs notions of centre and periphery, and challenges in particular a Eurocentric grand narrative of history. Weaving is also a metaphor for fiction, as is indicated by the pun on the word 'yarn' in this passage in *The Circle of Reason*, '[t]he essence of cloth – locking yarns together by crossing them – has not changed since prehistory,' which follows a passage a couple of paragraphs earlier that states, 'A loom is a dictionaryglossarythesaurus … the weaver, in making cloth, makes words' (CR, 74). It is to fiction, then, that Ghosh looks for an alternative rationality but in the long passage in *The Circle of Reason* when the weaving trope is first introduced, Ghosh recognises the fragility of the kinds of reason that weaving might represent, and its vulnerability to the power of technology and those who wield it, 'When the history of the world broke, cotton and cloth were behind it; mechanical man in pursuit of his own destruction … The machine had driven men mad' (CR, 57).

Amitav Ghosh's concern is not just, therefore, with the epistemic violence that erases other epistemologies but also the actual physical violence of the state and its technologies of power. In *Dancing in Cambodia, At Large in Burma*, as he wanders among the ruins of a Cambodia devastated by genocide, he reflects upon the paradox of a rationalism that could engineer the modern world through the mechanisms of modern government, and yet also devastate it, 'They [the Cambodians] had lived through an experience very nearly unique in human history: they had found themselves adrift in the ruins of a society which had collapsed into a formless heap, its scaffolding *systematically* dismantled, picked apart with the tools of a murderously rational form of social science' (*Dancing*,17–18, my emphasis).

This chapter has thus far examined how Ghosh explores the meta-physic of modernity with respect to science and social science, but the metaphysic also extends to what may be called the 'human' sciences such as history, anthropology, literary studies and so on. Ghosh's own academic training was in anthropology, which was a discipline that emerged in a colonial milieu – and, in very fundamental ways, was only made possible by it – alongside the natural and social sciences. But as part of the 'human sciences', its disciplinary status has always been somewhat ambiguous. As a 'science' it aspired to the rigorous methodology and objec-tivity of the natural sciences; and yet its authority rested on the subjective experience of fieldwork, on the personal testimony of the ethnographer. This tension between subjective and objec-tive knowledge, coupled with its colonial origins had a profound impact on the disciplinary protocols of anthropological know-ledge and its articulation through ethnography.

Perhaps more than any other discipline it has contributed to the translation of the metaphysic of modernity into an ideolog-ical formation that justified colonialism and continues to justify Eurocentrism. It does this by writing cultural descriptions of Other peoples and then organising the distribution of human cultures in space and time according to an ideological hierarchy which positions modern Western society as the cultural norm. All other cultures are arranged in relation to this reference point, both spatially and temporally: the modern *west* is deemed to constitute the historical 'now', and the *difference* of other cultures is measured in terms of their *distance* from it, spatially in terms of 'remoteness' or 'insularity', and temporally in terms of 'backwardness' or 'primitivism'. In other words, anthropology shores up the centrality of European culture by translating difference into distance; it is, in the words of Johannes Fabian, 'a science of other men in another Time'.[45]

The protocols of anthropological knowledge contribute to

what Fabian calls the 'denial of coevalness', which is an ideological disavowal of the fact that the contemporary world is made up of different cultures and societies which inhabit the *same* space and are as much part of the historical 'now' as the modern West, that their difference is not a sign of their primitivism or backwardness. Coevalness, on the other hand, imagines the world as plural and contested, and not as an expression of the universality of Western culture. The denial of coevalness is built into the writing up of anthropological knowledge even though the subjective experience of fieldwork recognises the coevalness of the researcher and those whom s/he is researching.[46] Whilst the gathering of anthropological knowledge *must* involve intersubjective encounters with the Other, the aspiration of the discipline towards 'science' impels ethnography towards the elimination of this subjectivity in the interests of 'objectivity' and 'rigour'. Intersubjective encounters – which may include conversations, jokes, arguments, gestures, and emotional and psychological investment in one's interlocutors – are translated into information and 'data', people into 'objects'. This is the function of what is known as 'the ethnographic present', which delivers a seemingly 'objective' perspective by removing the presence of the ethnographer; the participant-observer becomes less a participant, and more an observer whose perspective is external to the observed culture. The result is that the Other is represented as if frozen in time: the present tense objectifies the Other culture and denies it any sense of change, dynamism, and development. This in turn verifies the idea that such a culture is 'backward'; literally frozen in time, they are left behind by History.[47]

Anthropology thus acts as History's other side, as a kind of epistemological 'dustbin' which helps to hive off other cultures and their forms of knowledge through a rhetoric of *historical* supercession. It thus helps modern knowledge universalise itself by erasing the marks of its encounter with other knowledges, an erasure that is done in two complementary ways. First, through a literal excision by which other forms of knowledge are written out of the history of knowledge. Second, through a more metaphoric erasure that is paradoxically achieved through display, but display in a particular form: the exotic display of anthropological knowledge. In ethnographic texts, in museum displays and glass cabinets, 'other' forms of knowledge were displayed not as evidence of a 'simultaneity of different, conflicting, and contradictory forms of consciousness,' but as outdated, mythical, poetic, superstitious – the consciousness of 'other men in another time'.[48]

Anthropology is thus one of the key props on which western scientific universalism rests, and to challenge the metaphysic of modernity one must challenge anthropology and its proto-cols. One must, in other words, find new ways of writing about cultural difference that do not deny coevalness. This underscores Ghosh's attempt to engage with the 'subaltern' throughout his career and *In an Antique Land* represents this effort at its most sustained and successfully achieved.

If the authority of ethnographic discourse simultaneously rests on participant-observation and on the erasure of the ethnographer's presence in its writing up, *In an Antique Land* both reinscribes the presence of the ethnographer and reverses his authority.[49] The passages set in Lataifa and Nashawy are staged as intersubjective encounters, as dialogues and confronta-tions with interlocutors who refuse to be merely observed and instead interrogate *him* rather than the other way round. In a series of episodes that escalate into the narrator's furious alter-cation with the Imam, his ethnographic authority is contested and diminished. In fact, in a reversal of the procedure by which the ethnographer takes it upon him/herself to translate differ-ence into distance, it is *they* who distance Ghosh by translating his religious difference from them into an inexplicable and abso-lute Otherness. In an early episode, Ustaz Mustafa adopts the role of the knowing observer, ' "I have read all about India"', as a point of departure for the articulation of a series of stereotypes, 'There is a lot of chilli in the food and when a man dies his wife is dragged away and burnt alive … it's cows you worship, isn't that so?' (IAAL, 46, 47). Ghosh's encounters in Lataifa and Nashawy are written up as a repetitive cycle which constantly gravitates around a set of core differences such as cremation, cow-worship, and circumcision that serve to shore up the authority of Islam for the villagers in a reversal of the way that anthropology is used to shore up the authority of the West. In another episode, Ghosh's authority is diminished by the young Jabir who equates him with a child when he witnesses Ghosh's surprise at seeing ducks mating. Acquiescing in the ridicule by feigning ignorance of sex, he allows Jabir – at least temporarily – to position himself in a position of superiority, '"But he doesn't know a thing," said Jabir, "Not religion, not politics, not sex, just like a child"' (IAAL, 63). Samir Dayal has noted that this 'ironic self-deflation of the observer' may be an attempt to ground his writing of cultural difference in an ethical mode that respects the Other, a respect he implicitly finds wanting in standard ethnography.[50] Ghosh's authority is only restored in Jabir's eyes by the 'Indian machine' episode, which in the eyes of the *fellah* invests him with the 'delegated power of technology' (IAAL, 74). It is a reminder that Ghosh's formal experimentation is nevertheless merely a tempo-rary disturbance of the power relations that underscore the rules of anthropology. The metaphysic of modernity remains, in the final instance, intact not least in the eyes of the *fellah* them-selves. Despite this, Ghosh's ethical decision to refuse complicity with its discourse remains a valid one.

This recuperation of the intersubjective dynamics of the 'fieldwork account' not only challenges the objectification of the Other, but it also illuminates just how much is lost when field-work is written up as ethnography. Mary Louise Pratt has noted that the pressure to translate subjective experience into objective science does not, in fact, erase subjective accounts altogether but rather displaces them into 'prefaces' which operate as a legiti-mate space for narration of those aspects of fieldwork that do not constitute 'proper' – that is, scientific – knowledge. These prefaces also testify to the personal experience of the fieldworker and thus help establish the authority of the 'objective' account that will follow. Citing Malinowski's classic account in *Argonauts of the Western Pacific*, she notes that these prefaces usually begin with a scene of 'arrival at the field site'.[51] Ghosh, in contrast, begins his by dreaming of *leaving*. Moreover, the 'fieldwork account' also indicates how anthropology had its origins in travel writing, an origin it seeks to disavow as it becomes a 'scientific' discipline. But travelogues have shadowed 'professional' anthropology as an alternative discourse that nevertheless often shares its 'objectifying gaze'. Therefore subjectivity does not in itself constitute a resistance to the assumptions of ethnography. Indeed, travelogues are often more effective at disseminating those assumptions because they are more popular. European travelogues during the colonial period cemented the denial of coevalness by reserving the dynamism of travel for the European observer, thereby rendering the observed as static peoples and cultures. In addition to reinscribing intersubjectivity into *In an Antique Land*, the text is also a travelogue in which Ghosh is not the only traveller. Indeed, it soon becomes clear that the villagers are far from static and sedentary,

> The area around Nashawy had never been a rooted kind of place; at times it seemed to be possessed of all the busy restlessness of an airport's transit lounge. Indeed, a long history of travel was recorded in the very names of the area's "families" ... That legacy of transience had not ended with their ancestors either ... some men had passports so thick they opened out like ink-blackened concertinas. (IAAL, 173–74)

As James Clifford acknowledges, this complicates the concept of a 'field' itself, never mind the 'field account'. 'The anthropologist can no longer see himself as a (worldly) traveller visiting (local) natives. [Ghosh's] "ancient and settled" fieldsite opens onto complex histories of dwelling and travelling, discrepant cosmopolitanisms.'[52] Deconstructing the concept of the 'field' also disrupts the allochronic – Fabian's term for the denial of coevalness – logic of anthropology, which needs discrete and 'closed' cultures so as to organise them hierarchically in relation to the 'cosmopolitan' West. Here, Ghosh undermines that logic, showing Western cosmopolitanism to be only one among other cosmopolitanisms. Cosmopolitanism therefore rests not on the universalism of western knowledge but rather on the 'complex histories of dwelling and travelling' that are a feature of many other societies. Furthermore, if the notion of the 'field' is dismantled, then the identity of the West is too – that field known as the West is itself shown to be a construct that glosses over its own hybrid formation.

Ghosh also challenges the scientific pretensions of ethnography by evoking those modes of writing that have been expelled from ethnography in order to present anthropological knowledge as 'scientific'. The exclusion of 'rhetoric (in the name of "plain," transparent signification), fiction (in the name of fact), and subjectivity (in the name of objectivity)',[53] is precisely why *In an Antique Land* is so self-consciously literary, why it begins with a heavily rhetorical flourish – 'The Slave of MS H.6 first stepped upon the stage of modern history in 1942. His was a brief debut, in the obscurest of theatres … ' – and why, despite Ghosh's own insistence that it be categorised as a work of non-fiction, it is nevertheless appropriate to think of it as a 'fictive ethnography'.[54] The 'bucolic' narratives in Lataifa and Nashawy may indeed be accounts of actual events and experiences, but they are 'fictional' in the sense that they are 'fashioned' – and they are fashioned precisely in order to draw attention to their fictionalisation. This is principally achieved through narrative doubling, whereby themes and events in the 'historical' narrative that traces Ben Yiju and Bomma are echoed in the bucolic narrative or vice versa. Thus, for instance, there is the possibility of a blood feud in both narratives; in both we have the presence of romantic love – that between Ben Yiju and his wife, and that between Eid, the fellah, and his beloved – both of which transgress class and cultural barriers; there is a case of sibling rivalry in both narratives; and this doubling across time is itself paralleled by doubles across space: there are nearly identical stories of a modern road having to swerve past a shrine in both Egypt and India.[55] A comparison with Ghosh's article 'The Slave of MS H.6', which is one of the antecedents to *In an Antique Land* is instructive because none of these doubles are present in that text. However we might interpret these doubles in terms of Ghosh's overall project – which will be addressed in both Chapters 3 and 4 – one thing is clear: *In an Antique Land* is a clearly 'fictionalized' text that distances itself in its very form from the metaphysic of modernity as embodied in orthodox ethnography.

One final aspect of Ghosh's engagement with the protocols of ethnography is worth comment. Johannes Fabian has suggested that the method of participant-observation is based on an ideology of visualism, which believes that 'sight' is the 'noblest sense' and that 'knowledge is based upon, and validated by, observation'.[56] 'Among all the tenets of empiricism,' he adds, 'this one seems to have been the most tenacious'.[57] Visualism is thus one of the key features of the metaphysic of modernity, and Ghosh offers a challenge to visualism in both *In an Antique Land* and *The Calcutta Chromosome*. In the latter, occultism is used as a trope for the opacity of subaltern knowledge, which prioritises 'invisibility' over visibility. In *In an Antique Land*, Ghosh problematises the 'eye' of the observing 'I', thereby undercutting the epistemological basis of participant-observation. There is, in fact, an intriguing pun on 'sight' because Ghosh's visits to various 'sites' occasion failures of 'sight', 'There is nothing now anywhere within sight of the Bandar to lend credence to the great mansions and residences that Ibn Battuta and Duarte Barbosa spoke of' (IAAL, 243); or again, 'Fustat can be smelt before it is seen' (IAAL, 38). Leela Gandhi has perceptively noted that: 'History, in Ghosh's understanding, is almost always pathologised as a chronic condition of poor or bad visibility.'[58] Thus, Ghosh seeks 'the barely discernible traces that ordinary people leave upon the world' (17); Nabeel 'vanishe[s] into the anonymity of History' (353); and the metaphors of 'trapdoors' and 'foxholes' (16, 17). Undoing the dependence of 'insight' upon 'sight', Ghosh offers an opening into those cultural practices which do not privilege the visual, and sometimes even see the 'eye' as the least perceptive and most deceptive of organs.[59]

In all these ways, Ghosh wrestles with the colonial legacy and implications of anthropological knowledge. But in another sense, his work is deeply attached to one of its core principles, namely humanism. In fact, anthropology was instrumental in the articulation of modern humanism in the nineteenth century as *the* 'science of Man'. However, it paradoxically also divided 'humankind' and, in the course of its establishment as a 'science', helped to define 'humanity' in ways that served colonial interests. It thus reaffirmed rather than challenged Eurocentric and racist prejudices and in so doing exposed the transcendental humanism of nineteenth-century Europe as a convenient myth which could be used as a vehicle for certain political ideas, such as the 'civilising mission', that gave ideological cover to inhumane colonial practices. It is clear, however, that although Ghosh may want to deconstruct ethnographic discourse, he does not wholeheartedly want to throw the baby out with the bathwater. In fact his revised ethnography, by reinscribing the intersubjective encounters and restoring the principle of 'coevalness' between cultures, seeks to promote a renewed understanding of 'humanity' not as a transcendent myth but as an embodied, culturally bound and inescapably plural species. It is perhaps not surprising, therefore, that he challenges the metaphysic of modernity by deploying one of its most alluring and humanistic forms – the novel. But if this seems somewhat paradoxical, then it must be remembered that the novel has a somewhat ambivalent relationship to the metaphysic of modernity. It is simultaneously one of its exemplary forms and marginal: it is 'non-scientific' and therefore not a 'truth-bearing' discourse. On the contrary, Ghosh cherishes it precisely for its unscientific nature, believing it can thereby capture the truth of humanity in ways that elude or are overlooked by 'science'. Indeed, he has said that it is precisely fiction's ability to slip beyond the 'metaphysical' that interests him, and this is why he gave up anthropology, 'At one point in my life I was doing anthropology. But I realized very early on that anthropology was not of interest to me in the end because it was about abstractions, the way you make people into abstractions ... my real interest is in the predicament of individuals.'[60]

This humanist vision draws on the notion of an 'encounter' that anthropological science routinely erases from its own discourse, because it sees in the trope of 'the encounter' a means by which to recuperate the plurality of being in the world, the richness of human diversity. Throughout Ghosh's work he dramatises the 'encounter' – of peoples, cultures, ideas, and epistemologies – in order to challenge the binary logic of modernity. For him, the encounter between a Self and an Other is not a binary phenomenon as it has been seen in modern Western philosophy since Descartes. Instead the encounter produces a 'third' term in the hybrid space *between* the one and the other, a 'third' presence that is neither one nor the other but something else besides.[61] The boundary between Self and Other – which is precisely the place that ethnography dwells – is, according to the German philosopher Martin Heidegger, 'not that at which something stops but … that from which something begins its presencing'.[62] This something is the third term that loosens the binary opposition on which the metaphysic of modernity is constructed. This hybrid presence must be effaced if the binary logic of modernity is to be maintained, and thus the encounter must also be erased. The history of knowledge according to the West is one that systematically erases its encounter with other ways of thinking and being in the world because that is how it manages to see itself as 'universal'. These other knowledges are displaced and devalued: they become the opposite of knowledge.

Ghosh, however, suggests that Western knowledge is itself the product of those encounters – that beneath the binary rhetoric of universalism is a history of hybridity. The 'third' term silently haunts the gaps and fissures in the metaphysic of modernity and it emerges when knowledge is made to own up and confront its limits. Ghosh signals this third term by invoking numerous 'trinities': there are three sections to the *Circle of Reason*; there are three cities in *The Shadow Lines* – London, Calcutta, Dhaka – as well as three generations and three families; in *In an Antique Land*, the Indian Ghosh and the Egyptian *fellah* constantly refer to a 'third' (the West), and this is turn reflects the triangular geopolitical relationship by which Western power inevitably mediates the relationship between 'Third World' countries such as Egypt and India; there are also, in fact, three timelines in the text, not two as is often supposed – the medieval one, Ghosh's visit in 1980, and Ghosh's visit in 1988; in *The Calcutta Chromosome* there are three railway stations – Renupur, Sealdah, and Penn

Station – and three 'contemporary' researchers – Antar, Murugan and Urmila – who parallel three 'historical' ones: Ross, Mangala, and Laakhan; in *The Glass Palace* there are three families again – the Burmese royal family; Saya John's; and Dolly and Rajkumar's; and so on. The specific significances of these trinities will be explored in Chapters 3 and 4, but here we can say that the ubiquity of the figure of the 'trinity' in Ghosh's work signals two things. First, there is an 'excess' to the binary logic of modernity that will always emerge because the metaphysic of modernity can never capture, contain, or erase the plural ways of being in the world. Secondly, the hybrid space of the 'third' term is an ambivalent one, inevitably speaking against the metaphysic of modernity from within and through its prevailing forms of knowledge; Ghosh's fiction is therefore ineluctably bound to it even as it desires to move beyond.

Looking-glass borders

At the end of the main narrative of *In an Antique Land* (i.e. before the Epilogue), Ghosh recounts his abortive visit to the tomb of a local medieval saint, Sidi Abu-Hasira, in the nearby town of Damanhour. The Sidi had been Jewish, and his tomb therefore attracted a large number of Israeli visitors following the peace treaty signed by Egypt and Israel in the late 1970s. Being neither Jewish nor Israeli nor Egyptian nor Muslim, Ghosh is denied access and even arrested until a senior police officer establishes his identity and the reason for his visit. Ghosh realises that 'there was nothing I could point to ... that might give credence to my story – the remains of those small, indistinguishable, intertwined histories, Indian and Egyptian, Muslim and Jewish, Hindu and Muslim, had been partitioned long ago' (IAAL, 339). The tomb represents 'an anomaly within the categories of knowledge represented by those divisions' (340) – hence the presence of the Egyptian state's security apparatus. The episode thus illustrates the policing of identities by modern nation-states whose histories have been reconfigured in order to 'confirm a particular vision of the past' (95). Or, to put it in a slightly different manner, it highlights how 'the map of modern knowledge' is pressed into the service of nation-states.

The figure of the 'map' draws attention to the spatialisation of the 'metaphysic' of modernity into a geo-political system. The sense of absolute Otherness that Western scientific rationality projects onto different systems of knowledge therefore has political consequences that have shaped the modern world. The notion of a pure and authentic cultural identity – a Self – that is posited against an absolute Other was most influentially realised in the formation of nation-states and national traditions.[1] Anomalies in these traditions – such as the Sidi's tomb – serve as embarrassing and disruptive reminders of pre-modern, pre-national pasts that nationalists would prefer to forget because nation-states imagine themselves to be the political expression of 'natural' and primordial cultural units.[2] *In an Antique Land*, like most of Ghosh's work, constitutes a sustained critique of such claims.

It is worth examining this episode in a little more detail as it sheds some light on the particular shape and force of Ghosh's engagement with nationalism throughout his career. Having introduced the motif of the 'map of modern knowledge', Ghosh goes on to demonstrate how 'the patterns of the Western academy' had been rearranged to conform to it. Searching for information about the Sidi in Western libraries under the headings of 'religion' and 'Judaism', he can find no mention of the saint until he looks up sections on 'folklore'. We shall return to this significant distinction between 'religion' and 'folklore' in due course, but for now it is worth concentrating on the way in which Ghosh shows us how 'religion' is realigned along national traditions. This has been a key theme throughout *In an Antique Land* and Ghosh's deployment of the term 'partition' when discussing the 'partitioning of the past' is extremely significant. For Ghosh, indeed for most Indian intellectuals, the term 'partition' carries resonances that extend well beyond the literal meaning of the term, invoking as it does the catastrophic events that accompanied the 1947 Partition of the Indian subcontinent into the two nations of India and Pakistan at the moment of independence from colonial rule. The resulting triangle of associations between 'religion', 'nationalism' and 'partition' in an episode which brings to a head some of the most pressing concerns of the narrative perhaps obliquely indicates how his critique of nationalism in *In an Antique Land* has its source and motivation in anxieties generated by the politics of identity in the Indian subcontinent. Such anxieties predate *In an Antique*

Land, and they inform nearly all of Ghosh's writing from *The Shadow Lines* onwards.

The Shadow Lines probably represents Ghosh's most direct confrontation with nationalism and national identity. It is unsurprising, therefore, that the motif of the map appears throughout the text – the Bartholomew Atlas, the *A–Z*, the floor plans of houses, real and imagined – as the vehicle for some of its most significant episodes. Perhaps the most important of these occurs when the narrator, after having discovered the connection between his uncle Tridib's death and the riots he had been caught up in as a child in Calcutta, takes his Bartholomew Atlas and, with the aid of a 'rusty old compass', begins to draw geometric circles that teach him the 'meaning of distance' (SL, 227). Positioning his compass needle on Khulna (now in Bangladesh, but in East Pakistan at the time of Tridib's death) and placing Srinagar in Kashmir on its circumference, the narrator traces 'an amazing circle' that takes in almost all of South and South East Asia (and large parts of China too). He soon realises that distance is as much a figurative concept as it is a physical one, that it depends as much on how space is imagined as it does on the fact of space itself, 'within the tidy ordering of Euclidean space, Chiang Mai in Thailand was much nearer Calcutta than Delhi is; … Chengdu in China is nearer than Srinagar is. Yet I had never heard of those places until I drew my circle, and I cannot remember a time when I was so young that I had not heard of Delhi or Srinagar' (SL, 227). What distances Chiang Mai or Chengdu from Calcutta is not their geographical proximity or otherwise to Calcutta but rather their location outside the mental map of the nation-state and the borders that demarcate its space from that of its neighbours.

A nation is, therefore, much more than a portion of earth surrounded by borders that contain within them a 'people' to whom the nation belongs. It is a mental construct, a space that is imagined into being that houses – as we shall see, this too is a key motif in the novel – what Benedict Anderson has felicitously called an 'imagined community'.[3] The term 'imaginary' should not be taken to imply that nations are therefore 'unreal' or mere fabrications. Rather, it should be seen as a social and psychic glue, a faculty that binds together elements that may be socially and spatially separate. As Anderson points out, people in any given nation may not ever see each other and they may live hundreds, sometimes thousands, of miles apart but they can imagine they share an 'identity' – in the sense of a similarity – because of a 'silent communion' in their minds.[4] Nations are *both* 'real' and 'imaginary', material and immaterial. It is for this reason that Ghosh suggests that the borders that separate them are 'shadow lines'. The novel illustrates this by teasing the nationalist literal-mindedness of the narrator's grandmother who 'wanted to know whether she would be able to see the border between India and East Pakistan from the plane' (148).

As the embodiment of the nationalist imagination in the novel, the grandmother's categorical and disciplined mind, which 'liked things to be neat and in place' (149), parallels a vision of geopolitical space which sees a 'special enchantment in lines … hoping perhaps that once they had etched their borders upon the map, the two bits of land would sail away from each other' (228). However, since it is an 'imaginary' concept, the reality of the nation is articulated through language, and the relationship of the nation to the space it inhabits is thus in some ways as arbitrary as the relationship between words and the world they attempt to describe. The 'map' upon which the nation is inscribed is, like a text, merely a representation of the world, a metaphor of space and not space itself. Therefore the physical space of the nation, and the location of its borders – as represented by the map – may not necessarily coincide with the 'imagined community' that is brought into being through the language of nationhood, to the perplexity of the grandmother who cannot comprehend 'how her place of birth had come to be so messily at odds with her nationality' (149). The arbitrariness of borders, and the gap between maps and reality, could have been personally vouched for by millions of people during the Partition of 1947 as they found themselves on the wrong side of a border hastily drawn up by Cyril Radcliffe and his Boundary Commission, which partitioned an entire subcontinent without leaving its offices in Delhi by using (out-of-date and inaccurate) maps.⁵ Some towns were even bisected down the middle. In a moment of lucidity, the senile Jethomoshai points this out in no uncertain terms, 'It's all very well, you're going away now, but suppose when you get there they decide to draw another line somewhere? What will you do then?' (211). In the face of this, the belief 'in the reality of nations and borders … that across the border there existed another reality' (214) is shown to be a psychological defence, an attempt to salvage something from the unspeakable horrors that accompanied Partition, as the grandmother reveals when she contemplates the implications of arbitrary borders, 'But if there aren't any trenches or anything, how are people to know? I mean, where's the difference then? … What was it all for then – Partition and all the killing and everything – if there isn't something in-between?' (148–9).

In fact, national identity is by no means the only type of identity that is 'imaginary'. Theorists of subjectivity and identity have argued lately that *all* identity is 'imaginary'. Our sense of selfhood is a construct fashioned through language, discourse and narrative. The 'shadow lines' of the novel therefore encompass personal and subjective identities as well as collective social and political ones. These are linked in *The Shadow Lines* by the metaphor of the mirror and a number of corresponding symmetries. Thus, for instance, the shadow lines between nations are referred to as 'looking-glass borders' (65, 219, 228); Dhaka airport is 'so like the one she had just left' (190); whilst the trope of the mirror is most notably deployed elsewhere in the text through the figure of the 'twin'. The first of these 'twin' references occurs on the very first page as the narrator tries to imagine what the eight-year-old Tridib must have looked like, 'since I had nothing to go on, I had decided that he had looked like me' (3). Sexual identity is referenced by the narrator's desire for his cousin Ila, who is so like the narrator that '[he] could have been her twin' (31), and this in turn is enveloped into the narrator's comparison of himself with Nick Price, 'a spectral presence in my looking glass', whose position as the narrator's (more successful) sexual competitor is complicated by the colonial relationship on the one hand – 'always bigger and better, and in some ways more desirable … I would look in the mirror and there he would be … always a head taller' (49) – and their common masculinity on the other, which elicits sympathy from the narrator when he discovers the truth about his relationship with Ila, 'I wanted to get up then and hold him … he did not know the part he had played in my life, standing beside me in the mirrors of my boyhood' (186). Even siblings are referred to in terms of the mirror when the narrator observes his grandmother beside her sister, Mayadebi, 'they were holding hands over my head … in exactly the same way, as though there was a mirror between them' (35).

This persistent indexing of the various identities explored in the novel with reference to the metaphor of the mirror brings to mind the theories of the French psychoanalyst Jacques Lacan. According to Lacan, the development of a person's identity is initiated when the infant passes through what he describes as 'the mirror stage', which Lacan uses as a metaphor for the subject's entry into the Symbolic order: the linguistic system that makes 'sense' of the world and ourselves. By entering the system of language, which Saussure suggests creates meaning only by the differential relation of signs to each other, the 'self' acquires identity by becoming aware of 'difference'.[6] Identity is therefore enabled by and constructed through language, and the coherence of our sense of 'self' is mediated through the narratives we tell about ourselves, both personal and collective. Hence the novel's fascination with the power of the imagination, of memory, and of stories, 'Everyone lives in a story, he says, my grandmother, my father, *his* father, Lenin, Einstein, and lots of other names I hadn't heard of; they all lived in stories, because stories are all there are to live in' (179). The proliferation of narratives in the novel testifies to their ubiquity and ineluctability; there is no 'outside' to narrative in *The Shadow Lines*. They are 'all there are'. The recurring motif of imagined 'houses' – from the invention of the Price's house by Ila and the narrator in the basement of the Raibajar house, to the narrator's description, from memory, of the Price's house to his incredulous hosts, to the imagining of the 'upside-down house' by the grandmother and Mayadebi – reinforces this sense of identity being an 'imaginary' construct because 'home' is one of the most powerful metaphors in language for identity; we say that we are 'at home' when we feel most comfortable with ourselves and our surroundings.

However, if the imagination is the basis for individual and collective identities, the novel also suggests it is the basis for the *overcoming* of identity,

> I knew that the sights Tridib saw in his imagination were infinitely more detailed, more precise than anything I would ever see. He said to me once that I could never know anything except through desire, real desire, which was not the same thing as greed or lust; a pure, painful and primitive desire, a longing for everything that was not in oneself, a torment of the flesh, that carried one beyond the limit's of one's mind to other times and other places, and even, if one was lucky, to a place where there was no border between oneself and one's image in the mirror. (29)

The tension in this passage as it moves from associating the imagination with a 'precision' that is able to document ('to know') 'details' and the 'ordinariness of their difference' towards the transcendence of difference in the final phrase, once more calls to mind Lacan's theories of subjectivity and the paradox of identity formation. He suggests that prior to the 'mirror stage' the infant exists in a state of pure 'being' and is unaware of any difference between itself and the world. Lacan calls this the Imaginary state of being (which should not be confused with the social 'imaginary' in the sense outlined above). The 'mirror stage' initiates a split – symbolically represented by the reflection in the mirror – that enables a sense of self to emerge by inducing a recognition of its difference from the Other (the image, the world, and things in it). The mirror stage thus prepares the infant for its entry into the Symbolic order when its identity will be produced by the chain of differences that enable language to make 'sense' thereby allowing the 'subject' to make sense of itself. In the process of entering the Symbolic order and acquiring an identity, therefore, the sense of pure 'being' that existed prior to the mirror stage is lost but the desire for the sense of 'plenitude' it offered remains as a residue within identity that is secreted in the unconscious. Our sense of identity is split between a recognition, through language, of difference (which gives the self 'meaning') and an impossible desire to recover the plenitude and 'unity' of the Imaginary state, which can only be achieved by the transcendence of difference.

Lacan follows Freud in suggesting that collective identities such as nationalism approximate this sense of plenitude by offering a limited transcendence of difference through narcissism. For Freud, a collective identity such as nationhood is an 'ego-ideal' that offers us an image of ourselves that we in fact lack. Lacan concurs but inflects it with his linguistic insights. The main point – on which both Lacan and Freud agree – is that narcissism, which collapses the distinction between 'oneself and one's image in the mirror', is motivated by *desire*. Tridib's reasoning here thus shadows quite precisely psychoanalytic theory in showing how the imagination might help one pass *through* difference towards collectivity, just as the metaphor of the mirror that he invokes in this passage operates throughout the novel in a dual manner, illustrating both the formation of identities and differences *and* gesturing towards an underlying sameness. What remains at issue is the nature of the 'collectivity' that Tridib has in mind, or the 'sameness' that the novel gestures towards.

Most critics have seen Tridib as either a figure of abstract cosmopolitanism, an advocate of a universal and transcendent liberal humanism, or an equally cosmopolitan postmodernist. Either way, he represents a position that is critical of nationalism. Certainly, one could read this passage along with others – specifically, when Tridib mentions that he would like to meet May 'in a place without a past, without history, free, really free' (141); or his attachment to the story of *Tristan and Isolde*, 'about a man without a country, who fell in love with a woman-across-the-seas' (183); or his use of the imagination as a surrogate for global travel, 'Tridib had given me worlds to travel in and he had given me eyes to see them with' (20) – and conclude that Tridib does indeed represent a figure of universal humanism. Equally, however, one could argue that he is the figure most associated in the novel with the persistent 'mystery of difference'. As Jon Mee notes, 'Tridib's aspiration to think across the differences of time and space is interwoven with a powerful sense of the materiality of location. He thinks *across* cultures rather than beyond them.'[7] In other words, his 'global' imagination respects differences even as he traverses them. Mee suggests that this echoes Dipesh Chakrabarty's post-colonial and post-modern attempt to think through differences without assimilating them to some higher 'master code'.[8] This may be indicative of that characteristic tension throughout Ghosh's work between postmodernism and humanism. However, as indicated in chapter 1, that tension is itself determined by Ghosh's ambivalence towards nationalism. After all, transcending difference in the name of a higher unity is also symptomatic of *nationalism*. Furthermore, it could be pointed out that the *respecting* of differences is not alien to the nationalist imagination either; indeed, it sees internationalism as its necessary obverse condition.[9] What is being argued here, therefore, is that the tensions within the novel between postmodernism and humanism are enveloped by a more fundamental *ambivalence* between a critique of nationalism on the one hand and an affiliation to a particular kind of nationalism on the other.

This tension may be manifest in what Sujala Singh sees as a discrepancy between the text's 'questioning of nationalism in relation to sub-continental politics', and an uncritical acceptance of English nationalism's rhetoric about its 'finest hour' during the Second World War.[10] In particular, she draws attention to the narrator's favourable appraisal of wartime England, 'I wanted to know England not as *I* saw her, but in her finest hour – every place chooses its own, and to me it did not seem an accident that England had chosen hers in a war' (57). 'This unquestioning endorsement of England's 'finest hour',' Singh argues, 'reads like a parody of England's mythic exultation of itself as a country that had saved the world but lost an Empire because of the war.'[11] She adds, 'How does one make sense of this earnest identification with the glories of wartime England by a student of colonial history?'.[12] The argument is, at first sight compelling, but on closer inspection perhaps it identifies a discrepancy when in fact there is none. Indeed, a purely naturalistic response to her question might be that the narrator has imbibed such ideas from his grandmother's belief that national identity is predicated on war and bloodshed, 'It took those people a long time to build that country; hundreds of years, years and years of war and bloodshed. Everyone who lives there has earned his right to be there with blood: with their brother's blood, their father's blood and their son's blood. They know they're a nation because they've drawn their borders with blood' (76). A more literary response might be to suggest that the 'England at war' narrative operates as a ironic reflection of this rhetoric of sanguinity espoused by the grandmother, and present in nationalist discourses everywhere, which use metaphors of consanguinity – the notion of the nation as a family; with its Fathers and Mothers; as a fraternal bond – and memorialise death in war, as can see from the near ubiquity of cenotaphs and tombs of unknown (and thus representative) soldiers.[13]

From this perspective it can be seen that the novel undertakes a deconstruction of such rhetoric. First, from the very first page of the novel, one notices a curious reversal of the usual associations that accompany the notion of a blood relationship, 'The truth is that I did not *want* to think of her as a relative … I could not bring myself to believe that their worth in my eyes could be reduced to something so arbitrary and unimportant as a blood relationship' (3). Ordinarily, of course, blood relationships are seen as anything but arbitrary. In this, once again, the narrator echoes his grandmother who has a particular distaste for family attachments, which we are meant to believe stems from the experience of witnessing her father and uncle quarrelling, 'In later years it always made my grandmother nervous when she heard people saying: We're like brothers. What does that mean? She would ask hurriedly. Does that mean you're friends?' (121). For her, the absence of 'family feeling' is compensated by 'larger and more abstract entities' such as nationhood, which she explicitly figures in familial terms, using the rhetoric of consanguinity, 'War is their religion. That's what it takes to make a country. Once that happens people forget they were born this or that, Muslim or Hindu, Bengali or Punjabi: they become a family born of the same pool of blood' (76). The spilling of blood thus performs an alchemy that transforms differences into solidarity, strangers into family. Real family ties are, in this schema, relatively inconsequential. It is therefore ironic that the spilling of Tridib's blood is a consequence of her attempting, after a lifetime's disregard for 'family feeling', to align her actual family with her imagined one. A further irony is that although Tridib's death confirms her nationalist views – which she later projects onto the war with Pakistan in 1965, 'We're fighting them properly at last, with tanks and guns and bombs' (232) – it was not because of war between nations but in fact a consequence of nationalism being unable to overcome those sub-national or non-national differences – Hindu, Muslim etc. – that its rhetoric of consanguinity attempts to transcend. In effect, the novel dismantles the rhetoric's credibility.

Given that the 'England at war' narrative functions as a reflection of such a rhetoric its 'nationalist' dimensions are also ironically dismantled. English nationalism is shown to be as much of a fabrication as Indian nationalism. Indeed, in order to reinforce the point, Ghosh inserts the disruptive figure of the migrant, which draws into question the identity of the 'England' itself. His narrative specifically locates England's 'finest hour' in Brick Lane, and amongst its central cast of characters is a Jewish-German woman, Francesca Halévy. Indeed, Brick Lane is shown to have been home to successive generations of immigrants, including Italians, Jews, Poles and lately Bangladeshis; the various palimpsests that confront the narrator – the 'stern grey anti-racism posters … buried now under a riot of posters advertising the very newest Hindi films' (98); the 'large chapel-like building' that had once been a synagogue and is now a mosque; and the house that had once been home to Alan Tresawsen,

Francesca Halévy and Mike, an Irishman, which has become the
Taj Travel Agency – all testify to the rich layering of the cultural
geography of the East End. The 'England' that experienced its
'finest hour' during the Second World War is thus shown to be
shot through by cultural differences that abrasively rub against
the grain of English nationalism. This strand of the narrative
is, therefore, an integral part of the architecture of the text's
critique of nationalism.

Where, then, might we locate the tension between the
text's critique of nationalism and its (guarded) espousal of it?
It emerges in the uncertainty that can be detected in the novel
about whether it is mounting a universal critique of nationalism
that is applicable to all nations – exemplified by the England at
war episode – or nationalism *in the subcontinent*. Of course, it is
trying to do both. But *The Shadow Lines* seems to suggest that
its critique of nationalism in the subcontinent requires attention to specific elements that do not apply to other nationalisms
elsewhere and thus cannot be generalised. The narrator speaks,
for example, of 'the knowledge that normalcy is utterly contingent … that *sets apart* the thousand million people who inhabit
the subcontinent from the rest of the world … it is the *special*
quality of loneliness that grows out the fear of the war between
oneself and one's image in the mirror' (200, my emphasis). This
passage even hints that the motif of the mirror is specifically
applicable to the subcontinent, which is clearly in tension with
its application elsewhere in the text in relation to other nationalisms, 'it's the same over there – in Germany – though of course
in a much more grotesque way. It was odd coming back here
– like stepping through a looking glass' (65). Nevertheless, it is
an impression that is supported by a closer look at the pivotal
'compass' episode. The narrator draws 'another amazing circle',
this time centred on Milan. This one also encompasses a great
many nations. He then tries to imagine what kind of event could
occur in any of the vast number of places within that circle that
might 'bring the people of Milan pouring out into the streets.
I tried hard but I could think of none. None, that is, other than
war' (228). This is in direct contrast to the subcontinent where

an event like the theft of the Prophet's hair in Srinagar does induce a popular response two thousand miles away. The implication is clear: there is something 'special' about social relations in the subcontinent that complicate and transgress the 'looking-glass borders' of its nations, which instead of separating them actually, and ironically, binds them closer together in an 'irreversible symmetry' (228). This emphasis on the 'special quality' of the subcontinent actually recovers a key nationalist argument during the colonial period – that of the distinctive civilisation of the Indian subcontinent. This distinctiveness 'proved' that India was indeed a nation.[14] Writing from a post-colonial vantage point, however, the argument reappears in Ghosh's novel accompanied by a large dose of irony.

From this angle, the parable of the compass reveals a different interpretation to that with which this discussion of *The Shadow Lines* began. For alongside the 'symmetry' of the 'looking-glass borders' in the subcontinent, there is also an asymmetry that distinguishes these nations – India, Pakistan and, latterly, Bangladesh – from their neighbours. Thus, 'Hanoi and Chungking are nearer Khulna than Srinagar, and yet did the people of Khulna care at all about the fate of mosques in Vietnam and South China (a mere stone's throw away)? I doubted it. But in this other direction, it took no more than a week ... '(227). In other words, the logic of distance *does* hold true in one direction (moving away from the Indian subcontinent towards South-East Asia) but not in the other. But what is it that diminishes the distance between Srinagar, Khulna and Calcutta? It is not nationalism since it is clear that the political and social elites in both India and Pakistan 'believed in the power of distance no less than I did' (222). Nor is it religion as such because the passage makes it clear that the people of Khulna would not care for their co-religionists in Vietnam and China as they do for those in India (or, inversely, Pakistan). No, it is some 'other thing' (214), which emerges during the 'pathological inversion' of a riot that paradoxically indicates 'the indivisible sanity that binds people to each other independently of their governments' (225).

This 'sanity' gestures towards relationships that cannot

be spoken of because they cannot be accommodated into the 'vocabulary' of 'war and friendship' that articulates relationships between nation-states. Whilst such a vocabulary can provide 'weighty testimony to the eloquence of war', it cannot speak of this 'other thing', which exceeds the logic of the nation-state and resists its attempt to 'claim the monopoly of all relationships between peoples' (226). When the riots are reported in the newspapers, they are assimilated into the vocabulary of nation-states and their meaning is accordingly translated so that 'horror and outrage' precede satisfaction at 'quelling the disturbances' and the restoration of 'order' – which represents, in fact, the nation-state reasserting its authority over social discourse. The paradoxical effect is to thicken the silence that empties the riots of their significance as 'normalcy' is resumed. The narrator therefore sees his attempt to come to terms with the significance of Tridib's death as a 'struggle with silence'; like others, his social vocabulary is determined by the language of the nation-state, 'and things which did not fit my vocabulary were merely pushed over the edge into the chasm of silence' (214). Since it is 'beyond words', the 'other thing' that is the root cause of Tridib's death can only signify as an absence, 'a gap, a hole, an emptiness' (213); its only available language is the 'madness' of a riot.

This silence, and the manner in which it is described, once again calls to mind the theories of Jacques Lacan. Since 'reality' is constructed through language and discourse, it can only do so by repressing that which might disturb or disrupt the reality it seeks to construct. Since these repressed disturbances cannot be spoken of in the language that represses them in the first place, Lacan argued that the very structure of language reveals in its gaps and silences, in the disturbances of its logic, that which has been repressed.[15] This, he suggests, is where we will find the unconscious, which means that the unconscious is *present* in language itself, and its pressure is felt at those symptomatic points when the logic of language comes under strain, breaks down or cannot speak (e.g. 'pointed silences'). Silence thus operates here as a Lacanian figure of the unconscious. The Marxist theorist Louis Althusser and the literary critic Pierre Macherey have shown how Lacan's ideas can be applied to the cultural and political fields, demonstrating that the significance of a text or of an ideology lies not only in what it says but also in what it *does not or cannot say*, in what it conceals.[16]

Following this line of thought, then, one can suggest that the 'other thing' is the repressed political unconscious of the language of nationhood in the subcontinent. In other words, the languages of nationhood in the subcontinent – the idioms of state, of identity, of governance – must repress this 'other thing' because it threatens to undermine the very principle of nationhood itself. It is an Other that secretly resides within the Self and its presence can only be effaced by a severe psychological and ideological repression that is nevertheless omnipresent and serves as a constant, though unacknowledged, reminder of the failure of nationalist discourse in the subcontinent. As an echo of Partition, the communal riot (through which it 'speaks') serves as a reminder that Partition – which according to the protocols of nation-state is seen as a necessary and foundational moment in the history of the nation – achieved nothing. Each communal riot is a reminder that Partition resolved nothing. Far from being necessary, it is shown to have been unnecessary, its horrors unmitigated by the consolation of success, and that is why 'normalcy is utterly contingent' in the subcontinent (200). The communal riot can thus be read as a moment of disclosure that reveals the unconscious communal logic that is secreted within the discourse of nationhood in India and Pakistan, even though that discourse – especially in India – consciously disavows communalism.[17]

It is at this point that we can finally identify what the 'other thing' of which the narrator of *The Shadow Lines* cannot speak is. It is not religion *per se* but the intimate *relationship* of religion to nationalism in the subcontinent. Indeed, for all its concern with nationalism, the full force of *The Shadow Lines* is only apparent when it is read as an attempt to come to terms with *communalism*. One must remember that the novel emerged out of Ghosh's personal and first-hand experience of the anti-Sikh communal riots in Delhi in 1984 following the assassination of the Indian Prime Minister, Indira Gandhi. The fact that he could

not articulate a critique of communalism without also interrogating nationalism in the subcontinent merely underscores
the point.

For although nationalism and communalism in India have
customarily been characterised as oppositional discourses, much
recent work suggests that far from being essentially opposed
to one another, they were in fact construed as such after the
development of secular Indian nationalism in the 1920s.[18] Prior
to that, the construction of national identity by Indian nationalists developed along broadly 'communal' lines. Thus Gyan
Pandey writes that until the 1920s, 'the nation of Indians was
visualised as a composite body, consisting of several communities, each with its own history and culture and its own special
contribution to make to the common nationality. India ... was
conceived of as a collection of communities'.[19] Far from being
nationalism's Other, 'communalism' was by and large implicated
in, and even a determinant of, the development of early Indian
nationalism. It is this existence of a strong strain of communi-
tarian sensibility that led, perhaps inevitably, to a nationalist
historiography which accentuated those communal divisions.
This nationalist construction of the Indian past, tinted as it
was by strong communal influences, was firmly in place and
fully articulated by the time that secular nationalism emerged
in the 1920s so that even beyond the development of secularism it was never seriously called into question. As a consequence, the gradual extension of 'representative' politics led
community leaders to construct united 'Hindu' and 'Muslim'
and 'Sikh' etc. communities, and political identities within
India thus became increasingly codified along communal lines.
These were, to a great extent, already developed when, in the
late 1920s, secularism challenged the 'composite' idea of Indian
identity with its own idea of individual citizenship. The undif-
ferentiated concept of citizenship can be said, in many ways, to
have been created as a means of containing communal difference. However, even though secularism was a conscious effort
to overcome the increasing communal divisions within the
nationalist movement as well as in society at large, the problem

remained largely unresolved because the conceptualisation of secularism was extremely limited. This, to a large extent, still determines the vulnerabilities and anxieties of secularism—and secular nationalism—in post-colonial societies such as India.[20] Communalism, far from being nationalism's Other, is in fact its Double, its twin.

It is only when we read *The Shadow Lines* within the context of this intimate relationship between communalism and nationalism that the full significance of the motif of the mirror emerges for it reveals that India and Pakistan are locked in a narcissistic embrace from which neither can pull back. It is, however, narcissism of a particular kind. We have seen that narcissism is involved in the formation of all national identities, but in general it functions as a means of creating an ego-ideal, a self-image which can help define the Self against the Other. In the case of India and Pakistan, the Other *is* the Self. To put it another way, nationhood in the subcontinent is self-divided, 'the war between oneself and one's image in the mirror' (200). When one fears or hates the Other, one is in fact fearing or hating oneself. Narcissism in the subcontinent is thus inverted.

It is for this reason that Ghosh meditates almost obsessively in *The Shadow Lines* and elsewhere on symmetries in the subcontinent: 'As for the two governments, they traded a series of curiously symmetrical accusations' (SL, 225); 'there were exactly mirrored stories of Hindus and Muslims coming to each others' rescue' (IAAL, 209), and in *Countdown*, Ghosh's report on the nuclear stand-off between India and Pakistan, he repeatedly returns to moments of symmetrical action and reaction. This concern reaches its focal point in his account of the 'ritual' of lowering the national flags at the border post of Wagah. So perfect is the symmetry of the ritual – 'both armies reserve their tallest and most imposing-looking men for these border squads ... Their steps were perfectly co-ordinated on both sides ... Then the flags were lowered in exactly symmetrical lines of descent' (C, 85–6) – that Ghosh is moved to describe it as a 'sublimely comic ... pantomime' (85) and a 'parodic' enactment of enmity.

In trying to mount a critique of both nationalism in general and a critique of nationalism in the subcontinent, *The Shadow Lines* reveals an asymmetry in its appraisal of nationalism that indicates an ambivalent tension in its ideological position. Its critique of nationalism is undertaken in the name of a universal humanism, whereas its critique of nationalism *in the subcontinent* has as its target *communalism* and is undertaken *on behalf of* a secular, syncretic nationalism. This much is clear in Ghosh's representation of the Hazratbal shrine in Srinagar as a symbol of communal harmony and syncretic unity:

> The mosque became a great centre of pilgrimage, and every year multitudes of people, Kashmiris of every kind, Muslims, Hindus, Sikhs, and Buddhists would flock to Hazratbal on those occasions when the relic was displayed to the public ... (220) There were some incidents of rioting ... but the targets of the rioters were not people ... but property identified with the government and police ... in the whole of the valley there was not one single recorded incident of animosity between Kashmiri Muslims, Hindus and Sikhs. There is a note of surprise – so thin is our belief in the power of syncretic civilizations – in the newspaper reports which tell us that the theft of the relic had brought together the people of Kashmir as never before ... On 4 January 1964, the Mu-i-Mubarak was 'recovered' ... the city of Srinagar erupted with joy ... and Muslims, Hindus and Sikhs marched together. (221)

Whilst his representation of the pluralistic appeal of the shrine is borne out by historical research, Claire Chambers has argued that his representation of the events in 1963–64 idealises communal relations during the incident by eliding some of the specific historical and political dimensions that attended the crisis and responses to it.[21] Following Suhdir Kakar, Chambers sees Ghosh reiterating a secularist romanticisation of community relations in India, 'which has tended to downplay the dark side of Hindu-Muslim relations'.[22] Whilst there is some truth to this, it is perhaps a little unfair to suggest that *The Shadow Lines* ignores the 'dark-side of Hindu-Muslim relations', given that the kernel of the narrative is a communal riot. Indeed, the remarkable achievement of the novel is that it reveals the residue of this 'dark-side' within the discourse of nationalism in India. The integrity of the text lies in the fact that *despite* Ghosh's obvious affiliation to a syncretic version of nationalism the novel nevertheless discloses a truth that discomforts that affiliation. At one point the narrator says that to give meaning to 'these other things' would be a 'risk we cannot take any more than we can afford to listen to madness' (223). And yet, the novel does indeed take this risk. The narrator's 'struggle with silence' thus, in some measure, represents Ghosh's struggle with himself.

The Shadow Lines is, however, only an initial moment in this struggle. The appeal of syncretism is explored more thoroughly in his next book, *In an Antique Land*, and between the two texts there is more than just this relationship. In fact, it could be said that *The Shadow Lines* constitutes an *urtext* for *In an Antique Land*, a departure point for Ghosh's subsequent exploration of the problem of identity in the modern world, and particularly the 'post-colonial' world. The canvass is larger, the scope of the question more ambitious, as indeed is the quest for its answer. Beneath these, however, the core motivations and anxieties are similar, if not the same. For *In an Antique Land* can be read as an allegory of the politics of identity in the subcontinent as much as an exploration of the problematics of identity in modernity.

To this end Ghosh stages an allegorical encounter between himself, a Hindu, and the Muslim *fellaheen* of Egypt which generates a series of anxieties and problems that frame the questions to which the other narrative strand – the historical quest – offers a response. Although these encounters are framed in terms of a national difference between Egyptians and Indians, they are in fact articulated in terms of a religious encounter between a Hindu and Muslims. The main points of difference that are repeatedly recounted by the incredulous villagers are cow-worship, cremation, and circumcision. Each time, the interrogating *fellah* invokes the protective aura of Islam to indicate their disbelief at what they see as the barbarity of Hindu customs and the superiority of Islam. Usually, these are accompanied by an attempt at conversion. The first of these encounters occurs early in the narrative, between the narrator and Ustaz Mustafa, a title which indicates that he is not a *fellah* but rather a salaried government employee 'educated in modern, rather than traditional, forms of learning' (45). Ghosh rebuffs Mustafa's attempt to convert him by inviting him to the village mosque, and when Ghosh later reflects on his reluctance to enter the mosque there is an indication that his refusal may in fact be overdetermined by anxieties germane to his experience of religion in India, 'I began to wonder why I had not accepted ... he had meant well ... A part of me had wanted to go – not merely the part which told me that it was, in a sense, my duty, part of my job. But when the moment had come, I'd known that I wouldn't be able to do it: I had been too afraid, and for the life of me I could not understand why' (49). One might suggest that it is not due to his fear of conversion but rather to the wariness that accompanies Hindu-Muslim relations in India. The crossing of the mosque's threshold represents, in some part of Ghosh's unconscious, a transgression of the norms of communal discourse.

From this moment the bucolic narrative introduces successive episodes where the Hindu Ghosh's relation to his Muslim interlocutors is replayed, and eventually it spirals towards a climax as Ghosh, unable to bear the burden of interrogation any longer, flees a suffocating room, the cloistered atmosphere perhaps a metaphor for his sense of anxiety. This episode hinges on yet another discussion of circumcision, which in Arabic is designated by the term 'to purify'. That it is a discussion of 'purification' is perhaps yet another oblique hint at the allegorical nature of the episode because Pakistan literally means 'the land of the Pure'. The text then immediately recounts the same riots that had been the cause of Tridib's death in *The Shadow Lines* with the difference being that this time it is narrated as a direct experience whereas in the previous novel Tridib's death is shrouded by many layers of mediation. At the end of this excursus, Ghosh speaks of his inability to explain 'an Indian's terror of symbols' (210), to the *fellah* because 'theirs was a world that was far gentler, far less violent, very much more humane and innocent than mine' (210). It is worth remembering that the 'less violent ... humane and innocent' world of which he speaks is the Middle East, a region that has throughout the twentieth century experienced more social and political turbulence than any other. This idealisation perhaps serves not as an indicator of ignorance on Ghosh's part but as a foil which renders that contrast with the subcontinent all the more vivid. Once more we hear the refrain first raised in *The Shadow Lines* concerning the exceptionalism of the subcontinent.

The double-helix structure of *In an Antique Land* juxtaposes the bucolic narrative with the historical one and enables a contrast between the rigid conceptions of identity in the contemporary world and the fluid, syncretic medieval world of the western Indian Ocean trade. As Javed Majeed rightly observes, this medieval world becomes a 'zone of imaginative release', that provides a 'critical perspective on the exclusive identities of modernity'.[23] Even Ghosh's description of medieval 'slavery' serves this purpose, for master–slave relations 'would have appeared, perhaps, not as demeaning bonds, but rather as links that were in some way ennobling – human connections, pledges of commitment, in relationships that could just as well have been a matter of a mere exchange of coinage' (263). Before having arrived at this appraisal, Ghosh had suggested that medieval slavery is perhaps better explained not through the discourse of domination, subordination or exploitation but rather through 'its role as a spiritual metaphor' (260), which places it adjacent to the spiritual practices of the Sufis and the Vachanakara saint-poets of South India. Among devotees of these cults, the worshippers become 'slaves, searching for their master with a passion that dissolved selfhood' (261). All in all, 'the medieval idea of slavery tends to confound contemporary conceptions, both of servitude and of its mirrored counter-image, individual freedom' (259). If, as Paul Gilroy has argued, modern slavery is *constitutive* of modernity rather than a premodern hangover or aberration, then the force of Ghosh's 'subtle abduction' of the term 'slave' lies in its implication that the central principle of modern identity – the sovereign, individual self – is itself the flip side of the inhuman nullification of identity that is modern slavery.[24] By contrast, medieval slavery, as represented by the saint-poets, 'was the paradoxical embodiment of perfect freedom; the image that represented the very notion of relationship, of human bonds, as well as the possibility of their transcendence' (261). Whilst some critics have queried the historical accuracy of Ghosh's conceptualisation of medieval slavery and accused him of romanticisation, it is perhaps better to think of it as a deconstructive ruse that enables him to shed a critical perspective on modernity.

It is also worth noting that this critical perspective reconstructs the premodern world of 'accommodation and compromise' as a mirror image of *post*modernity. Its hybrid languages, such as the trading argot 'that was possibly compounded largely of Perso-Arabic and north Indian elements' (281) or Judeo-Arabic, which is 'a colloquial dialect of medieval Arabic written in the Hebrew script' (101), are indicative of polyglot, multicultural societies which consisted of overlapping and reciprocal cultural relationships. The merchants and traders, in particular, possessed a 'startlingly diverse network of associations' (277) that spanned three continents, anticipating the globalised economy of today. There is a note of awe in Ghosh's acknowledgment that 'Madmun's friends deserve to be counted amongst the most well-travelled men of the Middle Ages, perhaps of any age before the twentieth century' (157), and he clearly admires their cosmopolitanism. This mapping of postmodern attributes onto premodernity suggests that modernity itself is something of a historical detour, as symbolically represented by the stories of the roads and canals that must swerve past miraculously indestructible shrines. It is not only its formal experimentation, therefore, that marks the text's affiliation to postmodernism. Its themes, motifs and structuring ideas are also paradigmatically postmodern. Nevertheless, like *The Shadow Lines*, *In an Antique Land* exhibits the tension between a postmodern repudiation of modernity and its espousal as a refuge against the fragmentations of contemporary life. Once again, it is played out through an ambivalence over the value of nationalism.

The contrast between the two strands of the narrative highlights a historical rupture that Ghosh suggests was initiated by European colonialism. The medieval world of accommodations was soon 'devoured by that unquenchable, demonic thirst that has raged ever since', and the contemporary narrative demonstrates that the post-colonial world is still struggling to cope with its legacy. One of the principal consequences has been the imposition of a grid of exclusive national and religious identities that squat like palimpsests over the syncretic pluralism of that lost world. Unlike Ben Yiju and Bomma, therefore, Ghosh feels that he needs a 'sense of entitlement' (19) to be in Egypt in the first place. In this he is no different from all the others in the post-colonial world who have inevitably succumbed to a 'metaphysic of modern meaning' that has partitioned the past and allocated a 'choice of Histories' (95).

But running against the grain of this, *In an Antique Land* tracks a number of continuities that have surreptitiously survived the rupture by passing through 'a vast network of foxholes where real life continues uninterrupted' (15–16). Principal among these is the linguistic continuity between the Judeo-Arabic of Ben Yiju's time and the local dialect of Nashawy and Lataifa (104–5), and the continuing economic relationship between the Indian coastal town of Mangalore and the Persian Gulf, 'thousands of its residents are now employed in the Persian Gulf … In this, as in many other intangible ways, Mangalore remains true to its medieval heritage' (245). Thus, although it seems like Judeo-Arabic is known to only a 'handful of scholars' (103) or that Mangalore has 'lost virtually every trace of its extraordinary past' (245), the 'foxholes' of history enable small fragments of the vanquished premodern world of accommodations to be retrieved.

The tension between rupture and continuity is in turn mapped onto an even more significant distinction between 'High' and 'popular' culture. The High religious traditions of modernised, Sanskritised, Brahminical India and of modern Islam both emerge from the rupture of modernity and observe

the exclusions it brought about by dismissing popular religion as 'superstition' and/or by excising the history of popular
cross-cultural, inter-religious activity so as to trim their traditions according to the 'map of modern knowledge' and thereby
'confirm a particular vision of the past' (95). Conversely, Ghosh's
text cherishes popular culture as a site of resistance to the exclusions of modern religious and cultural identities. Just as the
'High' modernist Hindu and Muslim traditions observe and
confirm the historical rupture of modernity, and the exclusions
that accompany it, popular culture and folk religion transgress
them. Ghosh tells us, for instance, that it was likely that during
Ben Yiju's long stay on the Malabar coast he would have found
'a small patch of level ground' with the indigenous inhabitants
in 'popular traditions and folk beliefs' that have always existed
alongside the 'High' religious traditions of the Middle East and
South Asia (263). In the continued observance of the 'mowlid'
(carnival) of Sidi Abu-Hasira, or the subversive survival of a
Bobbariya-bhuta idol that 'slipped the spirit of an Arab Muslim
trader past the watchful eyes of Hindu zealots and installed it
within the Sanskritic pantheon' (274), one notices the persis-
tence of the overlapping, syncretic traditions that emerge whenever peoples of different cultures live in close proximity. Their
obduracy defies 'the enforcers of History' (342).

At the level of the popular, therefore, continuity through
time is accompanied by parallels across space. The result is a
number of uncanny 'doubles' that bind the present to the past,
and the Middle East to India. Ustaz Sabry explains to the *fellah*
that 'Our countries [India and Egypt] were very similar' (134),
and that 'the people of Egypt and India have been like brothers
for centuries' (186), and, sure enough, there is a story of a detour
around a shrine which refuses to yield to modern engineers in
both Egypt (139) and Malabar (265); in both the medieval and
the modern narratives there is the possibility of a blood feud,
the loss of a beloved child (Shaikh Musa's and Ben Yiju's), a
transgressive love affair, sibling rivalry, and, of course, in both
narratives the central character(s) is a displaced person – Ghosh
and Bomma in Egypt; Ben Yiju in India.

What is the significance of the 'double' in *In an Antique Land*? In Chapter 4, we shall discuss in more depth the significance of the 'uncanny double' with respect to Ghosh's understanding of and critical engagement with History. Here, it can be read as a sign of ambivalence because it is at this point that the text's critique of the exclusivity of modern national identities overlaps with its allegiance to a particular line of thought within Indian nationalism. In other words, by marshalling the 'popular' as a site of resistance and critique he also invokes 'popular' or 'folk' culture in exactly the same manner as certain key spokesmen for a syncretic view of Indian nationalism. The key is the association of the 'popular' with the metaphor of 'weaving', which as we have seen is one of Ghosh's most persistent and important motifs. Malabar is in an area of southern India called Tulunad, which we are told is 'rich in folk traditions and oral literature … [and] like so many other parts of the subcontinent, it forms a cultural area which is distinctive and singular, while being at the same time closely enmeshed with its neighbours in an intricate network of differences' (244). This last phrase – 'intricate network of differences' – is one that recurs throughout Ghosh's writing in various proximate forms and in each case it signifies distinct yet similar identities that are in some relationship of intimacy. Usually, Ghosh is referring to social and cultural identities but he also uses it to describe the cousins Nabeel and Ismail, 'There was a kind of complementarity between them, a close-stitched seam of differences' (148). The use of the word 'complementarity' suggests that whenever Ghosh deploys this term the intimacy he has in mind is not conflictual but rather open and reciprocal.

It is this reciprocity that stitches together the high and popular cultures of Tulunad into a syncretic unity, 'As in much of India, the religious fabric of Tulunad was woven from an equal mixture of local forms of worship … and the high Sanskritic tradition … that shaded gently and imperceptibly into each other. Indeed, under the benign cover of that shade, there was a good deal of trafficking between the two pantheons' (252). The reminder, on both occasions, that Tulunad was in no way exceptional, that this situation is replicated throughout the subcontinent, indicates a franchise within certain conceptions of 'India' as a whole. We can contrast this to the slightly different emphasis Ghosh puts on the relationship between high and popular culture in the Middle East, 'In some profound sense, the Islamic high culture of Masr had never really noticed, never found a place for the parallel history the Geniza represented' (95). The investment in a particular idea of Indian nationhood as 'benign' is scattered throughout Ghosh's fictional and non-fictional work, often only appearing between the lines of an argument or in implicit contrast to other forms of nationalism, as expressed, for example, in this line from his important essay, 'The Global Reservation: Notes Toward an Ethnography of International Peacekeeping': 'for those of us who look upon the UN as a bulwark against the wave of *ethnic* nationalism that is sweeping the world'.[25] The qualification hints at other forms of nationalism that do have some value, even in this essay which is more critical of nationalism than most of Ghosh's work.

In his affiliation to syncretic Indian nationalism, Ghosh follows some notable Indian thinkers who felt this vision of nationhood could constitute a model for the rest of the world, particularly Jawaharlal Nehru and Rabindranath Tagore. Indeed, Nehru frankly admitted the influence of Tagore, and Ghosh's debt to both is clearly apparent in some of the turns of phrase and metaphors used by both men when describing India's syncretic genius. Note, for example, the proximity of the following, taken from Tagore's critical lectures on nationalism, to Ghosh's own discourse, 'India has been trying to accomplish her task through social regulation of differences, on the one hand, and the spiritual recognition of unity, on the other.'[26] Or again, 'our former governments were woefully lacking in many of the advantages of the modern government. But because those were not the governments by the Nation [*sic*], their texture was loosely woven'.[27] The negative reference to 'Nation' here should not be taken to imply that Tagore did not believe in the kind of civilisational unity that others would term 'nation'; rather, his idiosyncratic terminology sought to distinguish that syncretic unity – 'a

natural regulation of human relationships'[28] – from the notion
of the modern nation-state. Nehru disagreed about the role of
the state but shares essentially the same vision about India's
syncretic history. In Sunil Khilnani's words, 'Nehru saw cultures
as overlapping forms of activity that had commerce with one
another, mutually altering and reshaping each other. India was a
society neither of liberal individuals nor of exclusive communities or nationalities, but of interconnected differences.'[29] Unsur-
prisingly, his language also finds echoes in Ghosh's discourse, as
we can see in this extract from his magisterial *The Discovery of
India*, '[India is] an ancient palimpsest on which layer upon layer
of thought an reverie had been inscribed, and yet no succeeding
layer had completely hidden or erased what had been written
previously.'[30] The palimpsest is also one of Ghosh's most important metaphors for history (as we shall see in Chapter 4), and his
etymological quests in *In an Antique Land* perhaps echo Nehru's
attempt in *The Discovery of India* by attempting to 'strip away
[its] dense layer of accretions' (IAAL, 291).

This recuperation of a particular kind of nationalism sits
ambivalently alongside a postmodern, post-nationalist cosmopolitanism in *In an Antique Land*. The 'allegorical' reading of the
text offered here has tried to show how the continuing appeal
of such syncretic visions of nationhood is related to Ghosh's
ongoing attempt to come to terms with the politics of identity
in the subcontinent, and in particular the enmeshing of religious and national identities that has traumatised the political
imagination of the subcontinent since Partition. It is significant,
in this respect, that Ghosh chooses syncretism as opposed to
other possible secular vocabularies because it observes religious
differences even as it attempts to provide a language through
which to negotiate them. Unlike some other secularist positions,
it does not dismiss religion altogether. That would not be politically viable, and it would contradict Ghosh's attempts to respect
difference. Often, discourses of 'respect' and 'tolerance' such as
liberalism or most current conceptions of multi-ethnicity and
multiculturalism depend on a secular dismissal of religion either
as an irrelevance or as an irrational obstruction to be overcome.

Ghosh's writing, on the other hand, is conspicuous for its serious and sympathetic engagement with religion as a valuable and deeply cherished aspect of identity. It is precisely for this reason, however, that he must repeatedly return to the problem of the relationship between religious identity and politics and the ways in which this relationship has manifested itself in the modern history of the Indian subcontinent. *In an Antique Land*, like most of Ghosh's texts, thus illustrates the acute dilemmas of the post-colonial intellectual and the limits of both postmodernism *and* nationalism in addressing them. The elegiac tone of the text, and its emphasis on the catastrophic and irreversible nature of historical defeat suggests a certain paralysis in Ghosh's ability to imagine a substantially improved future. The eschatological overtones of the final passage in the epilogue, with its hellish evocation of History engulfing an almost biblical exodus out of Iraq indicates the extent to which a nightmarish past weighs heavily on this text even as that same past also offers a 'zone of imaginative release'.[31]

In *In an Antique Land* Amitav Ghosh's ambivalent analysis of the politics of identity in the post-colonial world traces contemporary dilemmas back to the decisive and disruptive impact of European colonialism. His critique of exclusive modern identities, including national identities, is thus intimately bound up with a critique of colonialism and its effects. In *The Glass Palace*, he sketches something akin to a pre-history of nationalism in Asia by dramatising its emergence in the context of the upheavals engineered by war and conquest on the one hand, and trade and economic exploitation on the other. It is not without significance, therefore, that the main narrative takes place between 1885 and 1942. The former date is, of course, when Britain conquered Burma, annexed it into its Indian empire and sent its King into exile. However, 1885 also coincides with the formation of the Indian National Congress, which would become one of the principal vehicles of anti-colonial resistance and national liberation. At the other end of the main narrative, 1942 coincides with the Quit India movement, the final and decisive push towards independence organised by Congress and the last of the three great civil disobedience agitations led by Mahatma Gandhi. In that sense, then, it constitutes if not the end then at least the beginning of the end of British colonialism in Asia.

Against this backdrop, the novel charts the unmaking and remaking of individual and collective identities and examines the self-fashioning and self-alienation that followed in the wake of colonial defeat. Once again, defeat is a key structuring principle. As a response to colonialism, this epic historical novel attempts to represent:

> an enormous multiplicity of experience and of history. For me, at some point, it became very important that this book encapsulate in it the ways in which people cope with defeat, because this has really been our history for a long, long time: the absolute fact of defeat and the absolute fact of trying to articulate defeat to yourself and trying to build a culture around the centrality of defeat … But around defeat there's love, there's laughter, there's happiness, you know? There are children. There are relationships. There's betrayal. There's faithfulness. This is what life is and I want my book to be true to that.[32]

Within the context of a grand historical defeat, then, *The Glass Palace* explores the complex dynamics of collaboration, complicity and resistance to colonialism and its aftermath. Its characters' identities and motivations, their ideas and desires are shown to be shot through with tensions as they negotiate their sense of self and evaluate their place in the colonial scheme of things. In documenting this complexity, and in its gathering together an abundance of achievements and disappointments, joys and sorrows, in short in attesting to the multi-dimensional experience of life in a colonial milieu, this most humanist of Ghosh's novels tries to salvage a small measure of redemption from the existential wreckage of defeat.

The dynamics that shape the characters' lives in *The Glass Palace* are played out in both the economic and political fields. Indeed, the novel demonstrates how the economic and the political were two sides of the same colonial coin and it explicitly figures economic exploitation of land, resources and people as a counterpart to political oppression. This is evident in the novel's representations of various spaces that are linked together by colonial power on the one hand and the capitalist economy on the other. The meticulous descriptions of the Burmese interior – its jungle, its villages, its lifestyles – that accompany the equally exhaustive accounts of the timber industry are paralleled by the fastidious descriptions of the Morningside estate in Malaya, and the logistics of the rubber plantation. Indeed, trees are a significant motif in the novel and, in a sense, they stand as surrogates for the colonised peoples with whom they share the environment. Ghosh illustrates how this environment is exploited, but he also documents its resistance. The symbolic dimension of these spaces is evident when Matthew tells Uma, by then a prominent nationalist leader, that the estate is 'my little empire … There's law, there's order, everything is well run … But it's when you try to make the whole machine work that you discover that every bit of it is fighting back' (GP, 233). Despite the advice of scientific experts, Matthew prefers the explanation of the plantation's coolies who believe that some trees do not produce rubber because they are fighting back on their behalf, because 'every rubber tree in Malaya was paid for by an Indian life'. The same is true of the jungle. A ghost story told by Saya John's friend Doh Say about the wrath of an elephant on behalf of his dead *oosi* (rider) assumes a symbolic significance as we discover that the *oosi* had died because of the aggressive practices of the local agent of the timber company, a young Englishman by the name of McKay (97–103).

Although the economic is shown to be intimately entwined with the political, the two arenas of public service and private enterprise are shown to follow divergent trajectories until the larger logic of global historical events sweep all of the colonial subjects into a maelstrom of upheaval during the Second World War. *The Glass Palace* traces a narrative of private opportunity for a select few whilst the fate of colonialism's public servants gestures towards a lack of opportunity for the great mass of peoples as a consequence of political subordination. On the one hand, there are the entrepreneurs like Saya John and Rajkumar. On the other, there are the political figures like The Collector, the King and Uma. It is one of the great achievements of the novel that it can sympathetically portray a character like Rajkumar – whose rise from an illiterate orphan to the height of wealth and prosperity is admirably shown to be a result of his tenacity, courage, and business acumen – whilst not losing sight of the fact that this takes place within the context of a larger subjection that exacts a heavy political and economic penalty.

The success of Saya John and Rajkumar is based on a shrewd appraisal of the rules of the colonial game. In particular, it is their ability to absorb the colonial worldview, to subject themselves to its hegemony, that enables them to ascend to the pinnacle of colonial society. The novel signifies this through its attention to clothing as a marker of identity and attitude. Saya John, for instance, is introduced wearing European clothes (8), and he begins each of his business trips into the forested interior of Burma clad in a 'sola topee, leather boots, khaki trousers' (67). The narrator tells us that for Saya John, this was 'a ritual, a superstition', but it is more likely that Saya John was aware that his success as a busi-nessman depended on his performance of the role of a colonial *sahib* and the authority and assistance derived from it. Similarly, Rajkumar also undertakes a transformation of his identity – or at least signals it – as he prepares for the crucial business meeting which will determine the success or failure of his timber business. Saya John assists him as he changes out of his 'green *longyi* and scuffed *pinni* vest' (131) into a 'suit ... appropriately plain and black, and his tie neatly tied, the collar turned to just the right angle' (131). In this guise, Saya John sees not the orphan boy he had once known, 'an abandoned kalaa, a rags-clad Indian who had strayed too far from home', but rather 'a reinvented being, formidably imposing and of commanding presence' (132).

This emphasis on the performance of identity brings to mind recent theories of identity articulated from a post-structuralist perspective.[33] In particular, the critic Homi Bhabha has discussed colonial mimicry and suggested that it results in a hybrid identity that undoes the racialised oppositions on which the authority of colonialism rests. In his essay 'Of Mimicry and Man', he rehearses the dilemma of colonial educators in India who require 'a class of Indians native in blood and colour but English in tastes, in morals, and in intellect'.[34] Thus, in order to facilitate colonialism, there is a 'desire for a reformed, recognisable Other, *as a subject of difference that is almost the same, but not quite*'.[35] The hybrid identity of the colonial mimic man 'menaces' the structure of colonial discourse because the 'performance' of the colonial mimic man does not conceal an essential identity underneath that remains 'authentic' and stable, 'Mimicry conceals no presence or identity behind its mask.'[36] The hybrid identity of the mimic man discloses the lack of an essential difference between the identity of the English and the Indian precisely because it unsettles the location of such identities. Where does 'Englishness' reside? In 'blood and colour' or in 'tastes, in morals, and in intellect'? In acquiring English 'culture', have these Indian mimics become English? If so, what has happened to their Indianness? And what gives the English their identity if *anyone* can become English? The colonial 'mimic men' occupy a hybrid cultural space that is indefinable in static or essentialised terms because they are neither one thing nor the other but something else besides, an excess that cannot be contained within the terms 'English' or 'Indian'. This illustrates an ambivalence within those very terms that renders them uncertain.

In this instance, however, *The Glass Palace* does not endorse Bhabha's argument. The performance of a Westernised colonial identity for Rajkumar, in particular, is shown to be more like that of an actor donning a costume than the kind of 'performativity' that unsettles the very notion of identity as theorised by thinkers such as Bhabha and Butler. There is a sense that he is acting a role, that beneath the veneer of his costume is a more stable identity that is represented in his preference for a cotton vest and *longyi* over European clothes. Whereas Saya John may have begun his trips into the interior dressed in the uniform of a colonial adventurer, Rajkumar arrives at Ratnagiri – as a guest, it must be remembered, of a distinguished colonial official – sporting a 'half-chewed cheroot ... his crumpled longyi, his

greasy vest and his unkempt hair' (139). Even during dinner
at the Collector's Residence, Rajkumar's uncertainty over table
etiquette suggests a psychological resistance to the assimilation
of a European identity,'[e]ven now, after two years of dinners
and parties, he found it hard to cope with this atmosphere of
constrained *enactment*' (141, my emphasis), in marked contrast
to the Collector whose minute scrutiny of the dinner table is
of a piece with his thoroughly Anglicised sense of identity. To
a lesser extent, the same is true of Saya John, whose Christian
upbringing since his own orphan childhood may have facilitated
his greater ease with his hybrid identity, but who nevertheless
finds it impossible not to revert to indigenous garments in the
unforgiving environment of the Burmese jungle, 'At each stop
Saya John would shed an article of clothing, and within the space
of a few hours he would be dressed like Rajkumar, in nothing
more than a *longyi* and a vest' (68). His European garments, we
are told, are 'ill-fitting' (72) and he although he changes back
into them before visiting the young English company official
who oversees the teak camps, this act of shedding and then re-
assuming European dress nevertheless implies an unbridgeable
distance between them.

Public and political figures like the King and Queen of Burma,
on the other hand, are denied the opportunities granted – albeit
in controlled measure – to private individuals like Saya John and
Rajkumar. Whilst they are relatively free to peregrinate around
the vast spaces of the colonial arena, the King and Queen are
imprisoned in Outram House, trapped by the political logic of
imperialism, which has usurped their authority but nevertheless
remains nervous of their symbolic power to galvanise resistance
amongst the Burmese. In turn, their habits and attire symbolise
their unwillingness to divest themselves of their former identities. The King, we are told, had never been properly educated in
a modern European manner, and his knowledge of the world was
shaped by the customs and protocols of the Burmese court, and
his scholarly and spiritual inclinations as a Buddhist novitiate.
The political force behind him had been his Queen, and it is she
who insists that even in exile their household observes 'all the

old Mandalay rules – the *shikoes,* the crawling' (55). Although the Queen retains her Burmese clothing throughout her life as an indication of her refusal to succumb to the circumstances of her exile, her daughters undergo a slow transition towards a hybrid Indian-Burmese identity that is again signalled by a change in clothing, 'In their early years in India, the Princesses usually dressed in Burmese clothes ... But as the years passed their garments changed. One day, no one quite remembered when, they appeared in saris ... they learned to speak Marathi and Hindi as fluently as any of the townsfolk' (76–77). Significantly, Uma Dey would later arrive wearing a sari 'in the new style' (105), one invented by an Indian official to indicate a 'modern' Indian identity; this style of sari became an important signifier of Indian 'national' identity and a potent symbol in the struggle against the Raj.[37]

The Queen's obduracy is shown over the years to be based on more than personal pride and *hauteur.* It becomes part of a political logic of resistance, one that reaches fruition in the humbling of the Collector. As an official in the prestigious and powerful Indian Civil Service, the Collector represents precisely the type of educated colonial subject that Macaulay had in mind when he envisaged 'a class of Indians native in blood and colour but English in tastes, in morals, and in intellect' who would help facilitate colonial rule. His identity is shown to have thoroughly absorbed the colonial ideology of the civilising mission, as signalled by his 'finely-cut Savile Row suits' (104), his idealised memories of Cambridge, its 'cobbled streets and stone bridges' (159), his fondness for Schubert, and his presumption that his immersion in European culture offers him an Olympian vantage point from which to judge others, 'He had heard it said once that she [the Queen] had always really loved Thebaw. But what could they possibly know of love, of any of the finer sentiments ... these semi-illiterates who had never read a book in all their lives, never looked with pleasure upon a painting?' (152). His tragic fate enables Ghosh to explore the contradictions of colonial identity at both a personal and political level. As his career disintegrates around him, he reflects on the gap within himself between what he had been taught to desire, and the reality of his hybrid position 'in-between' social systems that undermine the rhetoric of the civilising mission. On the one hand, he becomes aware that the social and sexual relationships that he took to be emblematic of 'modern' civilisation – 'To live with a woman as an equal, in spirit and intellect' (172) – were 'not yet possible, not here, in India, not for us' (173). On the other, the Queen makes it quite plain to him that this chasm in his personal identity is a reflection of the realities of colonial rule. She turns his rhetoric inside out, disclosing his tenuous and contradictory position and the illusions that sustain it, 'Collector-Sahib, Sawant is less a servant than you. At least he has no delusions about his place in the world' (150.) As a servant of the Raj and a fully subscribed supporter of its civilising mission, he believes himself to be an agent of Progress and liberty. But the Queen reveals her 'gaoler' to be himself a prisoner, trapped within himself as much as by the circumstances of colonial dependency – by the discrepancy between the ideology in which he believes and the reality to which he must submit. Moreover, despite appearances, he too is not quite at ease with the demands of colonial mimicry; his identity is fragile, always tenuous, 'the position had brought him nothing but unease and uncertainty … There seemed never to be a moment when he was not haunted by the fear of being thought lacking by his British colleagues' (186).

The Collector clearly prefigures Arjun, a character whose ethical dilemmas as a soldier echo his mythical namesake from *The Mahabharata* who 'pauses in battle to question the purpose of war and the kingdom he is fighting for'.[38] The development of Arjun from loyal colonial subject to rebel soldier is the narrative centre-piece of the novel, its ideological core, and whilst the mythical Arjun eventually decides to follow the path of duty, *The Glass Palace* illustrates how for the latter-day Arjun duty is itself split, torn by colonialism into a dual, duplicitous, allegiance. The novel chooses to explore the effects of colonial hegemony by focussing on the British Indian Army because it is there that the contradictions of colonial ideology were most acutely felt. Indeed, as Ghosh observes in an essay that foreshadowed *The*

Glass Palace, the rebellion of soldiers like Arjun who eventually joined the 'forgotten' Indian National Army was not based on some nativist allegiance to a 'core' Indian identity but rather emerged out of their personal experience of these contradictions, 'The discovery of invisible barriers and ceilings [in the British Indian Army] disillusioned them with their immediate superiors, but it did not make them hostile to Western institutions. Rather, these encounters with racism served to convince them – as they had an entire generation of Westernized Indians – that the British colonial regime was not Western *enough*, not progressive *enough*.'[39] Thus they resist colonialism in the name of an ideology that was a fundamental part of colonialism itself, an ideology that spoke in dual registers, promising freedom on the one hand whilst denying it on the other.

The contradiction, as Ghosh notes, centred on race and the experience of racism. This was the most significant *impasse* in colonial ideology.[40] The Collector wryly observes that his downfall is predicated on race, both in the sense that the scandal of miscegenation violates racial taboos, 'they are tolerant in many things, but not this. They like to keep their races tidily separate'(173), and because he, as an Indian, falls foul of the racial divide. The scandal merely confirms his inherent unsuitability to assume leadership. If the rhetoric of the civilising mission encouraged mimicry – become like us and be free – it also threatened to undermine the racial divisions which justified colonial conquest in the first place (we are here because you are inferior). This contradiction generated a great deal of ambivalence and anxiety on the part of the coloniser as well as the colonised for it needed to be constantly contained by strategies that would maintain the distance of the Other; colonial mimicry always involved a slippage between 'almost the same but not quite' and '*Almost the same but not white*'.[41]

With respect to Arjun, therefore, Bhabha's theory of colonial mimicry is more applicable precisely because *The Glass Palace* concentrates on race as the key term in the debates between Arjun and his friend Hardy. Certainly, their hybrid identity is shown to be more akin to that envisaged by Bhabha than the novel's representation of Rajkumar or Saya John. Their performance does not conceal a prior identity, but rather their identity emerges out of their performance, 'they seemed to be inventing themselves for collective consumption ... Every meal at an officer's mess, Arjun said, was a glorious infringement of taboos ... every mouthful had a meaning – each represented an advance towards the evolution of a new, more complete kind of Indian' (278–9). It is precisely because of this, however, that their identity is fragile. Any sign of an 'alternative' Indianness threatens to dismantle it, which is why mention of Hardy's love of *chapattis* results in a pointed, embarrassed silence (280). The colonial hybrid identity is not a comfortable resolution of disparate influences but an uneasy, anxious and fragile space of accommodation that enables one to construct a place for oneself in the colonial scheme of things, but at the same time threatens to dismantle that scheme and one's place in it.

It is the unravelling of this sense of a self that has been carefully but anxiously constructed that leads to Arjun's eventual self-alienation and paralysis. By pointing out the racial logic of colonial rule, and their subordinate status within it, Hardy snips away at the threads that hold Arjun's sense of identity in a precarious balance. As a soldier, that balance is boosted by the institutions of command, by the simpler consolations of allegiance and duty. This acts as a bulwark against the complexity of Arjun's colonial position, a simple mask that protects him from the uncertainties within. Hardy reminds him what was inscribed over the entrance to their Military Academy, '*The safety, honour and welfare of your country come first, always and every time*' (330), but then goes on to ask:

> this country whose safety, honour and welfare are to come first, always and every time – what is it? Where is this country? The fact is that you and I don't have a country ... why was it that when we took our oath it wasn't to a country but to the King Emperor – to defend the Empire ... Yaar, if my country really comes first, why am I being sent abroad? There's no threat to my country right now – and if there were, it would be my duty to stay here and defend it.

Hardy's logic is impeccable and it opens a breach in the defences that maintain an identity like theirs. The duplicitous nature of colonial ideology is itself responsible for this aporetic split in their loyalties. They stand, uneasily, in between. In the heat of war they are forced to make a choice and they both choose to fight against the very system that had made them who they are, Arjun somewhat more reluctantly than Hardy.

Arjun's choice, however, is a negative one. He does not make it out of a positive affirmation of an alternative identity, but rather because the entire edifice of his sense of the world, its structure, its ways of operating, and his place within it have been shown to be nothing more than an illusion. In his correspondence with Dipesh Chakrabarty, Ghosh discusses this predicament for Indian colonial soldiers, and raises once more Tagore's story 'The Hungry Stones', which had been such a significant intertext to *The Calcutta Chromosome*. The refrain 'It's all a lie' in that story, he suggests, indicates Tagore's own unconscious registering of the dilemmas of colonial identity.[42] Ghosh reads the story as 'a fable for switched identities' and the refrain recognises the fragility of identities that move back and forth within themselves, condemned never to reach that moment of stillness that 'identity' promises. Arjun realises that his identity is a mirage, that he is alienated from himself, and he thus suffers from a psychological breakdown that is similar to the psychoses documented by Frantz Fanon in *Black Skin, White Masks*. Fanon suggests that the colonial subject – the racialised Other – is condemned to seeing itself not as s/he would like to see it, but through the lens of the colonial Other, the white European. And what they see is not a person but a 'thing' – a signifier of blackness, of inferiority, of barbarism.[43] Arjun, too, realises, 'It was as if I wasn't really a human being – just a tool, an instrument' (407). This causes psychological damage because it contradicts that other side of colonial ideology through which the colonial subject comes to see him- or herself as a modern 'individual'. For Hardy, however, there is the refuge of nationalism and his later success is projected as a consequence of his positive affirmation of an alternative. He becomes a 'national figure', an 'ambassador and high ranking official in the Indian government'(480). Again, this echoes Fanon who advocates nationalism in *The Wretched of the Earth* as a positive first step in the decolonisation of the mind. The denouement of *The Glass Palace* thus displays once more Ghosh's sympathies with anti-colonial nationalism as an emancipatory force in the modern world.

These sympathies are, however, qualified by the novel's recognition that anti-colonial resistance – whether from the nationalist perspectives characterised by Hardy and Uma, or from the socialist one articulated by Dinu – is bound up in a larger defeat because it is complicit in the logic of a universal Western modernity to which all peoples can and should aspire. This animates the leaders of the Indian Independence League as much as the colonial authorities they despise. It is echoed in the sentiments of the soldiers who joined the Indian National Army because they felt that the problem with colonial rule was that it was not Western enough. The novel charts the consequences of this larger defeat by recounting the failures of Burmese nationalism and the repressive post-colonial governmentality of the Burmese military regime, whose slogan 'The Burmese way to socialism' exemplifies the manner in which the emancipatory promise of modernism has been used to justify oppression, by nationalists and socialists as much as by colonialists.

Once again, however, Ghosh does not go so far as to denounce all nationalisms. The novel also makes it clear that the failures of Burmese nationalism can be traced to the assassination of Aung San, after which insurgency after insurgency broke out until the establishment of the military dictatorship. In *Dancing in Cambodia, At Large in Burma*, Ghosh observes, 'Aung San may indeed have been the only Burmese leader who could have averted the civil war. A few months before his death he had negotiated a landmark treaty with several minority groups ... The treaty ... lay the groundwork for what could have been a viable federal union.'[44] Later in the text, after having observed the Karenni guerrilla insurgency in the forested hills of northern Burma, he reflects that the ethnic separatisms may be justified because 'Burma's borders are undeniably arbitrary, the product of a capricious colonial history', but '[o]n balance, Burma's best hopes for peace lie in maintaining intact the larger more inclusive entity' that its current borders represent. Within that framework there needs to be a process of 'national reconciliation' between the various ethnic groups.[45] This small echo of India is yet another reminder that Ghosh's political affiliations remain bound to an idea of a multi-ethnic, syncretic nationalism.

In every single one of his texts Amitav Ghosh demonstrates a concern with migrants, refugees and displaced persons. By tracking them he strives to achieve a historical perspective that regards movement 'as a mode of being in the world'.[46] Paul Carter goes on to say that, 'The question would be, then, not how to arrive, but how to move, how to identify convergent and divergent movements; and the challenge would be how to notate such events, how to give them a social and historical value.'[47] Part of the value of such a perspective lies in its ability to contest and deconstruct notions of fixed and discrete cultures, identities, and landscapes. *The Glass Palace* and *In an Antique Land*, in particular, can be seen as complementary contributions towards a literary and historical mapping of the Indian Ocean as a unity that dramatically reconfigures how we come to see relationships between the societies and peoples that inhabit it, both at its shores and in the hinterlands behind them.[48] As Stephen Howe has pointed out, 'For most of recorded history, cultures, civilisations and economies are better defined by oceans than by land masses. Until very recently the sea connected where mountains and deserts divided.'[49] This maritime mapping challenges the partitioning of the past undertaken by nationalisms for whom 'culture' and 'identity' are invariably defined by the rigidities of land and not the fluid, open spaces of the ocean. Ghosh's Indian ocean challenges the binary logic that upholds such ideas by emphasising a triangular relationship between the Middle East, the South Asian peninsula, and South East Asia. Indeed, K.N. Chaudhuri says that the Indian ocean can be said to be constituted by *four* great civilisational fields: the Iranian-Arabic, the Hindu, the Indonesian, and the Chinese.[50]

Ghosh converges land masses that are otherwise seen as divergent into a common history by tracking the incessant movements that have bound the ocean in what the Irish poet Seamus Heaney, himself undertaking a similar enterprise for the North Sea, has called 'the netted routes of ancestry and trade'.[51] Ghosh's Indian ocean is crisscrossed by journeys – Alu's desperate flight to al-Ghazira in *The Circle of Reason*; those of Ben Yiju and Bomma between Egypt, Aden, and Malabar; Rajkumar's childhood in a *sampan* plying the swampy coastline between Bengal and Burma; the ships that transport the characters back and forth between Rangoon and Morningside; the journeys undertaken by the indentured Indian labourers who service the colonial economy in Burma and Malaya, and so on. His imaginative geography of the Indian ocean calls to mind the work of Paul Gilroy, whose 'Black Atlantic' similarly traced a counter-history of modernity represented by the merchants, sailors, soldiers, adventurers, pirates, political rebels, religious visionaries and social reformers who shuttled back and forth between Africa, America, and Europe.

For Gilroy, these movements problematise the notion of 'identity' as expressed through the nationalist metaphor of 'roots'. Instead, they demonstrate the fluid mobility of identity as an ongoing *process* of fashioning and re-fashioning that is captured by the metaphor of 'routes'.[52] Roots speak of identity as 'fixed', an expression of an unchanging 'essence' that can be defined in terms of race, culture, gender, sexuality, religion and so on. Often, such as in nationalism, this identity is metaphysically attached to a place. For Gilroy, however, identity is a moveable feast, shaping and being shaped by the changing contexts of our lives, and the flux of our social interactions with others. Nothing dramatises this more than the act of physical movement, which traverses – and thereby destabilises – those discursive formations that seek to 'ground' our identity. Identity thus emerges through the interplay between 'roots' and 'routes'.[53]

The Glass Palace explores this interplay through a minor but nevertheless audible and significant chord that echoes throughout the novel – the concept of 'home'. 'Home' is one of the most powerful metaphors of identity, and the relationship it signals with place – where we feel ourselves to be most 'at home' – makes it one of the key terms in the nationalist lexicon. To migrate – to move from one home to another – renders that relationship unstable. In a narrative so full of journeys, it is unsurprising that 'home' should be displaced so many times. Rajkumar, a young Bengal orphan, comes to see Burma as his home; after her marriage, Manju moves from Calcutta to Rangoon and on arriving, proclaims, 'I'm home' (301); but it is perhaps Dolly who most of all exemplifies the portability of identity through the multiple locations of her 'home' – she is brought from her native village to the court of Mandalay, which she comes to think of 'home'; after nearly 20 years in exile, she comes to feel that Outram House is 'home to me now' (112), and that 'If I went to Burma now I would be a foreigner' (113); on her return to Rangoon, Kemendine House becomes her home. After that, she never again feels 'at home'. Her temporary residence in Calcutta after her forced departure from Rangoon is accompanied by an increasing desire to follow the Buddhist renunciation of 'home' and identity altogether, which she does by becoming a Buddhist nun. These displacements disrupt the settled geographies of the self imposed by national traditions and undermine the belief that identity is rooted in a particular place. Perhaps nothing illustrates this better than the ironic reversal of attachments exemplified by the turn of events following the King's death: 'of the four Princesses, the two who'd been born in Burma both chose to live on in India. Their younger sisters, on the other hand, both born in India, chose to settle in Burma' (213).

For Gilroy, the concept that binds together the disparate 'webbed network' of the Black Atlantic is diaspora. Part of a cognate family of terms that have been deployed within cultural and social theory against national definitions of collective identity, history and culture, its relative appeal to a generation of critics seeking to dismantle the exclusivist rhetoric of nationalism lies in its ability to evoke identities that are 'historically specific but ultimately bound to a shared global and ethical destiny'.[54] Unlike, say, transnationalism, which keeps intact the structure of nationalist thought by analysing relationships between a 'home' nation and a 'host' nation, diaspora suggests a multi-lateral formation that complicates the difference between 'host' and 'migrant' communities, who both share a 'diaspora space' without priority being given to the former.[55] Diaspora relationships exceed notions of identity grounded in binary structures of thought such as nationalism. The difference between 'home' and 'away' is rendered complex, ambiguous and uncertain.

Ghosh certainly evokes the diaspora space of the Indian ocean, and to do so he invokes the metaphor of the family, which is unmoored from nationalist discourses of consanguinity – as demonstrated in *The Shadow Lines* – and deployed as an indicator of that dense web of relationships that intersect and exceed nationality. In so doing, he chafes against what he sees as a reductive strain of literary criticism that sees the 'family' as an allegorical term that necessarily signifies nationhood in 'Third World' literature.[56] In both his correspondence with Dipesh Chakrabarty and numerous interviews, Ghosh has stressed that for him the family is important as 'one way of *not* writing about the nation'.[57]

He is, however, aware that diaspora can paradoxically strengthen nationalist imaginings even as it unsettles them. For diasporic communities often imagine the consolatory fiction of a 'lost' homeland more rigidly in order to fortify themselves against the flux of uncertainties that accompany life in a diaspora space. These in turn can have material political effects through what Benedict Anderson has called 'long distance' nationalism.[58] In the contemporary world, a number of nationalist movements have received financial and political sustenance from their diaspora communities.[59] In *The Glass Palace*, it soon becomes clear that those soldiers in the Indian National Army that had been recruited from amongst the plantation labourers in Malaya possess an almost fanatical allegiance to its cause because, 'they were fighting for a country they had never seen … what was India to them? … India was the shining mountain beyond the horizon, a sacrament of redemption – a metaphor for freedom in the same way that slavery was a metaphor for the plantation'

(521–22). This fervour is, however, merely the obverse of the callous exploitation that had helped form the modern Indian diaspora in the first place. Unlike the medieval diaspora so affectionately traced in *In an Antique Land*, *The Glass Palace* recounts an altogether more sordid tale of the central role of Indian indentured labourers in the operations of the colonial economy. The account of their journey from India to Burma and beyond is recounted in detail (125–128), evoking the horrors of the 'middle passage' endured by black African slaves who also financed the prosperity of Euro-American modernity with unpaid labour. Ghosh does not therefore overlook the dark side of diaspora; his concern for the counter-history of diaspora as represented by his focus on the ordeals of indentured labourers and refugees shows how, for him, migration is not always an opportunity or cause for celebration.

The function of diaspora as a key term in his search for alternatives to nationalism is thus modulated, as always, by a certain ambivalence that results from Ghosh's acknowledgment that as a lived reality, as opposed to a theoretical abstraction, diaspora is a multi-dimensional phenomenon. It is this engagement with life as it is lived out in the precarious zones of the modern world that qualifies his espousal of post-nationalist idioms in both his fiction and non-fiction. In Ghosh's accounts of his travels through perhaps the most devastated of these zones, Cambodia, one finds these ambivalences over post-nationalism played out most visibly. In 'The Global Reservation' he shows how the UN's putatively global discourse of humanitarianism is itself enmeshed in the legacies of nationalism and ethnic absolutism; moreover, he shows that any post-national political order that emerges from it will not – indeed, cannot – simply erase or transcend ethnic and cultural difference but must rather work through them somehow. The political order that Ghosh sees emerging will be shaped by the fact that the 'UN represents the totality of the world's recognised nation-states, and the fundamental logic of its functioning is to recreate the image of its membership wherever it goes'.[60] This will 'probably result in a two-tier system of nation-states. In the first of these, the boundaries of the nation-state, as traditionally understood, will become increasingly blurred' as the UN, by order of the politically powerful nations, increasingly intervenes in the affairs of these states in the name of 'global order'. Conversely, the boundaries of nations in the other tier – those giving the orders – will become 'increasingly rigid'. Thus the nation-state, which had been so 'eagerly embraced by the peoples of the colonised world, as the embodiment of liberty, will become, effectively, the instrument of their containment'.[61]

This essay represents Ghosh's most thorough attempt to work through the political logic of modernity in the post-colonial world as it is emerging in this century. Its conclusions clearly signal Ghosh's own belief that the game is up for nationalism as a vehicle for liberation. Indeed, it echoes his fictional analysis of the nation-state as obstructive and divisive. However, as Ghosh recounts his experiences in Cambodia, there is nevertheless a sense that the *absence* of the state is a cause for extreme concern. This is clearer in the longer, expanded account that constitutes the first essay in *Dancing in Cambodia, At Large in Burma*. As he ventures into the interior of Cambodia he notes the effective absence of any central authority; in its place lies the capricious terror of banditry and guerrilla warfare. Thus, if the governmentality of the post-colonial nation-state is often figured as a menacing and threatening presence, here its absence indicates that it nevertheless possesses a certain aura of stability and order. It remains a bulwark against the kind of chaos chronicled in *The Shadow Lines*. If, as 'The Global Reservation' argues, the emergent political order will be limited by the continuing legacy of the nation-state, then perhaps this indicates a recognition on Ghosh's part that since a properly post-national world cannot yet be imagined into existence, the best alternative remains the syncretic nationalism advocated by Tagore and Nehru.

Tiny threads, gigantic tapestries

If a certain kind of rationality – scientific, empiricist, positivist – constitutes the 'grammar' of the metaphysic of modern meaning, then its syntax is History. History makes sense of modernity; it takes the 'grammar' of its metaphysic and makes it speak in 'proper' sentences that articulate modernity's principal themes: rationalism, enlightenment, liberty, the individual, the state, civil society, the rule of law, democracy, social justice and, above all, Progress. It does this through narrative. The word 'history' contains within it both the sense of 'events that have happened in time' and the narration of those events; it is both event and discourse. That is precisely what a narrative is – the ordering of events in time through discourse. Although there have been attempts to impose 'scientific' rigour on the discipline of History by minimising narrative in favour of analytical or 'dissertative' modes of writing, some element of narrative is unavoidable.

Just as the metaphysic of modernity supposes that scientific rationality can be infinitely extendable to cover all aspects of lived experience, so too can History be expanded to encompass all of reality. Everything has 'a' history – ideas, people, cultures, things, nature, and so on – which ultimately takes its place in the larger scheme of things which the historian Robert Berkhofer has called 'the Great Past'.[1] But this Great Past, conceived as 'a complex but unified flow of events' does not just exist independently, awaiting the historian's intervention; in fact, the historian already presupposes that the Great Past forms one 'Great Story' so that his/her 'history' of whatever aspect of it can take its place within the 'total historical context from which they are said to be a part'.[2] He goes on to add, 'Historical methods can operate only if historians conceive of contextual plenitude as a continuum of structured events organized according to the same narrative logic they employ in their own synthetic expositions, which supposedly mirror the past.'[3]

It is in this sense that we can speak of History as a meta-narrative (i.e. a 'higher' narrative) whether or not it is formally written up as a narrative account. However, like the scientific Reason from which it derives its rationale, the putative universalism of this 'total past' is an ideological veil, a self-projection onto the past (and, spatially, across the globe) of the particular concerns of a particular society at a particular moment in time, namely modern Europe. History is intimately tied to Euro-centrism even when it does not seem like it. As the historian Dipesh Chakrabarty has pointed out, writing History involves inscribing onto the past – *any* past – some local variant of the themes of European modernity, '"Europe" remains the sovereign, theoretical subject of all histories, including the ones we call "Indian," "Chinese," "Kenyan," and so on … all these other histories tend to become variations of a master narrative that could be called "the history of Europe".'[4] This is because the logic of historicism is oriented towards an explanation of how European modernity came into being as the *telos* – the 'end' purpose – of History 'first in Europe, then elsewhere'. [5] In terms of human history, these other pasts are channelled through the categories of European social science and their correspondence to or divergence from the European norm can thus be measured and placed on a sliding scale of difference that is usually figured in terms of 'distance', 'deviation' or 'lack'.

Throughout his career, Amitav Ghosh has sought to locate marginal, lost, or suppressed stories from the 'other' pasts that have yielded to the historical necessity posited by the meta-narrative of History – those 'barely discernible traces that ordinary people leave upon the world' (IAAL, 17) – in order to recover the 'tiny threads' that are 'woven into the borders of [its] gigantic tapestry' (IAAL, 95). The metaphor is an ambiguous one, confirming the centrality of the 'Great Past' even as it reorients its gaze towards the margins. What exactly does the 'tapestry' signify? What is it a metaphor of? Of the grand *narrative* of History? Or the sum of all events in time *prior* to their ordering and assimilation into historiography, which establishes some events as central and defining and others as marginal ("tiny threads")? The force of the metaphor seems to depend upon an acceptance of the former (i.e. History as totality) as a *necessary condition of marginality*, thereby accepting the self-identification of that History as central, definitive, and universal, even as Ghosh attempts to focus on the partial and discontinuous elements that disrupt that totality and render it perpetually incomplete.

We shall return to this ambiguity in due course as yet another indicator of that crucial ambivalent tension in his work between a postmodern postcolonialism which seeks to challenge and dismantle the ideological and institutional parameters of modernity, and a humanist postcolonialism that seeks to keep them largely intact. For now, however, it is worth noting that each of his major works direct their narrative energy toward 'marginal' or unofficial episodes in the historical record. In *The Circle of Reason*, Ghosh explores the histories of science and pseudoscience and their deployment in the colonial milieu; in *The Shadow Lines*, he examines the ways in which nation-states in the subcontinent are compelled to 'forget' the communal riots that disrupt their 'official,' state-centred histories, which sit like palimpsests above other histories of community, identity, and belonging; in *In an Antique Land*, Ghosh attempts to recover the forgotten history of the medieval Indian Ocean trade, that 'world of accommodation' that has been obscured by the 'the map of modern knowledge', in order to challenge the exclusive national identities that make the very possibility of such a history unthinkable – once again, the figure of the palimpsest emerges here as a highly significant metaphor in Ghosh's writing, one that alludes to the 'sly allegory on the intercourse between power and the writing of history' (IAAL, 82); in *The Calcutta Chromosome*, Ghosh mischievously deconstructs once more the history of modern science by rewriting an 'alternative' history in such a manner as to reinscribe the excised contributions of non-western knowledge systems and colonised peoples; *The Glass Palace* focuses on two overlooked episodes during the Second World War, which is perhaps the most extensively researched and represented period in history: the history of the Indian National Army in Malaya, and the 'Forgotten Long March' of Indian refugees from Burma in 1941;[6] and in his latest novel, *The Hungry Tide*, refugees are also the centre of attention as he recalls a marginalised episode in the coercive history of the modern post-colonial Indian state, namely the Morichjhāpi incident – which recalls his treatment of (post)-colonial governmentality in *The Circle of Reason*, and echoes *In an Antique Land* both through its central metaphor of the tide 'silting over the past' (the palimpsest once more), and the fortuitous recovery of a personal document that 'leaves some trace' of the incident on 'the memory of the world' (HT, 69).

In its own way, each of these texts challenges the Eurocentrism of History, sometimes by simply concentrating on non-European histories (though he never simply ignores the West, aware as he is that it constantly haunts non-European lives), at other times by deconstructing the Eurocentric historical record, as is evident, for example, in *The Calcutta Chromosome*, or in *In an Antique Land*, which contests the usual emphasis on non-European 'lack':

> Within the Western historiographical record the unarmed character of the Indian Ocean trade is often represented as a lack, or failure, one that invited the intervention of Europe, with its increasing proficiency in war. When a defeat is as complete as was that of the trading cultures of the Indian Ocean, it is hard to allow the vanquished the dignity of nuances of choice and preference. Yet it is worth allowing for the possibility that the peaceful traditions of the oceanic trade may have been, in a quiet and inarticulate way, the product of a rare cultural choice – one that may have owed a great deal to the pacifist customs of the Gujarati Jains and Vanias who played such an important part in it. (IAAL, 287)

Indeed, as the great historian of the medieval Indian Ocean trade, K.N. Chaudhuri, has pointed out, 'The phenomenon that is in need of explaining is not the system of peaceful but that of armed trading.'[7] Turning the tables on Europe, *In an Antique Land* challenges the principle of a European norm even as it recognises Europe's victory and mourns the vanquished traditions of a lost past.

Reversal is, in fact, one of the key stratagems by which Ghosh reappraises the historical significance of past events. The technique is evident in most of his novels but it can be illustrated best by analysing one of his essays entitled 'Empire and Soul: A Review of the *Baburnama*' (1997). It does not involve a simple inversion of the Eurocentric perspective as is common in many nativist anti-European or anti-colonial discourses; rather, the technique consists of a series of gradual recalibrations that effectively shifts the balance of emphasis away from Europe. It begins by suggesting that the autobiography of the founder of the Mughal imperial dynasty is 'one of the true marvels of the medieval world', and reminds us that Babur, who is known in the West as a warrior and ruler, was also a writer who 'did something that very few writers have done' by producing one of the few literary masterpieces 'without precedent and without imitators'.[8] Ghosh invokes Cervantes as a parallel, but does not collapse the distinction between Babur's own literary tradition and the 'Western tradition' to which the Spaniard belonged. Babur's self-fashioning through a 'narrative of self-discovery … [which] yields nothing to the confessional memoir of the 1990s', long predated the celebrated European 'discovery of the Self'(97). From here, Ghosh then introduces a number of minor reorientations – for example, the geographical recalibration of the 'centre', 'For Babur, Samarkand was the epitome of civilisation, the centre of the world's urbanity' (92); the rehabilitation of Jenghis Khan, who is often thought of in the West as the epitome of barbarity; the observation that, contrary to Western perceptions of backwardness, 'the women in his book are strong-willed and independent' (98) – until a series of explicit echoes of *In an Antique Land* are initiated by a self-reflexive meditation on the uses and abuses of history, 'History is notoriously not about the past' (102). He suggests that by writing out the 'accommodations' (105) that the Mughal rulers had encouraged – which had made modern Hinduism possible in the first place – contemporary Hindu nationalists are revising history in a manner similar to the Eurocentric historians who had erased the 'culture of accommodation' (IAAL, 288) of the medieval Indian ocean trade. This convergence with the concerns of *In an Antique Land* are brought to a head at the conclusion of the essay, which observes that 'while Babur was fighting his epic battles in the Indo-Gangetic plain', the Portuguese were making their decisive armed intervention into the Indian ocean at the Battle of Diu in 1509. In a piquant reversal of the Eurocentric perspective, Ghosh adds that 'Babur either had no knowledge of the Portuguese presence in western India or *he thought them beneath notice*' (107).

However, Ghosh acknowledges that 'in the long view' the history of the subcontinent 'as a whole' was more decisively shaped by the arrival of the Portuguese than by Babur's conquests. Even as he challenges Eurocentrism here, he restores Europe's primacy. Indeed, he inverts the metaphor of the 'detour' that he had used in *In an Antique Land* to suggest that European modernity, with its various chauvinisms, was merely an interruption of a longer history of accommodation and compromise. In that text it was modernity that was the aberration; here it is the Mughal period that is 'no more than a lucky time-out' (107). In both texts the 'medieval' functions as a critical perspective on modernity, but in both there is also a considerable ambivalence as to the value of that modernity and of the History that it brings into being. Both testify to the difficulty of challenging Eurocentric history whilst also writing historically because, in a sense, historical consciousness *compels* the historian to think of 'Europe' as the theoretical subject and 'centre' of History as such.

This is precisely the point of departure for Dipesh Chakrabarty's *Provincializing Europe: Postcolonial Thought and Historical Difference*, a book which Ghosh admires and over which he entered into a significant and detailed correspondence with

Chakrabarty. Although they had never before met or corre-
sponded, Ghosh and Chakrabarty share a common affiliation
to the Subaltern Studies project. Chakrabarty is a major figure
in Subaltern Studies, and it is not difficult to establish Ghosh's
alignment with the project; he has acknowledged that 'they and
I came out of a similar moment in the intellectual life of India',
and he is personally acquainted with several of the historians
that have participated in the project. Beyond that, the historical
concerns that have shaped Ghosh's work throughout his career
overlap considerably with the Subaltern Studies project from its
very inception, and Ghosh has indeed contributed to one of the
celebrated volumes of essays published by the group. This was
the long essay entitled 'The Slave of MS. H.6', that prefigured
In an Antique Land.[9]

Originally conceived as an attempt to account for 'the
contribution made by the people *on their own*, that is, *independently of the elite* to the making and development of [Indian]
nationalism', the project had to struggle from the outset with
some theoretical tensions that would significantly shape its
future direction, and its relationship to the disciplinary protocols of history itself.[10] On the one hand, they would attempt
to 'recover' histories of 'the people' that were excluded from,
forgotten about, or suppressed within the 'elite' narratives of
Indian nationalism. On the other hand, this effort constantly
confronted the limits of its own possibility. For if the subaltern is
absent from the historical record, how then can his or her experiences and historical contribution be 'recovered'? Their existence,
such as it is, can only be detected as textual traces in the historical records, records conceived and elaborated by and for the elite
(both colonial and nationalist), which inevitably mediates and
refracts the subaltern so that his or her motivations for acting as
they did are rendered opaque. To 'recover' a history of subalterns
would thus seem to involve the impossible task of identifying
a 'consciousness' that is invisible to the historical eye. In the
words of another contributor, 'the desire to recover the subaltern
subject became increasingly entangled in the analysis of how
subalternity was constituted by dominant discourses', and this

in turn has led later Subalternists to reconsider historical know-ledge itself as being implicated in the processes of domination (both actual and discursive) that erased the subaltern in the first place.[11] In other words, the logic of Subaltern Studies has been moving it towards a recognition that 'history' is itself part of the problem.

In this respect, *Provincializing Europe* is the most sustained effort to date at re-evaluating historical knowledge. As we have seen, Chakrabarty has noted that part of that effort involves acknowledging that historicism is inevitably bound with Euro-centrism. But he adds that it must also involve an interroga-tion of the fundamentals of historical consciousness so as to 'return us to a sense of the limited good that modern historical consciousness is'.[12] This is because the radical plurality of the world that is signalled most acutely by the intractable differ-ence of the subaltern cannot be conceived until historicity itself is rendered suspect. For despite the historian's avowed atten-tion to the concrete and particular, historicism in fact encour-ages abstraction, and moves inexorably towards the assimilation of 'difference' (the singular, the concrete) into a transcendent total narrative (the Great Story) that 'leaves nothing aside or behind'.[13] Its urge towards totality involves smothering differ-ence under a blanket of sameness because it 'translates' all experience into the metaphysic of modern meaning. In other words, history explains discrepant world-views and experi-ences ('life-worlds' is the term Chakrabarty uses) through the 'universal' logic of modern knowledge. An insurgent tribal may, for instance, have been motivated by the promptings of gods and spirits but a historian will explain his rebellion by 'rationalising' it through the explanatory mechanisms of secular knowledge – psychology, ideology, power, the state, distribution of wealth, and so on – which provide the key to historical meaning.[14]

Chakrabarty suggests that, according to historical thinking, it is time itself which mediates and ultimately negates all differ-ences by assimilating them into a higher unity. Since it is part of the ensemble of modern knowledge, history shares with the natural and social sciences a view of time as

> godless, continuous, and ... empty and homogenous ...
> this time is empty because it acts as a bottomless sack:
> any number of events can be put inside it; and it is homo-
> geneous because it is not affected by any particular events;
> its existence is independent of such events and in a sense
> it exists prior to them. Events happen in time but time is
> not affected by them ... It is part of nature. (*Provincial-
> izing Europe*, 73)

Historical time is thus seen as 'not a cultural code of representation but ... something more objective', and is therefore homolo-
gous to the abstract 'language' of Newtonian science. Just as the
difference between the Hindi word *pani* and the English word
water can be mediated by the overarching abstraction 'H_2O', so
too does historical time yield a transparent 'objectivity' with
regard to human differences. By contrast, Chakrabarty argues
that time is not natural at all, a position supported by Einstein
himself who arrived at his Special Theory of Relativity (1905)
only when 'it came to me that time was suspect'.[15] As such,
discrepant life-worlds cannot be easily translated into a univer-
sally applicable secular idiom of History; what it cannot accommodate in its bottomless sack are those radically different ways
of thinking and being that presuppose non-secular conceptualisations of time and space.

Subalternity therefore encompasses more than just subordinated social groups whose experiences have not been documented; it refers to entire ways of being in the world that remain
radically 'untranslatable' into forms of historical consciousness.
Chakrabarty calls these 'subaltern pasts', which are 'moments
or points at which the archive that the historian mines develops
a degree of intractability with respect to the aims of professional history ... Elite and dominant groups can also have
subaltern pasts to the extent that they participate in life-worlds
subordinated by the "major" narratives of the dominant institutions.'[16] For example, the Bengali cultural practice of *adda*,
which involves a gathering of friends 'for long, informal, and
unrigorous conversations', indicates how, amongst the Bengali
elite in the early- and mid-twentieth century, there were life-

worlds that were relatively unmoored from capitalist modernity and thus somewhat outside the explanatory paradigms of social history. In the course of Chakrabarty's long analysis it becomes clear that *adda* shares an intimate relationship to Bengali literary modernism and the cosmopolitanism that is such an important feature of Bengal's modern vernacular culture.[17] One is reminded of Tridib's cosmopolitanism in *The Shadow Lines* and his attendance at an *adda* in Gole Park.[18] What the narrator's grandmother, who is subsumed within a historicist vision of the world as seen through the eyes of capitalist modernity, interprets as Tridib's *louche* and unproductive behaviour can be given a subaltern history which in fact sees the unproductivity (in capitalist terms) of such occasions as evidence of an alternative and tangential life-world submerged just beneath the visible contours of Bengali modernity. Chakrabarty argues that the *adda* therefore became a site within which colonised Bengalis could negotiate their dwelling in modernity on their own terms.

If subalternity represents the limit of historical representation, doing 'subaltern history', therefore, involves more than attempting to recover histories of the subalterns. It is not a case of filling out the historical record so as to achieve a more complete account of the past because that is already anticipated by the 'bottomless sack' of historicism. Rather what is required is a 'double task': on the one hand, subaltern history must pursue social justice, and in order to do this one has to speak the language of modernity because '[one] cannot argue with modern bureaucracies and other instruments of governmentality without recourse to the secular time and narratives of history and sociology'.[19] On the other hand, it must respect the radical untranslatability of subaltern difference and in order to do that subaltern history must resist history's totalising urge and instead focus on 'fragments' that are not part of a greater totality. This involves dismantling the 'secular time and narratives of history and sociology'. The 'double task' of subaltern history therefore involves, in Chakrabarty's words, the 'struggle to hold in a state of permanent tension a dialogue between two contradictory points of view', so as to 'take history, the code, to its limits in order to make its unworking visible'.[20]

It may well be that this 'double task' is impossible but Gayatri Chakravorty Spivak has suggested that one of the strengths of deconstruction is its ability to operate in the realm of paradox, 'transforming conditions of impossibility into possibility'.[21] One is reminded here that Ghosh's very first novel, *The Circle of Reason*, deployed paradox as a deconstructive tool that exposed modern scientific Reason to be itself paradoxical. It could be suggested, therefore, that Ghosh's fictive engagement with history throughout his career is a profound attempt to undertake the double task of taking history to its limits in order to open up a space for different life-worlds to emerge.

The question remains, however, as to how subalternity can be represented historically if, by definition, it exists beyond historical representation. At this point, the problem of doing subaltern history moves from being a theoretical problem to being a problem of form. If, in theoretical terms, the subaltern figure operates as an intractable disturbance which opens up the mechanisms of history to inspection, the correlate question is 'what does this look like on the page?'. For if we agree with Spivak that the subaltern cannot speak in the sense that s/he cannot represent him or herself in discourse and still remain subaltern, it is nevertheless true that the manner in which the subaltern appears as a 'textual effect' within discourse affects the ways in which that discourse relates to the issue of subalternity.[22] It is at this point that Amitav Ghosh's texts can be seen as perhaps the most radical attempt to 'do' subaltern history. His major works, in the very act of fictively exhuming subaltern pasts, *make visible* the methodological processes that submerged those pasts in the first place. In so doing, they put into doubt the value of the historical enterprise without, however, abandoning it altogether.

If, in recent years, most historians have conceded that 'objectivity' in historiography is an impossible dream, they nevertheless steadfastly hold on to an empiricist view that there is a deeper objectivity which pertains to the 'sources' that constitute the grounds of historical knowledge. If, at one level, they agree that history is a matter of subjective interpretation, they argue that, at a deeper level, these interpretations can be measured against the evidence, the 'facts' as presented in the historical record, the archive. There is therefore a split between what Berkhofer calls the 'representationality' of historical writing, and the 'referentiality' of the evidence, 'Hence the statements so customary in the profession that history is both science and art, both a reconstruction and a construction ... factual because of reference to (f)actuality, literary because of its synthetic (re)presentation.'[23] For orthodox historians, the documents in the archive are somehow different from other texts, possessing an empirical value that exonerates them from the burden of representation; in such documents, 'reality' is directly 'present', – they 'refer' to actuality rather than 're-present' reality.

It is difficult to see how the 'evidence' contained in the sources somehow possess a different kind of textuality to representational forms such as historiography or, for that matter, fiction. The post-structuralist critique of historicism interrogates both the *grounds* of historical knowledge (in the form of evidence) and the *production* of historical knowledge (in the form of historiography) in terms of the intertextuality that links the one to the other, and the relationship of that textuality to the 'real' world. If 'history' raises questions about textuality and reference/representation, then this in turn must be related to the nature of language itself. For Derrida, 'Historicity itself is tied to the possibility of writing', and therefore must operate under conditions of *différance*.[24] *Différance* points to the impossibility of an exhaustive and fixed meaning, and de-mystifies the 'fantasy that the past may ... be exhaustively and truthfully represented' since the historical sign by virtue of it being a linguistic sign necessarily involves an excess of meaning, or what Derrida calls 'supplementarity'.[25] The past is thus never fully 'present' in the archive.

If, for orthodox historians, the archive is that point at which theoretical debate is terminated, for others it is precisely the point at which 'History' is most fully revealed to be enmeshed in an infinite tissue of intertextual relations that problematises the 'truth' that historical knowledge can deliver. For that 'truth' is perpetually menaced by the 'supplement' – that which 'exceeds' historical discourse: the subaltern. It is unsurprising, then, that the archive has been the object of intense theoretical scrutiny amongst subaltern historians, and Ghosh too invokes the archive as a key organising principle in at least three of his novels: *The Shadow Lines*, *In an Antique Land*, and *The Calcutta Chromosome*.

The endless chain of signification in which the archive – and textuality itself – is embedded propels Ghosh, the historian, on his quest to find the subaltern figure of Bomma in *In an Antique Land*. It is a quest that can only be undertaken by solving numerous etymological puzzles, and yet the solution of each one yields not the truth but instead a new set of puzzles. It has been suggested that there is something inherent in the practice of etymology itself, an anti-historicist element which identifies and exposes discontinuities.[26] Etymology – ironically, the search for a word's meaning(s) – fragments and disrupts any attempt to define a total and exhaustive meaning and of its nature recovers difference from within the historical sign. For Ghosh, this aspect of etymology is particularly useful; he talks of the difficult nature of historical accessibility due to the 'giddying spiral of meanings' that Arabic words 'spin out' (IAAL 161). He consistently engages in etymology, such as his search for the slave Bomma's name, and the medieval meanings of slavery. Of Bomma Ghosh says, 'my unravelling of the Slave's history had been blocked by an intractable etymological puzzle: the mystery of his name' (IAAL 246), but the trail eventually leads him across 'a wide swathe of Tulu culture and history' (IAAL 251), which is 'rich in folk traditions and oral literature but does not possess a script' (IAAL 244). As Keith Jenkins has pointed out, the historian's emphasis on 'primary' evidence privileges textual evidence – the 'document' – and 'the really significant questions are those answerable by empirical and archival research'.[27] One of the effects of this was effectively to excise 'oral cultures' from

History but Ghosh's etymology illuminates a 'subaltern past' beyond the reach of the archive.

The limits of the archive are also explored in the pivotal section of *The Shadow Lines*. As the narrator tries to piece together two seemingly discrepant events – the death of his uncle Tridib in a communal riot in Dhaka, and his own frightening close encounter with a riot in Calcutta – into a coherent historical narrative, he is constantly frustrated by the archival record of those events, which seem to bear only tangential evidence of what his memory had assumed to be an incontrovertible 'truth'. Whilst the archives do, in the end, allow him to establish the chronological simultaneity of the two events, and to conclude that there was some causal relationship between them and the theft of the 'Mu-i-Mubarak' relic in Srinagar, the 'meaning' of those events – both in a personal and public sense – remains elusive. Whilst there is plenty of comment about the riots for a few days, ' By the end of January 1964 the riots had faded away from the pages of the newspapers, disappeared from the collective imagination of "responsible opinion", vanished without leaving a trace in the histories and bookshelves. They had dropped out of memory into the crater of a volcano of silence' (226). But, 'It is not ... the silence of an imperfect memory. Nor is it a silence enforced by a ruthless state ... it lies outside the reach of my intelligence, beyond words' (SL, 213). The riot is figured here as a 'subaltern past', which cannot be spoken of in the language of historicity precisely because it disrupts the logic of modernity, and the political logic of the nation-state, 'The theatre of war, where generals meet, is the stage on which states disport themselves: they have no use for memories of riots' (226). The 'event' that had such a profound effect on the narrator's life, that swallowed up the lives of his uncle and great-uncle as well as many hundred others, cannot figure as part of the 'history' of the nation, which takes the public biography of the state as its 'subject'; it is a 'fragment' that remains unassimilable into the 'whole' that this history represents. It remains intractable, inexplicable in the languages of modernity, of secularism, of political science, history or sociology.[28]

Against the silence of the archive, *The Shadow Lines* coun-
terpoints memory as another channel into the past, one that in
some ways is more adequate than 'history' but in other ways
less so. The 'truth' of the past that is delivered by memory is of a
different kind to that delivered by the historians. Indeed, there is
a suggestion in the novel that 'history' is not synonymous with
collective memory but is instead a particular form of relationship with the past that privileges certain kinds of narrative about
it, whilst memory, whether personal or collective, conceives of
the past in different ways. History, which is based on the archive,
on the document, on some relation to institutional power, cannot
grasp the experiences that are undocumented, for, as we have
seen, the questions it seeks to answer are presupposed by the
evidence it sees as significant. The subaltern historian Gyan
Pandey has theorised in detail the deficiencies of historiography
when it comes to representing communal riots in the subcontinent in terms similar to those adduced by Ghosh in *The Shadow
Lines*. He suggests that 'some of the most sophisticated writing
in the social sciences continues to reduce the lives of men and
women to the play of material interests, or at other times to
large impersonal movements in economy and society over
which human beings have no control … the emphasis placed
upon these factors often leaves little room for the emotions of
people, for feelings and perceptions'.[29] If part of the 'double task'
proposed by Chakrabarty is to hold together both 'analytical' and
'affective' histories,[30] then *The Shadow Lines* proposes memory
as a means of thinking about the past which, in contrast to the
'official' past composed by historians, is felt rather than known.
Memory's past operates tangentially to the recorded past of 'official' history, intersecting it and disrupting it, revealing its gaps
and fissures, its 'fragmentariness', despite its 'apparent solidity
and comprehensiveness'.[31]

This is not to say that Ghosh offers memory as a 'better'
or more valid means of accessing the past. *The Shadow Lines*
consistently represents memory as itself 'fragmentary', episodic
and incomplete. The narrator is only able to piece together the
'truth' of what happened to Tridib through the recollection

of others, and of Robi in particular. But the crucial moments surrounding Tridib's actual death are filtered through Robi's account of a recurring dream and this is subject to various distortions. Marginal details are recalled vividly, 'I can see little details sometimes: a green coconut, for instance, lying in the middle of the road … a slipper on the pavement – not a pair, just a single rubber slipper' (SL, 239), whilst whole dimensions of the experience remain inaccessible, 'May is screaming at us; I can't hear a word but I know what she's saying' (240). In the end, however, it still does not add up to a complete picture; the 'truth' of quite *why* Tridib leaves the safety of the car to face certain death is never resolved – it remains a 'mystery'. At other times, memory is shown to be susceptible to the distortions and compensations of fantasy, as is the case with Ila's account of her school friends who 'were always the most beautiful, the most talented, the most intelligent' (22) or when she recounts the young Nick Price's 'rescue' of her *alter-ego*, Magda, on whom she projects – and alters – her childhood memory of life in London. Furthermore, memory has the potential to freeze the past into a *tableau* that has difficulties accounting for or accepting change. The narrator, who is gifted with considerable mnemonic skills, is surprised when he first encounters the London suburb of West Hampstead, which he has imagined in his mind according to Tridib's memories of it, 'I had not expected to see what Tridib had seen. Of course not … knowing it to be lost in a forty-year-old past. But despite that, I still could not believe in the truth of what I did see' (56). The grandmother, too, is unable to accommodate the changed reality of the Dhaka she had known as a child. In the course of the journey from the airport to the new suburb in which her sister resides, she laments, 'I've never seen any of this. Where's Dhaka' (190). The episode ends with the narrator's reflection on the limitations of memory:

> She had talked to me often about that house and that lane. I could see them myself, though only in patches, for her memory had shone upon them with the interrupted brilliance of a lighthouse beam … people like my grandmother, who have no home but in memory, learn to be

very skilled in the art of recollection. For me, Kana-babu's
sweet-shop at the end of the lane was as real as the one
down our own road, yet I could not tell whether the lane
itself was paved or unpaved, straight or curved, or even
whether it had drains running along it. (190)

Such details, of course, are liable to elude historians too, so what
we see here is not some simple antithesis between memory
and history but rather a complex series of intersections that is
perhaps most accurately summed up by the French historian,
Pierre Nora. Noting how memory in modernity has itself been
altered by the emergence of history so that we are less able to
recall without 'archival' assistance – i.e. that our memory is
itself less self-sufficient, more dependent on material 'traces'
(whether private or public) such as letters, schedules, diaries etc.
– he remarks, 'What we call memory is in fact a gigantic and
breathtaking effort to store the material vestiges of what we
cannot possibly remember, thereby amassing an unfathomable
collection of things we might someday need to recall.'[32]

Silence as a metaphor for subalternity is also one of the
key motifs of *The Calcutta Chromosome*. In Chapter 2, we
saw how Ghosh deploys a deconstructive fictional strategy in
order to represent the unrepresentable. Here we can examine
how Ghosh represents the 'imperial archive' as an institutional
and ideological site that, according to Thomas Richards, 'was a
fantasy of knowledge collected and united in the service of state
and empire'.[33] Ross's biased and exaggerated *Memoirs* takes its
place in this archive alongside the recorded observations, opin-
ions, hypotheses and conclusions of colonial doctors, linguists,
anthropologists, historians, surveyors, civil servants and the like,
all of which helped compose a particular picture of the colony.
Like the Subaltern historians, *The Calcutta Chromosome*
suggests that this archive needs to be read 'against the grain'
in order to open up a space for subaltern pasts. This involves
reading 'between the lines' and identifying those moments of
disruption when colonial knowledge encounters an intractable
disruption in its logic.

The space 'in-between' is one of the key sites in the novel's representation of the colonial archive. The narrative commences with a disruptive moment in the archival process as AVA fails to recognise a fragment of an ID card and by the end of the first chapter we are told that the purpose of this exhaustive archiving is because the administrators of the International Water Council 'saw themselves as making History with their vast water-control experiments: they wanted to record every minute detail of what they had done ... Instead of having a historian sift through their dirt, looking for meanings, they wanted to do it themselves' (CC, 7). Instead of History, what the ID card springs open is a narrative unrecognisable to such administrators, a subaltern history that would be incredible to Murugan's hyper-rationalist colleagues. Indeed, when Murugan submits a scientific paper with the title, 'An Alternative Interpretation of Late-Nineteenth Century Malaria Research: Is There a Secret History?' he is labelled a 'crank and an eccentric' (35). It is significant that Murugan had been LifeWatch's 'principal archivist' because this suggests an ordered and categorical mind accustomed to the systematic processing of knowledge. It is only when this mind encounters an intractable disruption of such order – his first article on the subject is entitled 'Certain Systematic Discrepancies in Ronald Ross's account of Plasmodium B' – that he begins to glimpse the possibility of the subaltern past that is eventually revealed by the narrative of *The Calcutta Chromosome*.

It soon becomes clear from Murugan's account of his 'research' to Antar that he has read 'between the lines' of the archive on early malaria research, principally those documents left behind by Ross himself. Like the administrators of the Water Council, Ross 'writes everything down', because has 'decided he's going to rewrite the history books. He wants everyone to know the story like he's going to tell it' (51). But Murugan's interpretation does not oblige Ross by accepting his word at face value; instead, Murugan builds up an alternative narrative based on what Ghosh himself had noticed at the margins of Ross's *Memoirs* as he researched the novel, that 'most of the connections [he made] came from his servants'.[34] *The Calcutta Chromosome* thus literally emerges from the margins of the colonial archive and inserts itself 'between the lines' of the 'official' history of malaria, addressing the glosses, the gaps and the fissures in the historical record. The process is symbolically figured at the moment when Murugan finds his 'proof' in an uncatalogued letter that falls out from *between* the pages of a scientist's private papers that are stored in an archive in Baltimore (118–19). True to its own enterprise, however, the novel never actually reveals this 'subaltern' document for to do so would be impossible; it is lost in the ether of cyberspace, and AVA is only able to reconstruct 'a semblance of a narrative by running the retrieved fragments through a Storyline algorithm' (127). As it happens, the 'text was too corrupt to do a continuous image conversion. The best she could do was a verbal rendition' (127). Challenging the historian's reliance on the written document, one of the key pieces of evidence in the novel is only accessible through a medium which most historians find highly untrustworthy: oral testimony. In fact, when this testimony is 'transcribed' in the text of the novel (135–54), it is soon clear that the 'voice' is neither Murugan's nor Farley's (the writer of the original letter) but that of a third-person narrator who recounts it in a novelistic style. In this manner, Ghosh scrupulously refrains from translating the subaltern past into a 'document' that could be assimilated into the idioms of historical discourse.

It is at this point that fiction emerges as an alternative discourse for expressing subalternity, an opposition represented by the two seekers after the Silence, Phulboni the writer and Murugan the archivist/historian. Significantly, neither *actually* find what they are looking for, even though they know it is there but whereas Murugan tries to discover the history of the subalterns, Phulboni uses 'literature' and his 'telling' is in fact a non-telling: an encounter with the untellable that is signalled by the major trope in his work: silence. In other words, he tells the cult's secrets in the form of stories which, paradoxically, keep the secret intact precisely because fiction is not seen, in the modern division of knowledge, as a truth-bearing discourse in the way that history is. To be fair to Murugan, he does seem to be aware of his limitations, 'to know something is to change it, therefore in knowing something, you've already changed what you think you know so you don't really know it at all: you only know its history' (103–4). In other words, 'history' is not the history of the 'event' or 'thing'; rather it is the history of its history – the history of its representations. This is similar to what Foucault calls the 'phantasm' of history. Foucault suggests that an 'event' is only constituted as such through its repetition in thought as a 'phantasm', a Platonic 'bad copy' which is part of a series of repetitions. Foucault therefore recommends a new historical method, which he calls 'genealogy', that traces the series of repetitions; the object of inquiry is not the event but rather the phantasmic series.[35]

In this scenario, history is a palimpsest which obscures the past with a 'dense layer of accretions' (IAAL, 291). The palimpsest is one of the most frequent figures in Amitav Ghosh's writing, and in *In an Antique Land* the archive is itself explicitly figured as such, 'For more than eight centuries papers continued to *accumulate* inside the Geniza' (57, my emphasis). It is more metaphorically signalled by the rubbish dump that now stands on one of the most important sites in Cairo's history beneath which lie 'huge quantities of Chinese pottery and other riches: it was here that some of the earliest and most valuable fragments of Indian textiles have been found' (39) – traces of the history that Ghosh is trying to excavate. The palimpsest is invoked in *The Hungry Tide* when the bookish headmaster Nirmal uses the 'deep, deep time of geology' – one of the natural sciences from which historicism derives its notion of homogeneous, empty time – to suggest ironically that the tide country is better explained by myth than by geography, 'This map shows that in geology, as in myth, there is a visible Ganga and a hidden Ganga: one flows on land and one beneath the water' (HT 181). In *The Shadow Lines*, a pivotal passage describes the history of London's East End in terms of a series of migrant habitations, each obscuring the previous one like a palimpsest with only faint traces of the others showing through. The 'chapel-like' building that had once been a synagogue is now a mosque (SL 99), the 'stern grey anti-racism posters … buried now under a riot of posters advertising the very newest Hindi films' (98). This is echoed in *The Calcutta Chromosome*. Antar's building in New York is the site of numerous historical intersections, 'with one wave of migrants moving out and another moving in' (CC 16). More significantly, the central conceit of the novel also gestures towards the palimpsest. Behind the façade of a Romen Haldar or a Mrs. Aratounian lies a Laakhan and a Mangala. The plasmodium held to be responsible for these interpersonal transferences mutates in a manner which mimics the palimpsests of its hosts. Just as Mangala conceals herself in Mrs. Aratounian, for example, the malaria bug 'keeps altering its coat-proteins. So by the time the body's immune system has learned to recognize the threat, the bug's already had time to do a little costume-change before the next act' (250). Not for nothing does one character say that 'everything is other than what it appears to be, a phantom of itself' (153).

This leads us to another recurring motif in Ghosh's fiction: the figure of the phantom or ghost. The idea of the 'supernatural' is one that recurs throughout his work, and the full significance of the 'phantom' can only be understood in relation to the 'double task' that is attendant upon writing subaltern histories. Dwelling on how a subaltern historian should 'translate' that which eludes historical consciousness into forms of subaltern historiography, Chakrabarty suggests that the concept of translation 'must possess something of the "uncanny" about it'.[36] For example, translating the 'tool-worshipping jute worker's' understanding of labour, 'into the universal category of "labor" [which informs historical consciousness]' involves a double-take that 'must be enough like the secular category "labor" to make sense, yet the presence and plurality of gods and spirits in it must also make it "enough unlike to shock"'.[37]

Taking this as his point of departure, Bishnupriya Ghosh says that Amitav Ghosh 'mobilizes literary resources' for this purpose.[38] He is referring specifically to *The Calcutta Chromosome* but the point holds good for all the haunted moments in Ghosh's work. The slightly fantastic mode of *The Circle of*

Reason accommodates the supernatural more easily than the later texts – especially in the second section, in which a swirl of stories include a number of ghosts – but even in those there is at least *one* moment or point which gestures towards the phantasmagoric. May Price, for instance, describes the Victoria Memorial in Calcutta as 'a haunted site' that occludes 'some other meaning' (167), illustrating once more the interrelation between the phantasmic and the palimpsest and their role in the 'double-task'. In a novel that dwells on the ephemeral nature of memory, that relation is conjured up again when the narrator sees in the cellar 'the ghosts who had been handed down to me by time: the ghost of the nine-year-old Tridib ... the ghost of Snipe ... the ghost of the eight-year-old Ila ... the ghostliness was merely the absence of time and distance – for that is all a ghost is, a presence displaced in time' (178). In other words, the ghost is a signifier of the *presence* of the past (which is, by definition, absent). This dialectic between absence and presence informs the work of Ghosh the historian in *In an Antique Land* as he conjures up ghostly presences from the archive.[39] At one point, the presence of that past delivers an uncanny shock. As he learns medieval Judæo-Arabic, he finds many similarities between it and the dialect of Lataifa:

> Over the next couple of years, as I followed the Slave's trail from library to library, there were times when the magnifying glass would drop out of my hand when I came across certain words and turns of phrase for I would suddenly hear the voice of Shaikh Musa speaking in the documents in front of me as clearly as though I had been walking past the canal, on my way between Lataifa and Nashawy. (IAAL, 105)

The Glass Palace also introduces a supernatural episode, when a phantom elephant kills the planter *sahib* who had been responsible for its caretaker's death (GP 99–103). In *The Hungry Tide*, the worldly and rationalist Kanai encounters a ghost in the form of a tiger on the island of Garjontola. The episode disturbs his urban complacency and is the catalyst for a reappraisal of his life and beliefs but it is also memorable for the manner in which it produces its uncanny effect, first by prefiguring the possible presence of the tiger as Fokir shows Kanai what he suggests are footprints but which, to Kanai, appear little more than marks in the mud; the discussion between them then turns to the question of fear, which for Fokir is a mark of respect for 'the ways in which the tide country dealt out death' (HT, 328) but which Kanai thinks is just a game that Fokir is playing with him in order to frighten him – a power game designed to reinforce Kanai's sense of dependence on him. The reader is thus attuned to this fear when Kanai, alone and distressed, sees the tiger before him 'less than a hundred meters away ... watching him with its tawny, flickering eyes' (329). Its appearance is so sudden that, along with Kanai, the reader is jolted by fear. Less than a page later, however, the very existence of this tiger is rendered doubtful, 'Horen shook his head. "There was nothing there," he said' (330), and as readers we are left with a nagging uncertainty that hovers between the lingering fear brought on by the encounter and the relief that washes in with the apparent return of 'normality'.

In each instance, the 'phantom' or haunting is a metaphor that gestures towards those subaltern pasts that cannot otherwise be brought into discourse without co-opting them into the metaphysic of modern meaning. More than that, it signifies the *presence* of such pasts in a radically plural world that cannot be exhaustively mapped by such a metaphysic. In *The Hungry Tide*, the link between Ghosh's literary phantoms and Chakrabarty's project is made explicit – an echo perhaps of their earlier correspondence. The subaltern figure of Fokir is seen as 'a ghost from the perpetual past that was Lusibari. But she guessed also that despite its newness and energy, the country Kanai inhabited [i.e. modern India] was full of these ghosts, these unseen presences whose murmurings could never quite be silenced' (HT 220). Co-existing with 'history', subaltern pasts constitute what Chakrabarty calls a 'time-knot', which is his term for 'the plurality that inheres in the "now"'.[40] It is because subaltern pasts are never fully lost, because modernity, despite its best efforts, is even now entangled with these pasts – in other words, because they continue to haunt modernity – that the 'uncanny' encounter of these discrepant life-worlds is signalled by the figure of the phantom.

It is at this point that we can comprehend the full significance of the 'doubles' in *In an Antique Land* and *The Shadow Lines*. For the uncanny is a double-effect: it is both familiar and strange at the same time. In Freud's seminal essay 'The Uncanny', the concept is explained through his identification of the series of doubles that structure Hoffmann's story, 'The Sandman'.[41] Even in common parlance, we speak of doing a 'double-take' and we do so because when we undergo an uncanny experience our reality is momentarily destabilised and our consciousness is partially displaced by our 'unconscious'. And, as we have seen with regard to *The Shadow Lines* in Chapter 3, it is perhaps in the unconscious that we inhabit those fragments of subaltern pasts most intimately. Indeed, perhaps it would be truer to say that *they* inhabit us, even if we consciously seek to repress them in the name of being or becoming modern. It is appropriate, then, that the subaltern historian, in striving to achieve the 'double-task' of estranging ourselves from the habits of consciousness that we call 'historical', should attempt to induce the necessary effect of the uncanny by deploying the figure of the double.

If the double-task of the subaltern historian is to hold in productive tension both 'analytical' histories that utilise the conceptual categories of modern historical thought *and* 'affective' histories that account for the plural ways of being-in-the-world, then according to Chakrabarty this calls for a 'nonsociological mode of translation [which] lends itself more easily to fiction, *particularly of the nonrealist or magic-realist variety practiced today, than to the secular and realist prose of sociology or history'.[42] As is apparent in the emphasis given here, fiction is not *necessarily* better suited to writing subaltern histories; rather, certain *forms* of fiction are of particular value. The realist novel, for instance, shares with historiography a common genealogy in the metaphysic of modern meaning, its protocols of representation being exactly the same: an omniscient third-person narrator;

an empiricist and secular epistemology; deployment of homogeneous, empty time and chronological plotting: cause, effect, and sequence; and a plain prose style that emphasises 'transparency' so as to give the impression that the text is merely a window onto the world. As Chakrabarty suggests, fantastical or magic-realist modes of fiction might offer the best prospects, and Ghosh has indeed utilised elements of the fantastic mode in both *The Circle of Reason* and *The Calcutta Chromosome*. And yet, his other texts cannot be said to be fantastical; indeed, they conspicuously share some of the features of formal realism, particularly its plain prose style. In what ways, then, do such texts challenge the dominant protocols of historical and realist representation?

Ghosh's formal experimentations visibly display his sympathy for the postmodern challenge to realist historiography and fiction. The non-chronological, self-reflexive, multi-generic nature of texts such as *The Circle of Reason*, *The Calcutta Chromosome*, *The Shadow Lines* and, to a lesser extent, *The Hungry Tide*, is apparent but two of his texts stand out for contrasting reasons and deserve further comment. On the one hand, *In an Antique Land* is the most formally experimental and innovative of his texts, and it also constitutes his most sustained engagement with historiography. On the other hand, *The Glass Palace* is his most humanist and 'orthodox' work, a classical historical novel in the manner of the great nineteenth-century realists. Both open up interesting avenues of inquiry into the formal requirements of doing subaltern history.

In an Antique Land is, above all, a bravura *performance*. Its most formidable formal achievement is its self-conscious showcasing of the production of historical knowledge by making visible the figure of the historian as an actor in the theatre of knowledge. As Robert Berkhofer has suggested, orthodox historians attempt to achieve a reality-effect for their texts by concealing their presence, 'what is presented as (f)actuality is a special coding ... designed to conceal their highly constructed basis'.[43] Hence the third person narrative, which is a way of organising the text so as to give the impression that it is literally

'History speaking' and not a historian.[44] Ghosh, on the other hand, inserts himself into his narrative. He charts his own progress, the obstacles he encounters, the assistance he receives; like an actor he adopts various *personae* – a detective, a student, an etymologist, a genealogist. From its very first words, the text *stages* its encounter with History, 'The Slave of MS. H.6 first stepped upon the stage of modern history in 1942. His was a brief debut, in the obscurest of theatres, and he was scarcely out of the wings before he was gone again … ' (IAAL, 13). The evident theatricality emphasises the fact that history is a form of rhetoric, an attempt at persuasion, and although we may find Ghosh's subaltern history convincing, it is not due to its inherent 'truth' or due to the unimpeachable weight of facts that he accumulates. In fact, there is precious little evidence to bear the weight of such a detailed historical reconstruction. Moreover, the bulk of the historical narrative concerns not the subaltern Bomma but the far from subaltern Ben Yiju.

It is precisely for this reason that Ghosh dramatises his own efforts in order to demonstrate how much of his narrative is a reconstruction by a historian whose own investment in his narrative is laid bare – this being the function of the 'anthropological' counter-narrative that propels Ghosh in search of the lost 'culture of accommodation' in the first place. In the process, he also illuminates the limits of historical knowledge. The process by which he arrives at a name for the Slave demonstrates this particularly well. The archive gives Ghosh only the faintest of clues – a letter in the Geniza archive mentions him and the translation renders it as 'Bama'. A footnote explains that the translator, the great historian Goitein, had 'been informed by a specialist in Indian history that "Bama" was "vernacular for Brahma"' (246). Ghosh, however, has his doubts and he informs the reader of the minutiae of his own attempt to establish the Slave's name. What is significant is that the Slave's name, by a quirk of the language in which it appears in the archive, is a *space* (B-M-A) which needs filling; it is clear, however, that it cannot be filled conclusively. Ghosh stages his hesitancies and doubts throughout his search and thus marks a limit within his own discourse of the historical 'knowledge' he is apparently revealing. Even the 'specialist' he consults says that 'the Slave's name was *probably* "Bomma"' (250). If the name is the key to Bomma's identity and therefore his history, it is nevertheless still only a small step towards establishing the subaltern past it represents. Again, rather than covering his tracks, Ghosh confidently displays them, 'It took me a long time afterwards to check the steps in the argument and to work out the consequences ... for the history of the Slave' (254). He still admits, however, that the argument itself is 'speculative'.

This is not the only time that Ghosh offers a qualified assessment of his own historical narrative. Throughout, one might say that he only provides us with 'speculative proof', and the evidence, rather than being used to *settle* the matter, is instead a spur towards further speculation. There is a simultaneous need to establish the 'facts' as presented in the archive and a refusal to be bound by them. Perhaps the sinuous nuances of this endeavour are best captured in the wonderfully coy manner with which he concludes that Ben Yiju's marriage to his slave Ashu was because he loved her: 'If I hesitate to call it love it is only because the documents offer no certain proof' (230). This after he has admitted, 'There is no particular reason to connect Ashu's manumission with Ben Yiju's fatherhood yet it is difficult not to' (229). The limits of the archive – 'no certain proof' or 'no particular reason' – are at once both illuminated and transgressed. Ghosh prefers to leap into the realms of speculation than to withdraw from the stage because in a sense he has no other choice – this is what a subaltern history demands, this 'fictional' excess that 'supplements' the discourse of the historian. The supply of extensive footnotes also performs the double-task of calling attention to the limits of history and its necessary supplements. As Shirley Chew has pointed out, they 'make wonderful reading in themselves. Referencing and explaining the matter in hand, they also gesture towards other stories and other pathways.'[45] If the orthodox historian uses footnotes to verify his account by *returning* to the 'facts' in the archive, Ghosh's footnotes are points of *departure* into the 'chain of signification', which is precisely what the 'supplement' is according to Derrida.

Chakrabarty's admission that fiction may be more suited to representing subaltern pasts than historiography raises another question – 'But then what of history?' he asks.[46] He broaches here the difficult theoretical problem of the relationship of fiction to history. We have seen in Chapter 2 how Ghosh has used fiction deconstructively to rewrite history in *The Calcutta Chromosome*; on the other hand, we have argued above that fiction *as such* does not necessarily fit this bill. Whilst postmodernists have emphasised the fictionality of history, there is in fact another side to the question: what, if any, is the historical value of fiction? It has perhaps been put better by Salman Rushdie in his political fable *Haroun and the Sea of Stories* (1990), 'What's the use of stories that aren't even true?'[47] This is too vast a question to dwell upon here but we can touch upon it by considering the example of the historical novel.

For the great Hungarian critic Georg Lukács, the historical novel in the hands of a Scott, a Manzoni, or a Tolstoy addresses the great question of 'historical truth in the artistic reflection of reality'.[48] It does this not by the accumulation of details but through its form, which reflects 'the struggles and antagonisms of history, by means of characters who, in their psychology and destiny, always represent social trends and historical forces.'[49] He praises Scott, in particular, for the elaboration of plots that focus on a 'middling' hero who renders these large historical dynamics in 'typically human terms': 'Through the plot, at whose centre stands this hero, a neutral ground is sought and found upon which the extreme, opposing social forces can be brought into a human relationship with one another.'[50] The social interactions of this middling hero enable the author to portray 'a broad and many-sided picture of the everyday life of the people' and thus represent 'the unity of social existence that underlies this richness'.[51] As such, 'a total historical picture' emerges.[52]

For Lukács, who is known as one of the great Marxist humanists, the key point is that in the hands of a master historical novelist fiction can deliver the kinds of historical truth that can only be rendered non-fictionally by historical materialism (i.e. Marxism). The historical novelist can 'penetrate [historical] facts in order to elicit their inner connections,' and in some respects trump the historian by rendering the great historical process – 'mankind's journey of progress,' he calls it – in human terms as 'the crowning peaks of the contradictory, vying forces of popular life'.[53] Throughout the magisterial opening chapter of *The Historical Novel*, one notices the characteristic register of 'historical necessity' and 'totality'. Despite its brilliance, however, the argument is tendentious. It exists to support a particular Marxist-Hegelian mode of historicist analysis. From this perspective, historical fiction has value precisely because it *confirms* historicism; it brings to light not that which disrupts or disturbs the historicist conception of time but those elements of the past that exemplify the historical necessity of such a vision.

In many respects, *The Glass Palace* possesses all the formal features of the historical novel as identified by Lukács. Like Scott's novels, its protagonists are not 'great' persons in the sense of being historically significant. Such historical personalities are seen by Lukács as 'representative ... because his [*sic*] personal passions and personal aim coincide with this great historical movement [embracing large sections of the people]', but one of the features of the historical novel is that they exist at the margins of the narrative.[54] In *The Glass Palace* the 'historical' figures such as the King and Queen of Burma, Aung-San Suu-Kyi, and even Gandhi, are all relatively minor figures. The personal trajectories of the various protagonists encompass both the elite and popular spheres of life ranging from the coolies on the Morningside Estate to the courtly splendour of Mandalay. Moreover, large historical forces are indeed represented by many of the characters – Rajkumar, the face of capitalist modernity; Uma, the nationalist hero; Arjun, the agonised, hybrid colonial subject and the instrument of colonial coercion; Dinu, who represents the rise of socialist internationalism, and so on. On reading *The Glass Palace* one may indeed concur with Lukács that the hero 'is life itself and not the individual.'[55]

Of course, there are a number of subaltern pasts alluded to in the novel – those of the *oosis* and *hsin-ouqs* in the forests of Burma; the indentured coolies; not to mention Rajkumar's own early life as an destitute orphan. Each of these and others are touched upon but their assimilation into a historical novel of this sort sweeps them up into the vortex of larger historical forces and renders them as ancillary details of a narrative that has its centre of gravity elsewhere. Two moments in the text, however, deserve attention as possible points of resistance to the historicism of the novel. One is a narrative fragment – the 'loose-end' of Arjun's death in the Burmese jungle. In contrast to his friend Hardy, whose affiliation to nationalism enables him to dwell with comfort in a (post-)colonial modernity, Arjun's fate perhaps gestures to the subaltern pasts that remain entangled within it. There is no 'future' for him because the experience of war has slowly dismantled his modern identity and opened him up to the conflicting pasts that play themselves out to a stand-still. He *cannot* re-enter modernity because the fragments of those subaltern pasts are no longer repressed by his modern self. The entangled pasts that constitute his contradictory person-ality dissolve his sense of identity and he lapses into desperate incoherence. He has become subaltern, as it were, and he thus opens up a momentary critical perspective that allows Dinu to re-evaluate his own historicism. Watching Arjun disintegrate before his eyes he reflects 'was it possible for someone such as him, Dinu, to assume there was a greater reality, a sweep of history that could be invoked … ? He could no longer be confi-dent that this was so' (GP 519).

The second moment is the twist at the end that turns the entire narrative on its head and even renders its status as a historical novel uncertain. Without warning, what had seemed like a standard third-person omniscient narrative is suddenly interrupted by the 'author' – not the 'narrator' as such but another figure who hovers on the edge of fictionality … Jaya's son, Rajkumar's great-grandson, who may or may not be Ghosh himself. The narrative is his 'book', which he has clearly written in the third person, but by introducing himself as a character in his own narrative his presence is disclosed and the text is displaced slightly; it is now as much a family memoir as it is a historical novel. This meta-fictional gesture is somewhat similar to Ghosh's self-reflexive experiments with the narrator of *In an Antique Land* or *The Shadow Lines*. The generic indeterminacy that ensues renders the 'history' it represents problematic because it suddenly becomes an intimate family portrait, a subjective account of one's own past. It thus has the status of a personal testimony which, for the orthodox historian, is of lesser value than the 'official' document. It lies at the intersection of personal memory, family lore and 'public' history that was explored in *The Shadow Lines*. Just as in that text this intersection illuminated the limits of both 'history' and 'memory', so too does this minute gesture remind us that Ghosh is perhaps not yet prepared to accede totally to the claims of historicism.

Nevertheless, *The Glass Palace* and, to a lesser extent, *The Hungry Tide*, mark a significant shift in Ghosh's writing towards a more humanist and historicist point of view. It would be mistaken, however, to overlook the fact that a humanist sympathy for historicism has always been a significant characteristic of his writing. Even the most postmodern of his texts, such as *In an Antique Land* and *The Calcutta Chromosome* exhibit this ambivalence towards history, which is one reason why the 'tiny threads, gigantic tapestry' metaphor is such a significant one in terms of his entire *oeuvre*.

Contrary to the anti-historicist, anti-empiricist conception of history that we have seen him employ, there are many moments in *In an Antique Land* when Ghosh seems perfectly unaware of his historicist methodology. For example, the category of 'evidence' is sometimes utilised in a quite orthodox and unproblematic way suggesting a direct sense of historical recoverability, in which the problem of reference is quite overlooked. Thus he says of his own notes, 'I knew that if my own memories *had not been preserved* in such artifacts as notes and diaries, the past would not have much purchase on my mind either' (IAAL 320, my emphasis). There is also his use, at times, of etymology in a strictly historicist manner, attempting to settle on the 'origins' of words and names. Thus, the 'Arabic word 'sukkar' ... is itself *ultimately derived* from a Sanskrit source' (IAAL 269, my emphasis); or the word 'adobe' 'probably derives from the Arabic al-tub' (IAAL 37); or 'Fustat' from the 'Latin-Greek word "fossaton"' (IAAL 36). Complementing this is a desire to return to 'original' architectural sites, especially when those sites are themselves the storehouses of words, so that the Geniza 'still stands on the site today ... the very site which held the greatest single collection of medieval documents ever discovered' (IAAL 59). As Derek Attridge shows, etymology's 'Greek root means "discourse on true meaning" ... This view of etymology [i.e. the earlier the meaning the better] is one version of the wide-spread notion that words have *authentic meanings*', and though it can be used to unsettle dominant ideologies it can also be used to confirm a dominant ideology.[56] In the nineteenth century, the development of the positivistic science of philology at the apogee of European imperialism utilised such etymological prac-tices to impose a particular model of history – one which traced languages to a point of origin in the 'classical' cultures of antiq-uity – which helped fix 'the map of modern knowledge' (IAAL 342), with Europe at its unquestioned centre. This concern with origins necessarily implies a teleology that affiliates Ghosh's theoretical position here with the historicist 'map' he is trying to redraw. Perhaps most significant of all is his construction of numerous linguistic continuities between the rural communities of modern Egypt and Ben Yiju's medieval community. On the one hand it does, as I have suggested above, problematise the construction of historical discourse by evoking the uncanny; on the other hand, however, it 'assumes an unproblematic identity across time',[57] which posits a humanist concern with a tran-scendent human identity that operates on the humbler levels of history – all that is required is to 'strip away the dense layer of accretions' (IAAL 291) in order to uncover it.

Such ambivalence, however, is appropriate to a writer who has wrestled throughout his career with the 'double task' atten-dant upon writing subaltern histories. In English, it is difficult to speak of the paradoxical nature of this task without lapsing into pejorative evaluations. Doubleness, for example, is often seen as synonymous with 'duplicity' which carries within it the charge of dishonesty, of not being 'straight'. The task which Ghosh has set out to achieve, along with others, is one that seeks to challenge the view that paradox and contradiction is inherently a problem, a point of view that has as a corollary the desire to 'straighten out' the warps and fractures of a radically plural world into a monochrome modernity. Amitav Ghosh has perhaps attempted the difficult task of 'provincialising Europe' with more imagination and precision than even most subaltern historians. Dipesh Chakrabarty may have theorised the task at hand with the greatest rigour thus far but in Ghosh's texts we see the ambition realised most vividly. In this respect, he may have enjoyed the advantages open to a writer of fiction but his talents and inclinations have been channelled by a disciplined and critical imagination. His texts straddle the border between history and fiction and it is from this indeterminate site that they attempt the impossible double-task of writing historically about pasts that could not have been articulated through historical discourse in the first place.

Critical overview and conclusion

Amitav Ghosh has established himself as one of the most significant Indian writers of his generation. His work has earned considerable critical acclaim in the Indian subcontinent, Europe, America and indeed much of the world. His major novels have been translated into a number of languages and rewarded with literary prizes.[1] This has in turn helped Ghosh to reach a wide readership, particularly in the United States and the Indian subcontinent. Rather surprisingly, despite the strong critical endorsement of his novels in Britain, his profile there has never been quite so high, which perhaps reflects the inordinate influence of the Man Booker Prize for which he has (again, surprisingly) never been nominated.

In terms of academic criticism, Ghosh has enjoyed considerable attention from literary scholars in America, Britain, and the Indian subcontinent, who see in his writing perhaps the most sustained and coherent attempt to engage with some of the most politically contentious, and therefore theoretically important, contemporary issues. As indicated in Chapter 1, his work wrestles with the post-colonial predicament in ways that demonstrate a certain self-consciousness about the academic work that has developed in the latter decades of the twentieth century under the rubrics of 'critical theory', 'postmodernism' and 'postcolonialism'. Perhaps for this reason it was within academic circles that Ghosh's voice was first recognised as being the most prominent of all the post-Rushdie generation of Indian writers in English. The publication of *The Shadow Lines* was a significant milestone in this respect, coinciding as it did with the emergence of a critique of nationalism and national identity within what was then becoming established as 'postcolonialism'. *In an Antique Land* confirmed this first impression of Ghosh as a highly intellectual writer whose preoccupations largely overlapped with this new generation of critics, and whose innovative textual experiments offered new insights and openings into the cluster of conceptual and theoretical concepts that had been developed to describe, analyse and interpret the complex of colonial and post-colonial relations.

And yet there is surprisingly little published criticism on Ghosh when compared, for example, to Rushdie (though it must also be admitted that this is rapidly changing). To date, there are only two monographs on his work (including this one) and several volumes of essays, most of which have only been published in India and a larger number of articles in scholarly journals.[2] In addition, Ghosh's work has received critical treatment in some books which also deal with larger themes and other authors, the most notable of which is Tabish Khair's long chapter on *The Calcutta Chromosome* in his *Babu Fictions: Alienation in Contemporary Indian English Novels*.[3] In terms of unpublished research, a number of PhD dissertations have been completed in recent years that either focus exclusively on Ghosh or deal with one or more of his texts in relation to a wider thesis. The most noteworthy of these is by Claire Chambers, who has also published parts of the thesis in a couple of fine journal articles on *The Circle of Reason* and the relationship between science and pseudo-science, and *The Calcutta Chromosome* as post-colonial science fiction.

The extant criticism has been largely directed towards *The Shadow Lines*, *In an Antique Land*, and *The Calcutta Chromosome*. There is a notable divergence of interests here between the criticism that has emerged from the Indian subcontinent and that which has been produced in the Western academy. The former have tended to concentrate on *The Shadow Lines*, whilst the emphasis of the latter has been on *In an Antique Land* and *The Calcutta Chromosome*. This is perhaps an inevitable reflection of the subject matter of the respective texts on the one hand, and the preoccupations of the critics on the other. Given the focus of *The Shadow Lines* on questions of national identity and communalism in the subcontinent, it is not surprising to find that its impact in India has been enormous. It is a set text in most university curricula, and has been published by Oxford University Press as a critical edition for students complete with a selection of some highly significant and influential essays. Most of the volumes of essays that have been published in India are dedicated to *The Shadow Lines*, as a glance at the bibliography will indicate. Whilst there are some volumes of essays that examine Ghosh's writing as a whole they too reflect the overwhelming presence of *The Shadow Lines* within the Indian literary-critical imagination: they tend to bulge with essays on that novel – with *In an Antique Land* and *The Calcutta Chromosome* making up the supporting cast, and *The Glass Palace* and *The Circle of Reason* barely emerging out of the wings. In Western circles, however, the balance is shifted firmly towards the more experimental and postmodern *In an Antique Land* and *The Calcutta Chromosome*. Mapped onto this initial divergence, one notices a further divergence in the evaluation of Ghosh's writing. Although, on the whole, Ghosh's work has been favourably received, there is nevertheless a strong chord of dissent from a number of Indian critics who are generally positioned on the political left and espouse a more traditional Marxist criticism. By contrast, Ghosh's reception in the West has been almost unanimously enthusiastic.

Although a detailed consideration of the extant criticism on Ghosh's work is beyond the scope of this chapter, it is worth identifying a few issues that have emerged as significant points of debate. The first of these concerns Ghosh's representations of gender. With the exception of Nagesh Rao, most Western critics have tended to overlook gender in Ghosh's work, or deal with it tangentially in favour of the more obvious concerns with knowledge, history and the politics of religious and cultural identity – as, indeed, has this book.[4] But it is worth dwelling on this issue a little because Ghosh's representations of gender in *The Shadow*

Lines has been the subject of much critical debate in India. At its heart, this debate concerns the respective characterisations of the major male and female characters – the narrator, Tridib and Nick Price on the one hand, and Ila, the grandmother and May Price on the other – and the framing of their moral and political attitudes and choices within the narrative structure. Rajeswari Sunder Rajan, for example, argues that despite the novel's inversion of the usual passive/active signifiers it nevertheless associates itself with the passive male characters, who are evaluated positively, at the expense of the active female ones. In contrast to the narrator's admiration and respect for Tridib's cosmopolitanism stands the seemingly systematic satirical representation of Ila's cosmopolitanism; the grandmother, too, stands in contrast to Tridib as the embodiment of the nationalism that the novel so effectively critiques. Both suffer quite badly at the hands of the narrative, and because it is difficult to distinguish between the narratorial and authorial voices one may reasonably conclude that the perspective of the narrator is that of text itself: 'what remains with us at the end is the punishments visited on both [Ila and the grandmother], endings which have a curiously harsh air of retribution about them. The counterpart of the novel's romanticized homosociality [i.e. the relationship between Tridib and the narrator] is a covert misogyny directed at the grandmother and the beloved.'[5]

The novel's critique of nationalism is therefore highly gendered. Its espousal of Tridib's cosmopolitanism over Ila's reveals the text to be complicit in the framing of a post-national future in terms of a benign masculinity. This in turn associates an undesirable nationalism with femininity. Insofar as women become the sites where the notion of 'freedom' is played out – the grandmother's desire for political freedom from colonial rule on the one hand, and Ila's desire for personal freedom from (national) 'tradition' on the other – Ghosh repeats a certain nationalist gesture of using women as emblematic figures that do not signify 'womanhood' as such but something else, such as 'culture', 'tradition', 'nation', and 'authenticity'.[6] This, however, is precisely the point at which a possible counter-argument about the novel's gender politics might emerge. For Ila's significance as an embodiment of Western ideas about sexuality is shown to be nothing more than a projected image that belies an altogether different reality. Instead of the 'greedy little slut' who 'wants to be left alone to do as she pleases' (SL, 78, 88), she is later shown to be nothing like the kind of person both the grandmother and the narrator imagined her to be, 'I only talked like that to shock you, and because *you seemed to expect it of me somehow*. I never did any of those things: I'm about as chaste, in my own way, as any woman you'll ever meet' (SL, 184, my emphasis).

Two points emerge from this line of argument. The first is that contrary to Sunder Rajan's assertion that 'There is no suggestion of irony, resistant points of view, or other checks to the reach of [the narrator's] central vision', what we witness here is precisely a limitation of and resistance to his perspective that puts into doubt the easy identification of the narrator's point of view with that of the novel itself. In the gap that is opened up is a space for a critique of the narrator himself. Secondly, following on from this, one sees in Ila's words a convergence between the narrator's view of female sexuality and that of the grandmother. In other words, it is far from clear that the narrator does unequivocally espouse Tridib's transcendent cosmopolitanism. Indeed, as Jon Mee has shown, it is far from clear that Tridib's own cosmopolitanism is 'transcendent' at all.[7]

In the 'hotel bar' passage that is sandwiched between the grandmother's first attack on Ila and her second, when Ila pushes her uncle Robi's tolerance of her behaviour to breaking point, it becomes clear that both Robi and then the grandmother interpret her desire for personal freedom as a woman in purely sexual terms which are then translated into an affront to their 'culture'. Like others before them, they both see a woman's personal behaviour as being bound up with the integrity and authenticity of national identity. Her 'Western' behaviour is condemned precisely because it supposedly violates this arrangement. Ila's behaviour not only illuminates how nationalism thus reinforces patriarchy but it also shows how, despite their scepticism towards nationalism, both Robi and the narrator are shown to be implicated within its rigidly patriarchal construction of sexual and gender relations. As Suvir Kaul has perceptively noted when Ila later discloses her unhappiness with Nick, the narrator displays a 'minor cultural triumphalism' that is based no doubt on his continued investment in a nationalist view of gender relations.[8] In other words, the narrator's views on gender and sexuality reveal the contradictions of his own cosmopolitan desire.

Compared to *The Shadow Lines*, there has been relatively little debate about Ghosh's representation of gender and sexuality in his other texts. Why this is so is a matter for speculation but it is worth pointing out that the women have become more significant presences in Ghosh's texts. Whilst James Clifford's complaint that 'We hear little from women' in 'The Imam and the Indian' holds true, to some extent, of *In an Antique Land* as well, they certainly have more of a presence in the longer text.[9] It is *The Calcutta Chromosome*, however, that sees a feminine figure emerge for the first time in Ghosh's work as a central organising principle around which the text is structured. Mangala, as the doubly-subaltern leader of the counter-science cult, is central to the novel's attempt to revise the discourse of science thereby articulating, according to Suchitra Mathur, an 'alternate mode of being/knowledge that provides scope for third-world/women's agency'.[10] Both *The Glass Palace* and *The Hungry Tide* follow-up with women characters that are more detailed and more individualised than either Ila or the grandmother in *The Shadow Lines*, who sometimes appear to be sketched rather schematically. Dolly and Uma, for example, are not vehicles for any particular point concerning nationality, tradition and identity. They develop as characters and occupy as much of the emotional landscape of the *The Glass Palace* as their male counterparts. Though it would be fair to add that the central characters such as Arjun and Rajkumar are still men, the novel does not subordinate them to the male perspective. In *The Hungry Tide* the central character is a young woman, Piyali Roy, and she is supported throughout by a cast of female characters including Mashima, Kusum and Moyna that together create a text which is, to large extent, articulated from a feminine perspective. Whilst it is not possible to conduct a thorough examination of Ghosh's representations of gender in these later texts in this chapter, it is perhaps appropriate to indicate this as an area that demands further thought and research.

Another issue is the concern that some critics have about the political implications of Ghosh's writing. In particular, they see his work as espousing a postmodern idealism that abdicates the political responsibility to examine the 'material' conditions of post-colonial experience. As such, some of them argue that Ghosh does not face up to 'political realities'. Again, this criticism is voiced mainly by Indian critics and it is principally directed at *The Shadow Lines*. The most influential essay in this respect is perhaps A.N. Kaul's 'A Reading of *The Shadow Lines*', which is reprinted at the back of the critical edition of *The Shadow Lines*. He argues that the novel's point is that the shadow lines between nations is an 'illusion' and that 'frontiers ... do not exist'.[11] He adds that that novel, 'also sees as illusions so many other demarcations and categories of human experience and understanding', that the only thing it values is an 'amorphous romantic subjectivity' expressed through 'the primacy of the imagination'.[12] This leads him to conclude that '"Shadow lines" is a metaphor for evading rather than exploring political realities ... Realities do not go away just because you call them illusions'.[13]

It is clear that the argument presented in this book diverges fundamentally from Kaul's rather crude materialistic reading, which depends on a binary opposition between 'imagination' and 'reality'. As Jon Mee has argued in Ghosh's defence, Kaul 'seems to ignore the anthropological nature of the imagination explored in the novel';[14] moreover, it is perhaps significant that Kaul quotes Ernest Gellner's unequivocal statement that nationalism 'invents nations where they do not exist' rather than Benedict Anderson's nuanced definition of the nation being an 'imagined community' in which 'imaginary' is not a synonym for 'invented'.[15] Later, he proposes that the novel, despite 'the precise mention of dates and locations', espouses 'the idea of the non-reality of space and time' in order to draw attention to 'the sameness of the underlying essential experience'.[16] It is difficult to see how the novel both imagines space and time with precision *and* suggests that they are 'unreal' but in any case the real target of Kaul's ire is the novel's 'postmodern banalities', which ignore 'the operation of such divisive forces as racism, imperialism, and class exploitation'.[17] There is a pointed silence, however, about the divisiveness of nationalism – a significant omission that suggests Kaul is articulating a position from the Indian nationalist left.

Kaul's basic position has been repeated by many other Indian critics of *The Shadow Lines*, but it has also reappeared in Gauri Viswanathan's highly influential early essay on *In an Antique Land*, 'Beyond Orientalism: Syncretism and the Politics of Knowledge.' Viswanathan has criticised Ghosh's espousal of syncretism, which she suggests is a point of contradiction in Ghosh's argument because whilst Ghosh sees syncretism as 'a sign of revolt, persisting in the cultural practices of contiguous local communities, against the meretricious assertion of difference by the state', the history of syncretism as a concept is ironically shown, through her archaeology of its emergence in nineteenth-century England, to have been 'a fiction produced by the state as it absorbs religious and cultural identities into a unified national identity'.[18] Ghosh's adherence to syncretism thus leads to him being 'trapped by [his] inability to confront difference at the level of immediate, intersubjective encounters'.[19] This, she suggests, is why he is compelled to look to the past when he is faced with the Egyptian *fellaheen* who continuously interrogate his 'difference' in the present. Taking refuge in history is symptomatic of the inadequacies of syncretism as a response to political conflict, and 'can be read as an inability or even refusal to concede the reality of partition'.[20] In contrast to Kaul's depiction of Ghosh as a fully paid-up postmodernist, this critique of Ghosh's syncretism is, in effect, a critique of the political inefficacy of the secular humanism that he shares with Nehru.

From the other end of the critical spectrum, Robert Dixon has argued that *In an Antique Land* is far more effective in its cultural politics than *The Shadow Lines* precisely because the latter submits 'an untheorized and utopian belief in a common humanity', whereas the former's postmodernism 'allows him to avoid … "the slide towards essentialism"'.[21] Speaking from within the terms of a postcolonial theory that has assimilated the idioms of postmodernism and post-structuralism, Dixon believes that *In an Antique Land* manages to deliver the 'strategic essentialism' that Spivak had noticed in the Subaltern Studies project through 'a fluid and at times confusing deployment of the lexicons of both liberal humanism and post-structuralism … [which] is part of his strategic avoidance with either humanism or post-structuralism … In a theoretically elusive way he suggests that "real life" can only be grasped as a performance in the "theatre" of writing, which actually produces the presence it seems to describe.'[22]

Although Dixon acknowledges the tension in *In an Antique Land* between humanism and postmodernism here, it seems strange that he should conclude that Ghosh's strategy is to avoid affiliation with either. Dixon's phrasing may be seen, in fact, as an unwitting corroboration of Kaul and Viswanathan's disquiet about the political implications of Ghosh's work. Seeing the tension between postmodernism and humanism in *The Shadow Lines* as a 'fault' that needs to be resolved, the resolution he identifies in *In an Antique Land* does not involve a choice between one or the other but the *avoidance of both*. Ironically, this leaves the theoretical – and therefore political – status of Ghosh's texts unresolved. In fact, Dixon seems to suggest that Ghosh's texts float free of any affiliation – a position quite close to Kaul's assertion that Ghosh values an 'amorphous' imagination over material reality.

What Dixon does not seem to consider is the possibility that Ghosh's 'duplicity' does not indicate a 'refusal to be pinned down' by avoiding affiliation with either liberal humanism or postmodernism but instead denotes a strategic *commitment to both*. The central argument of this book has been that Ghosh's writing is characterised by an *ambivalent* tension between the modes of liberal humanism and those of postmodernism but all three of the critical positions outlined above attempt to resolve this tension, by characterising his work unequivocally as post-modernist (Kaul), humanist (Viswanathan), or by dissolving it altogether (Dixon). In the preceding chapters we have examined some of the reasons for Ghosh's ambivalence but we have yet to evaluate its political value. Does it imply that Ghosh is unable to make the necessary choices that constitute an effective political attitude? Or does it ask us to reconsider what constitutes 'the political' itself?

Those who dismiss Ghosh's writing as an abdication of political responsibility or a refusal to confront harsh political realities do so on the basis of a particular vision of what constitutes an effective or appropriate political behaviour or attitude. This vision is based on the fundamental premise that politics involves action – an active intervention into the affairs of the world. Any discourse is thus endowed with political significance to the extent that it can be acted upon. As such, politics involves the making of choices that enable one to follow through on a particular course of action. It is here that Ghosh's ambivalence creates something of a problem not because he avoids making a choice (as Dixon suggests) but rather because he simultaneously espouses more than one political position. In other words, Ghosh refuses to make a choice based on a binary model – he chooses both. According to the standard view, this dilutes the political efficacy of his work because in politics one cannot follow two opposing courses of action at the same time. Ambivalence is therefore seen as a sign of political weakness – it is read as vacillation, or paralysis, or even a refusal of politics itself.

But what is at stake in the idea that if one does not hold an unequivocal political position then one does not have the basis for a viable political praxis? Given that globalisation has resulted in accelerating the multiple contradictions inherent in modernity, how is it possible *not* to be ambivalent, especially if attending to the 'double task' demanded by a post-colonial politics that seeks social and political justice for the wretched of the earth on the one hand, whilst observing and respecting cultural difference on the other? This politics simply cannot be unequivocal because it must always contain within itself this inherent doubleness (which is not a 'duplicity'): one register that acknowledges the metaphysic of modernity, its institutions and its governing ensembles of knowledge such as the state, citizenship, equality, social science and the rule of law etc.; and, on the other hand, another register which exceeds and resists that metaphysic because it does not observe the forms of rationality that inhere in the emancipatory projects of modernity. Indeed, this politics recognises that those projects involve an epistemic violence against other ways of thinking and being in the world – hence the strategic value of an alignment with postmodernism – whilst also acknowledging the importance of modernity's universal frameworks in any struggle to establish social justice on a global scale.

This 'politics of ambivalence' must necessarily stand somewhat at odds with an 'activist' vision of politics because any negotiation of cultural difference involves keeping open the ethical possibility of 'doubleness'. In other words, Ghosh's attempt to choose *both* the political registers of modernity – humanism, secularism, syncretic nationalism, historicism – *and* those registers that resist or contest them – subaltern, postmodernism – signals a commitment to the 'ethical' dilemmas involved whenever one encounters the Other. What his politics of ambivalence refuses is the subordination of the ethical to the political, the means to the ends, theory to practice, and deliberation to action that the 'activist' view of politics sets up in a series of false oppositions that establish a particular conception of what constitutes 'politics'. This rhetoric of political activism, rather than keeping open the ethical negotiation of cultural difference, forecloses it by insisting on achieving ends at the expense of exploring the means. It goes without saying that these ends are not often those envisaged by subaltern groups themselves. Indeed, the activist view of politics in our time continues to reinforce the universalisation of European norms and categories. This is not to say that there is no need for political activism: there are clearly many occasions that demand decisive political interventions. It is debatable, however, whether novels are suitable ideological vehicles for such moments given the relative autonomy of the genre from the political field. Ambivalence, on the other hand, might be seen as an appropriate position for a novelist to adopt in a post-colonial context. It could be read as the register of an ethics that recognises the inescapable duality and impossible paradox of the post-colonial predicament.

It is perhaps not surprising, then, that along with ambivalence the main register in Ghosh's texts is that of irony. For irony involves a certain doubleness of perspective, and the many ironies in Ghosh's texts signal an ability to look both ways. Most of them are situational ironies and his usual tactic is to approach the situation from the perspective of those who are about to be ironised. This establishes a certain sympathy between the reader and the victim of the irony. At the same time, the irony is produced by a deliberate distancing of the reader's perspective, which allows them to see and know what cannot be seen or known by the characters being ironised. This double-effect is perhaps analogous to Dipesh Chakrabarty's call for histories that are both 'analytical' (distanced) and 'affective' (sympathetic).

Nor is it surprising that many of the key moments in Ghosh's texts involve the foregrounding of an ethical situation which remains unresolved. We shall focus briefly here on two similar episodes in *The Shadow Lines* and *The Hungry Tide* which dramatise the encounter between Western values and norms and those Others whom the West's rhetoric of political activism often ignores or injures as it establishes its own political standards as universal. In both cases, Ghosh does not seek to judge or apportion blame but he does demonstrate how a 'Western' urge to political intervention forecloses an ethical understanding of the 'local' standards of conduct. In *The Shadow Lines* it is May Price who demonstrates this disjunction between Western humanitarianism and the dynamics of communalism peculiar to the subcontinent. The text scrupulously delineates her humanitarian credentials in order to prepare the ground for the climactic episode that leads to Tridib's death. She is shown devoting her life to 'several worthy causes', fasting on a Saturday in solidarity with those in the world who go hungry, and using her free time to collect money for 'famine relief'. She is an admirable character who sees what she does as 'useful'. Later, she introduces Tridib to the merits of 'humane' intervention. As they drive out of Calcutta, she makes him stop the car in order to put an injured dog out of its misery. The stubborn refusal to accept the local norms of conduct that Tridib and the narrator exhibit introduces the smallest hint of Western condescension, which is significantly voiced by her opposition between speech and action, 'All you're good for is words. Can't you ever *do* anything?' (SL 170). Perhaps it is this activist rebuke to the passive Tridib that coils the psychological spring that leads to his disastrous intervention at the end of the novel. It is certainly the case that the condescension she voiced during the dog episode is repeated more vociferously and with greater emphasis. Articulating herself with the self-righteousness of someone who is secure in the knowledge that her values trump all others, she screams once more for action, 'Those two are going to be killed because of you – you're cowards, murderers, to abandon them like that' (SL 240). Is she to blame for Tridib's death? The novel withholds its judgment and perhaps indicates that we as readers must do so too. But in the decisive moment, it is clear that May herself does not. She assigns responsibility for what is going to happen to the Other – 'killed *because of you*' – thereby reserving for herself the prerogative of moral and ethical judgment. And yet, ironically, it may be said that it is *she* who is responsible for three and not two deaths. It must be stated once more that the text withholds its judgment. Are two deaths necessarily better than three? And should we not *try* to save a life even if we must thereby risk others? Are 'we' in the West better equipped to respond to these difficult dilemmas than others? These ethical questions remain unresolved and have perhaps even intensified in the uncertain and tense political climate of the early twenty-first century. *The Shadow Lines* perhaps offers us a way of approaching such questions without imposing any particular answers.

A similar episode occurs in *The Hungry Tide*, this time in relation to the politics of ecology and conservation. Again, Ghosh meticulously prepares the ground for the decisive episode. Using the mechanism of a rediscovered diary to introduce a flashback,

Ghosh outlines the conflict which led to the 'forgotten' massacre in 1970 of refugee settlers on the island of Morichjhāpi in the Sundarbans, the tide country of the Bay of Bengal. The diary enables Ghosh to introduce the conflict and its consequences not only in the familiar terms of a post-colonial governmentality that is quick to direct the coercive machineries of the state against its own citizens, but also in terms of a political disjunction between the demands of wildlife conservation according to a particular western model of ecology, and the needs of the local inhabitants who consider themselves to be an integral part of the local ecology:

> the worst part was not the hunger or the thirst. It was to sit here, helpless, and listen to the policemen making their announcements, hearing them say that our lives, our existence, was worth less than dirt or dust. 'This island has to be saved for its trees, it has to be saved for its animals, it is a part of a reserve forest, it belongs to a project to save tigers, which is paid for by people from all around the world.' Every day, sitting here, with hunger gnawing at our bellies, we would listen to these words, over and over again. Who are these people, I wondered, who love animals so much that they are willing to kill us for them? Do they know what is being done in their names? Where do they live, these people, do they have children, do they have mothers, fathers? As I thought of these things it seemed to me that this whole world has become a place of animals, and our fault, our crime, was that we were just human beings, trying to live as human beings always have, from the water and the soil. No human being could think this a crime unless they have forgotten that this is how humans have always lived – by fishing, by clearing land and by planting the soil. (HT 261–2)

For the inhabitants of the tide country, they are themselves part of the environment; their lives are dictated by the rhythms and force of the tides, by their relation to the soil and to the animals that surround them. The novel suggests that western environmentalism has, at least in some incarnations, a propensity to separate humanity from 'nature' – perhaps as a result of the binary western thinking that posits an opposition between 'culture' and 'nature' – and the tiger in particular is seen as a motif of this clash of perspectives. Whilst the tide country people fear and respect the tiger, they see it as just another inhabitant of the Sundarbans. They do not, however, romanticise the tiger nor do they believe that the tiger needs to be 'protected' from them. Indeed, they know that nothing protects them from the tiger. The tigers in the tide country are man-eaters and they live beside humans in a precarious balance that is signalled symbolically by the imaginary line that divides Bon-bibi's realm (human) from the demon Dokkin-rai's (the tiger). For either creature to cross that line is to invite confrontation.

When Piyali Roy witnesses the killing of a tiger, her sympathy for the tiger outweighs her concern for the human inhabitants of the village. It is the moment that her romantic vision of her fisherman guide, Fokir, is punctured. Like May, her tone is one of outrage and moral censure. Again, the politics that accompanies this position is an activist one, 'We have to do something, Kanai. We can't let this happen' (HT 293). Her companion, Kanai, an urbane and modern Indian, however, recognises what she herself cannot or does not see. Instead of action, he suggests that she try to see it from the villagers' point of view, 'Piya, you have to understand – that animal's been preying on this village for years. It killed two people and any number of cows and goats ... ' (HT 294). Locked as she is into a Western paradigm which sees humans as being different from animals, she believes that human beings must be responsible for their actions, whereas animals bear no responsibility for theirs, 'This is an animal, Kanai ... You can't take revenge on an animal' (ibid.). This is in contrast to Fokir, who sees the tiger much as he would see his human neighbours, 'He says, when a tiger comes into a human settlement, it's because it wants to die' (HT 295). Ghosh represents this episode in a manner that closes the customary distance between humanity and animals. The mob takes on a bestial appearance; on the other hand, through Piya's eyes the tiger is humanised, 'it was as if she could see the animal cowering inside the pen.' (294) For Western readers this perhaps displaces sympathy onto the animal; on the other hand we are told both during the episode and in the chapter that follows that tigers kill people as well. In an ethical debate between Kanai and Piya, he reminds her that 'It happens every week that people are killed by tigers ... If there were killings on that scale anywhere else on earth it would be called a genocide, and yet here it goes unremarked' (300). The reason for this, he argues, was because 'it was people like you ... who made a push to protect the wildlife here, without regard for the human costs' (301). Piya, however, retorts, 'Just suppose we cross that imaginary line that prevents us from deciding that no other species matters except ourselves. What'll be left then? Aren't we alone enough in the universe? And do you think it'll stop at that? Once we decide we can kill off other species, it'll be people next – exactly the people you're thinking of, people who are poor and unnoticed' (ibid.). Once again, the novel does not offer a resolution; its position is ambivalent but this lack of resolution is precisely what opens up the ethical debate – unlike the resolute and activist positions adopted by May and Piya, which close it off.

The importance of Amitav Ghosh's politics of ambivalence is not so much in its inherent political value or otherwise but rather in the way it offers us a means of revising what politics might mean in a globalised, post-colonial world. Its political value must therefore be seen within the context of the effort to 'provincialize Europe'. Is social justice of any value if, in order to achieve it, we must erase the other ways of being in the world that might help us visualise a more inclusive, globally just future if only we could somehow find the means to listen to them? And in order to listen to them, what must we do to our own ways of thinking and being? The pressure of these questions weighs heavily on Ghosh's work, and it is to his credit that he neither evades them nor does he attempt to resolve them. If we remain frustrated by this open-endedness then this perhaps reflects our need for the closure of ethical, political and imaginative possibilities in order to pursue a politics that gives us the satisfaction of appearing to do something. But, as we have seen in relation to the two episodes discussed above, doing 'something' is not necessarily the same as the ethical imperative to do the *right* thing. Amitav Ghosh has consistently tried to observe this ethical imperative, to keep open the channels of communication between ourselves and our Others so that we might begin to 'hear that which [we] do not already understand'.[23]

Notes

Chapter 1

1 *The New Yorker*, 73, 23 and 30 June, 1997. The photograph is reproduced in Arvind Krishna Mehrotra, ed. *A History of Indian Literature in English*, London: Hurst & Co., 2003, p. 319.

2 Amitav Ghosh, 'India's Untold War of Independence,' *The New Yorker*, 73, 23 and 30 June, 1997, pp. 104–21.

3 Interview with Neluka Silva and Alex Tickell, *Kunapipi*, 19:3, 1997, p. 171.

4 Ibid.

5 James Clifford, 'The Transit Lounge of Culture', *Times Literary Supplement*, 3 May 1991, p. 8.

6 Meenakshi Mukherjee, 'Maps and Mirrors: Co-ordinates of Meaning in *The Shadow Lines*' in *The Perishable Empire: Essays on Indian Writing in English*, New Delhi: Oxford University Press, 2000, p. 139.

7 Amitav Ghosh, 'The March of the Novel through History: the Testimony of my Grandfather's Bookcase' in *The Imam and the Indian: Prose Pieces*, Delhi: Permanent Black, 2002, p. 289. Hereafter cited in the text as 'The March of the Novel'.

8 Ranajit Guha, *An Indian Historiography of India: A Nineteenth Century Agenda and its Implications*, Calcutta: K.P. Bagchi, 1988, p. 42. See also Henry Schwarz, *Writing Cultural History in Colonial and Postcolonial India*, Philadelphia: University of Pennsylvania Press, 1997.

9 Edward Said, *Culture and Imperialism*, London: Chatto and Windus, 1993.

10 Amitav Ghosh, 'The Ghosts of Mrs. Gandhi' in *The Imam and the Indian*, pp. 46–62.

11   Suni Khilnani, *The Idea of India*, London: Penguin, 1998, pp. 199–200.

12   Ibid., 201.

13   Interview with Tehelka.com, 9 August 2000, cited in Claire Chambers, 'The Relationship between Knowledge and Power in the Work of Amitav Ghosh'. Unpublished PhD dissertation, University of Leeds, 2003, p. 252.

14   Interview with Frederick Luis Almada, *World Literature Today*, 76:2, 2002, p. 89.

15   The term is Dipesh Chakrabarty's and is introduced in chapter 4 in his *Provincializing Europe: Postcolonial Thought and Historical Difference*, Princeton: Princeton University Press, 2000. The term is useful as a reminder that not all subaltern histories are histories of subalterns in the sociological sense. This will be discussed in more detail in Chapter 4.

16   Steven Connor, *Postmodernist Culture: An Introduction to Theories of the Contemporary*, Oxford: Blackwell, 1989, p. 6.

17   Sugata Bose and Ayesha Jalal, *Modern South Asia: History, Culture, Political Economy*, London: Routledge, 1997, pp. 201–2.

18   Khilnani, *Idea of India*, p. 51.

19   The term 'governmentality' was coined by the French philosopher and historian Michel Foucault. Its implications for readings of Amitav Ghosh's will be discussed in detail in Chapter 2.

20   One of the key formative experiences of an entire generation of Bengali intellectuals who came of age in the 1960s and 1970s was the Maoist-inspired Naxalite insurgency in 1967, a militant peasant uprising that had its origins in the village of Naxalbari in Darjeeling, in northern West Bengal. It spread across West Bengal and even to other states such as Andhra Pradesh, inspiring as well as terrifying the urban Bengali middle classes. In the wake of Naxalbari, many Calcutta students affiliated themselves to Maoist ideas and organisations. The Naxalite insurgency is a very minor but perceptible echo in some of Ghosh's works: it is hinted at in *The Circle of Reason* by Rakhal's clandestine bomb-making, and indeed Alu's characterisation by the authorities as an 'extremist' is an indication of its presence in the narrative. In *The Shadow Lines*, the narrator mentions early on that 'everybody young was turning Maoist at that time.', p. 10. Although this was before the Naxalbari uprising, it indicates the degree to which Maoism circulated within the cultural imagination of certain sections of metropolitan Bengal.

21 For useful introductions to their work see Ranajit Guha and Gayatri Chakravorty Spivak, eds. *Selected Subaltern Studies*, New York: Oxford University Press, 1988; Vinayak Chaturvedi, ed. *Mapping Subaltern Studies and the Postcolonial*, London: Verso, 2000; and David Ludden, ed. *Reading Subaltern Studies: Critical History, Contested Meaning and the Globalization of South Asia*, London: Anthem Press, 2002.

22 Interview with Neluka Silva and Alex Tickell, p. 173.

23 Amitav Ghosh, 'The Slave of MS. H.6' in Partha Chatterjee and Gyanendra Pandey, eds. *Subaltern Studies: Writing on Asian History and Society, Vol. VII*, New Delhi: Oxford University Press, 1992, pp. 159–220.

24 Amitav Ghosh, *Dancing in Cambodia, At Large in Burma*, New Delhi: Ravi Dayal, 1998, p. 87.

25 See his essay, 'Naipaul and the Nobel', which can be accessed at his website www.amitavghosh.com.

26 Tony Davies, *Humanism*, London: Routledge, 1997, p. 24.

27 Schwarz, *Writing Cultural History*, p. 47; see also p. 36.

28 Amitav Ghosh, *Countdown*, New Delhi: Ravi Dayal, 1999, p. 106.

29 Sumit Sarkar, 'Renaissance and Kaliyuga: Time, Myth and History in Colonial Bengal' in Gerald Sider and Gavin Smith, eds. *Between History and Histories: The Making of Silences and Commemorations*, London: University of Toronto Press, 1997, p. 101.

30 Ranajit Guha notes that historiography actually predated the emergence of the novel in colonial Bengal in *An Indian Historiography of India*, p. 31.

31 The key figure in this respect was the scientist J.C. Bose, who appears as a figure of adulation for Balaram in *The Circle of Reason.*

32 Khilnani, *Idea of India*, p. 26.

33 Interview with Tehelka.com, 9 August 2000, cited in Claire Chambers, 'The Relationship between Knowledge and Power' p. 244. See also Ghosh's detailed correspondence with the Subaltern Studies historian Dipesh Chakrabarty concerning his book *Provincializing Europe*, 20 December 2000. This correspondence can be accessed at www.amitavghosh.com.

34 Sumanta Banerjee, *The Parlour and the Streets: Elite and Popular Culture in Nineteenth Century Calcutta*, Calcutta: Seagull, 1989, p. 149.

35 Ibid., 205–6.

36 Rabindranath Tagore, *Nationalism*, London: Macmillan, 1917, pp. 19; 22; and 23.

37 'The Ghosts of Mrs. Gandhi', p. 61.

38 Amitav Ghosh, 'Satyajit Ray' in Tabish Khair, ed. *Amitav Ghosh: A Critical Companion*, New Delhi: Permanent Black, 2003, p. 7.

39 Ibid., 6.

40 Interview with Frederick Luis Almada, p. 89.

41 Connor, *Postmodernist Culture*, p. 115.

Chapter 2

1 Amitav Ghosh, 'The Imam and the Indian' in *The Imam and the Indian: Prose Pieces*, Delhi: Ravi Dayal & Permanent Black, 2002, p. 4.

2 Gyan Prakash, *Another Reason: Science and the Imagination of Modern India*, Princeton, NJ.: Princeton University Press, 1999, pp. 12–13.

3 See Michael Adas, *Machines as the Measure of Men: Science, Technology, and Ideologies of Western Dominance*, Ithaca, NY: Cornell University Press, 1989.

4 For an analysis of 'diffusionist' theories of scientific development, see Deepak Kumar, *Science and the Raj: 1857–1905*, New Delhi: Oxford University Press, 1997. See also David Arnold, *Science, Technology and Medicine in Colonial India*, Cambridge: Cambridge University Press, 2000.

5 Prakash, *Another Reason*, p. 25; p. 30.

6 Ibid., 31.

7 Ibid., 32.

8 Kumar cites the example of Radhanath Sikdar, a member of the Indian Cartographical Survey team, who 'was the first to compute and find out in 1852 that a peak designated XV which had been observed from six different stations, was the highest point on earth'. On receiving this information, the Surveyor-General, Colonel Waugh, promptly named the peak after his predecessor, George Everest. Sikdar also wrote large portions of the standard Manual of Surveying, a fact frankly admitted by the authors, Smyth and Thuillier. In the second edition, however, Sikdar's name, and references to his contribution, was omitted. Kumar, *Science*, p. 59; p. 185.

9   Arnold, *Science*, p. 13.

10 Claire Chambers, 'Historicizing Scientific Reason in Amitav Ghosh's *The Circle of Reason*' in Tabish Khair, ed. *Amitav Ghosh: A Critical Companion*, New Delhi: Permanent Black, 2003, pp. 46–7.

11 There is an interesting parallel between Balaram's school and one established in Calcutta in 1871 by Keshubchandra Sen, a member of the reformist Hindu group known as the Brahmo Samaj and a prominent figure in the Bengal Renaissance. It was a free school that would educate 'shopkeepers, carpenters, blacksmiths, goldsmiths, weavers, masons, etc.' It too had two 'wings' – one teaching practical skills based on European technology to the sons of the *bhadralok* in the mornings; the other, sitting in the evening, taught the artisans the rudiments of European 'science'. See Sumanta Banerjee, *The Parlour and the Streets: Elite and Popular Culture in Nineteenth Century Calcutta*, Calcutta: Seagull 1989, p. 63. This perhaps unconscious echo of a key figure in the Bengal Renaissance in the less impressive character of Balaram illuminates his purpose in this section of the novel: he signifies the psychological dependency of the Bengal Renaissance – and the modern vernacular culture which emerged from it – on colonial ideologies of knowledge and culture.

12 Chambers, 'Historicizing Scientific Reason', pp. 50–3.

13 Claire Chambers, 'The Relationship between Knowledge and Power in the Work of Amitav Ghosh'. Unpublished PhD dissertation, University of Leeds, 2003, p. 22.

14 Arnold, *Science*, p. 63.

15 Claire Chambers, 'Postcolonial Science Fiction: Amitav Ghosh's *The Calcutta Chromosome*', *Journal of Commonwealth Literature*, 38:1, 2003, p. 60.

16 Interview with Neluka Silva and Alex Tickell, *Kunapipi*, 19:3, 1997, p. 176.

17 Arnold, *Science*, p. 13; p. 92; Chambers, 'Postcolonial Science Fiction', p. 58.

18 Urbashi Barat, 'Time in the Novels of Amitav Ghosh and Arundhati Roy: Technique as Meaning' in Syed Mashkoor Ali, ed. *Indian Writing in English: A Critical Response*, New Delhi: Creative Books, 2001, pp. 131–2.

19 Kumar, *Science*, p. 177.

20 For a stimulating discussion of the subaltern implications of Mani-

cheanism in *The Calcutta Chromosome*, which challenges the prevailing view of Manichean dualism within postcolonial studies, see John Thieme, 'The Discover Discovered: Amitav Ghosh's *The Calcutta Chromosome*' in Tabish Khair, ed. *Amitav Ghosh*, pp. 128–41.

21 For a more detailed discussion, see Chambers, 'Knowledge and Power', p. 253.

22 Ghosh's version is published as 'The Hunger of Stones' in *The Imam and the Indian*, pp. 326–39.

23 Interview with Tehelka.com, 9 August 2000 cited in Chambers, 'Knowledge and Power', p. 244.

24 Chambers, 'Postcolonial Science Fiction', p. 68.

25 James Clifford, 'Introduction: Partial Truths' in James Clifford and George Marcus, eds. *Writing Culture: The Poetics and Politics of Ethnography*, Berkeley: University of California Press, 1986, p. 2.

26 Chambers, 'Postcolonial Science Fiction', p. 58.

27 One may note, in passing, that despite its name 'chaos theory' does not in fact subscribe to a vision of the universe as contingent, random and chaotic. Quite the opposite, in fact. It suggests that beneath the apparent chaos of random events a pattern can be detected at a higher order of mathematical calculation. The parallels with religious belief, despite the distance in idiom, need not be spelled out.

28 Arnold, *Science*, pp. 68–9.

29 Kumar, *Science*, p. 12.

30 Michel Foucault, 'Governmentality' in Graham Burchell, Colin Gordon and Peter Miller, eds. *The Foucault Effect: Studies in Governmentality*, Chicago: Chicago University Press, 1991, pp. 87–104.

31 Ibid., 92.

32 Colin Gordon, 'Governmental Rationality: An Introduction' in *The Foucault Effect*, p. 10.

33 Michel Foucault, *The Order of Things*, London: Routledge, 1974, p. 19.

34 Ibid., 35; 34.

35 Ibid., 56; see also 54; 50; and 71.

36 Foucault, 'Governmentality', p. 99.

37 Ibid., 100.

38 Letter to Dipesh Chakrabarty, 20 December 2000. This can be accessed at www.amitavghosh.com. See also Bishnupriya Ghosh, 'On Grafting the Vernacular: The Consequences of Postcolonial Spectrology', *boundary 2*, 31:2, 2004, p. 200.

39 John Thieme, 'The Discoverer Discovered', p. 136.

40 Martin Leer, 'Odologica Indica: The Significance of Railways in Anglo-Indian and Indian Fiction in English' in Nanette Hale and Tabish Khair, eds. *Angles on the English Speaking World, Volume 1: Unhinging Hinglish: The Language and Politics of Fiction in English from the Indian Subcontinent*, Copenhagen: Museum Tusculanum Press, 2001, p. 58.

41 Yumna Siddiqi, 'Police and Postcolonial Rationality' in Amitav Ghosh's *The Circle of Reason*', *Cultural Critique*, 50, 2002, p. 176.

42 Elizabeth Deeds Ermarth, *Sequel to History: Postmodernism and the Crisis of Representational Time*, Princeton: Princeton University Press, 1992, p. 19.

43 G.J.V. Prasad, 'The Unfolding of a Raga: Narrative Structure in *The Circle of Reason*' in Viney Kirpal, ed. *The New Indian Novel in English*, New Delhi: Allied Publishers, 1990, p. 101.

44 Chambers, 'Knowledge and Power', p. 205.

45 Johannes Fabian, *Time and the Other: How Anthropology Makes its Object*, New York: Columbia University Press, 1983, p. 143.

46 In this respect, it is important to acknowledge that the 'field' is usually perceived as being 'distant'; the same kind of research, when undertaken 'at home' – i.e. in the West – is called 'sociology'.

47 See Fabian, *Time and the Other*; and Clifford and Marcus, eds. *Writing Culture*.

48 Fabian, *Time and the Other*, p. 146; see also p. 143.

49 For a detailed and stimulating comparison between Ghosh's DPhil thesis at Oxford, and its revision as *In an Antique Land*, see Neelam Srivastava, 'Amitav Ghosh's Ethnographic Fictions: Intertextual Links between *In an Antique Land* and his Doctoral Thesis', *Journal of Commonwealth Literature*, 36:2, 2001, pp. 45–64.

50 Samir Dayal, 'The Emergence of the Fragile Subject: Amitav Ghosh's *In an Antique Land*' in Monika Fludernik, ed. *Hybridity and Postcolonialism: Twentieth Century Indian Literature*, Tübingen: Stauffenberg-Verlag, 1998, pp. 116–17.

51 Mary Louise Pratt, 'Fieldwork in Common Places' in Clifford and Marcus, eds. *Writing Culture*, p. 31.

52 James Clifford, 'The Transit Lounge of Culture,' *Times Literary Supplement*, 3 May 1991, p. 8.

53 Clifford, 'Introduction' in Clifford and Marcus, eds. *Writing Culture*, p. 5.

54 Leela Gandhi, '"A Choice of Histories": Ghosh vs. Hegel in *In an Antique Land*' in Khair, ed. *Amitav Ghosh*, p. 57.

55 Anshuman A. Mondal, 'Allegories of Identity: "Postmodern" Anxiety and "Postcolonial" Ambivalence in Amitav Ghosh's *In an Antique Land* and *The Shadow Lines*', *Journal of Commonwealth Literature*, 38:3, 2003, pp. 19–37.

56 Fabian, *Time and the Other*, p. 106; see also p. 107.

57 Ibid., 108.

58 Gandhi, '"A Choice of Histories"', p. 69.

59 The Hindu concept of *maya* is one such example. Insight into the true nature of existence is not predicated on 'seeing things as they truly are' because sight is itself part of the condition of 'illusion'. An interesting discussion of the priority given in premodern and non-secular cultures to acoustics over visibility can be found in Talal Asad, *Formations of the Secular: Christianity, Islam, Modernity*, Stanford: Stanford University Press, 2003.

60 Interview with Frederick Luis Almada, *World Literature Today*, 76:2, 2002, p. 85.

61 See Homi Bhabha's conceptualisations of 'hybridity' and 'third space' in his *The Location of Culture*, London: Routledge, 1994.

62 Martin Heidegger, 'Building, Dwelling, Thinking' cited in Bhabha, *Location of Culture*, p. 1.

Chapter 3

1 There is a large literature on nations and nationalism that spans a number of disciplines. Key texts are Benedict Anderson, *Imagined Communities: Reflections on the Origin and Spread of Nationalism*, London: Verso, 1983; Ernest Gellner, *Nations and Nationalism*, Oxford: Blackwell, 1983; Anthony D. Smith, *Theories of Nationalism*, London: Duckworth, 1971, and *National Identity*, London: Penguin, 1991; and Eric Hobsbawm, *Nations and Nationalism Since 1780: Programme, Myth, Reality*, Cambridge: Cambridge University Press, 1992. A good introductory reader is Gopal Balakrishnan, ed. *Mapping the Nation*, London: Verso, 1996.

For a critical overview of the key conceptual debates see Anshuman A. Mondal, *Nationalism and Post-Colonial Identity: Culture and Ideology in India and Egypt*, London: RoutledgeCurzon, 2003, pp. 11–43.

2   See Ernest Renan, 'What is a Nation?' in Homi Bhabha, ed. *Nation and Narration*, London: Routledge, 1990, pp. 88–22.

3   Anderson, *Imagined Communities*, p. 6.

4   Ibid.

5   A good account can be found in Sugata Bose and Ayesha Jalal, *Modern South Asia: History, Culture, Political Economy*, London: Routledge, 1997, pp. 165–200.

6   Jacques Lacan, 'The Mirror Stage as Formative of the Function of the I' in *Ecrits: A Selection*, London: Routledge, 1989, pp. 11–18. Lacan revised Freudian psychoanalysis in the light of the linguistic theories of Ferdinand de Saussure, whose ground-breaking lectures on language as a sign-system were posthumously published as 'Course in General Linguistics' in 1916. Abridged and reprinted in Julie Rivkin and Michael Ryan, *Literary Theory: An Anthology*, 2nd edn., Oxford: Blackwell, 2004, pp. 59–71. For Saussure, the meaning of any given linguistic sign is based on its difference from all other signs. 'Cat' means what it does because it is different from 'bat' or 'tree' and so on. The implication is that meaning does not inhere in the sign but is rather the effect that emerges from the differential relation between signs within the total system of signs in any given language. Meaning is therefore 'relational'.

7   Jon Mee, '"The Burthen of the Mystery": Imagination and Difference in *The Shadow Lines*' in Tabish Khair, ed. *Amitav Ghosh: A Critical Companion*, Delhi: Permanent Black, 2003, p. 91.

8   Ibid. I discuss Chakrabarty's work in detail in Chapter 4.

9   In the sense that any single nation sees itself as part of a global community of nations. Internationalism is thus inherent in the idea of nationalism.

10   Sujala Singh, 'Inventing London in Amitav Ghosh's *The Shadow Lines*', *Kunapipi*, 21:2, 1999, p. 18.

11   Ibid., 17.

12   Ibid.

13   On memorials and tombs of unknown soldiers, see Anderson, *Imagined Communities*, pp. 99–11.

14   For more detail, see Mondal, *Nationalism and Post-Colonial Identity*, chapter 2.

15   Jacques Lacan, 'The Agency of the Letter in the Unconscious or Reason since Freud' in *Ecrits*, pp. 161–97.

16   Louis Althusser, 'Ideology and Ideological State Apparatuses' in *Lenin and Philosophy*, London: New Left Books, 1971. See also, Pierre Macherey, *A Theory of Literary Production*, New York: Routledge, 1978.

17   Pakistani nationalist discourse, of course, has a different relationship to communalism because Pakistan as a nation is itself the realisation of communalism – it is the outcome of Muslim separatism. Nevertheless, Pakistan must also insist that Partition was in fact a resolution of the communal problem, otherwise its very *raison d'être* is undermined. The metaphor of the mirror thus holds true.

18   See Gyan Pandey, *The Construction of Communalism in Colonial North India*, New Delhi: Oxford University Press, 1990; Partha Chatterjee, *The Nation and its Fragments: Colonial and Postcolonial Histories*, Princeton, N.J.: Princeton University Press, 1993; Shahid Amin, *Event, Memory, Metaphor: Chauri Chaura 1922–1992*, New Delhi: Oxford University Press, 1996; Mondal, *Nationalism and Post-Colonial Identity*.

19   Pandey, *Construction of Communalism*, p. 210.

20   See Mondal, *Nationalism*, pp. 53–8; and Anshuman A. Mondal, 'The Limits of Secularism and the Construction of Composite National Identity in India' in Peter Morey and Alex Tickell, eds. *Alternative Indias: Writing, Nation and Communalism*, Amsterdam: Rodopi, 2005.

21   Claire Chambers, 'The Relationship between Knowledge and Power in the Work of Amitav Ghosh'. Unpublished PhD dissertation, University of Leeds, 2003, pp. 132–7.

22   Cited in Ibid., 129.

23   Javed Majeed, 'Amitav Ghosh's *In an Antique Land*: The Ethnographer-Historian and the Limits of Irony', *Journal of Commonwealth Literature*, 30:2, 1995, p. 46.

24   Paul Gilroy, *The Black Atlantic: Modernity and Double Consciousness*, London: Verso, 1993, p. 45; p. 218; the phrase 'subtle abduction' is Leela Gandhi's, in her '"A Choice of Histories": Ghosh vs. Hegel in *In an Antique Land*' in Khair, ed., *Amitav Ghosh*, pp. 70–1.

25   Amitav Ghosh, 'The Global Reservation: Notes Toward an Ethnography of International Peacekeeping' in *The Imam and the Indian: Prose Pieces*, Delhi: Permanent Black, 2002, p. 265, my emphasis.

26 Rabindranath Tagore, *Nationalism*, London: Macmillan, 1917, p. 15.

27 Ibid., 35.

28 Ibid., 19–20.

29 Sunil Khilnani, *The Idea of India*, London: Penguin, 1998, p. 169.

30 Jawaharlal Nehru, *The Discovery of India*, Delhi: Oxford University Press, 1988, pp. 38–9.

31 Majeed, 'The Ethnographer-Historian', p. 46.

32 Amitav Ghosh, Interview with Frederick Luis Almada, *World Literature Today*, 76:2, 2002, p. 89.

33 See, for example, Judith Butler, *Gender Trouble: Feminism and the Subversion of Identity*, London: Routledge, 1990, and Homi Bhabha, *The Location of Culture*, London: Routledge, 1994.

34 Lord Macaulay, 'Minute on Education', 2 February 1835, cited in Bhabha, *The Location of Culture*, p. 87.

35 Homi Bhabha, 'Of Mimicry and Man' in *The Location of Culture*, p. 86.

36 Ibid., 88.

37 See Emma Tarlo, *Clothing Matters: Dress and Identity in India*, London: Hurst and Co., 1996.

38 Maria Budhos, 'Questions of Allegiance', *Los Angeles Times Book Review*, 11 February 2001, p. 5.

39 Amitav Ghosh, 'India's Untold war of Independence', *The New Yorker*, 23 and 30 June 1997, p. 108. Original emphases.

40 Ghosh makes much of this in his correspondence with Dipesh Chakrabarty. See www.amitavghosh.com.

41 Bhabha, 'Mimicry', p. 89.

42 Letter to Dipesh Chakrabarty, 20 December 2000. See www.amitavghosh.com.

43 Frantz Fanon, *Black Skin, White Masks*, London: Pluto Press, 1986.

44 Amitav Ghosh, *Dancing in Cambodia, At Large in Burma*, Delhi: Permanent Black, 1998, p. 73.

45 Ibid., 100–1.

46 Paul Carter, *Living in a New Country: History, Travelling and Language*, London: Faber and Faber, 1992, p. 101.

47 Ibid.

48 Historians who have undertaken this effort include Fernand Braudel, *The Mediterranean and the Mediterranean World in the Age of Phillip II*, 3 vols., Berkeley: University of California Press, 1996; K.N. Chaudhuri, *Trade and Civilisation in the Indian Ocean: An Economic History from the Rise of Islam to 1750*, Cambridge: Cambridge University Press, 1985; Paul Gilroy, *The Black Atlantic*.

49 Stephen Howe, 'Sea Changes' [A review of *In an Antique Land*] in *The New Statesman and Society*, vol. 5, no. 222, 2 October 1992, p. 48.

50 Chaudhuri, *Trade and Civilisation*, p. 21.

51 Seamus Heaney, *North*, London: Faber and Faber, 1975, p. 13.

52 Gilroy, *The Black Atlantic*, p. 19.

53 Ibid. See also Stuart Hall, 'Cultural Identity and Diaspora' in J. Rutherford, ed. *Identity: Community, Culture, Difference*, London: Lawrence and Wishart, 1990, pp. 222–37.

54 Iain Chambers, *Migrancy, Culture, Identity*, London: Routledge, 1994, p. 39.

55 Avtar Brah, *Cartographies of Diaspora*, London: Routledge, 1996.

56 This, at times highly contentious debate, was initiated by Frederic Jameson's essay, 'Third World Literature in the Era of Multinational Capitalism', *Social Text*, 15, 1986, pp. 65–88.

57 Interview with Almada, p. 89.

58 Cited in Bruce Robbins, 'Introduction Part 1' in Pheng Cheah and Bruce Robbins, eds. *Cosmopolitics: Thinking and Feeling Beyond the Nation*, London: University of Minnesota Press, 1998, p. 11.

59 Irish, Hindu, and Israeli nationalisms, for example – amongst many others.

60 'The Global Reservation', p. 265.

61 Ibid., 266.

Chapter 4

1 Robert Berkhofer, 'The Challenge of Poetics to (Normal) Historical Practice' in Keith Jenkins, ed. *The Postmodern History Reader*, London: Routledge, 1997, p. 146.

2 Ibid., 145.

3   Ibid., 144.

4   Dipesh Chakrabarty, *Provincializing Europe: Postcolonial Thought and Historical Difference*, Princeton: Princeton University Press, 2000, p. 27.

5   Ibid., 7.

6   In fact, the history of the Indian National Army is a *lacuna* within a *lacuna* – the overlooked contribution of soldiers in the British Indian Army, such as Ghosh's father, in the fight against the Japanese in South-East Asia. In films such as *The Bridge on the River Kwai* one struggles to see an Indian face despite the fact that Indians made up the majority of the soldiers on the Asian front. Ghosh has written a moving and extensive non-fictional piece on the Indian National Army in Malaya: 'India's Untold War of Independence', *The New Yorker*, 23 and 30 June 1997, pp. 104–21.

7   K.N. Chaudhuri, *Trade and Civilisation in the Indian Ocean: An Economic History from the Rise of Islam to 1750*, Cambridge: Cambridge University Press, 1985, p. 14.

8   Amitav Ghosh, 'Empire and Soul: A Review of the *Baburnama*' in *The Imam and the Indian: Prose Pieces*, Delhi: Permanent Black, 2002, p. 90. Subsequent references are indicated in the text.

9   Amitav Ghosh, 'The Slave of MS. H.6' in *Subaltern Studies: Writing on Asian History and Society: VII*, eds. Partha Chatterjee and Gyanendra Pandey, Delhi: Oxford University Press, 1992, pp. 159–220.

10 Ranajit Guha, 'On Some Aspects of the Historiography of Colonial India' in Vinayak Chaturvedi, ed. *Mapping Subaltern Studies and the Postcolonial*, London: Verso, 2000, p. 2, original emphasis. This was the manifesto of the project, the first essay in the first volume of *Subaltern Studies*.

11 Gyan Prakash, 'Subaltern Studies as Postcolonial Criticism', *American Historical Review*, 99:5, 1994, p. 1480.

12 Chakrabarty, *Provincializing Europe*, p. 112.

13 Elizabeth Deeds Ermarth, *Sequel to History: Postmodernism and the Crisis of Representational Time*, Princeton: Princeton University Press, 1992, p. 28.

14 Chakrabarty, *Provincializing Europe*, pp. 102–9.

15 Albert Einstein, cited in Ermarth, *Sequel to History*, p. 16.

16 Chakrabarty, *Provincializing Europe*, p. 101.

17 Ibid., 180–213.

18   Interestingly, Chakrabarty notes that Ranajit Guha had told him that in the Calcutta of his youth, 1930s, he and his friends met in parks for their *adda* because they were removed from parental surveillance. He also notes that the physicist Satyendranath Bose took part in a literary *adda* that used to meet on a rooftop. Both parks and rooftops are sites that are singled out for mention in the literary topography of *The Shadow Lines* and their significance in relation to the history of *adda* is worth some attention.

19   Ibid., 86.

20   Ibid., 254; 96.

21   Gayatri Chakravorty Spivak, 'Subaltern Studies: Deconstructing Historiography' in *In Other Worlds: Essays in Cultural Politics*, London: Routledge, 1988, p. 201.

22   Ibid., 207. See also Spivak, 'Can the Subaltern Speak?' in Cary Nelson and Lloyd Grossberg, eds. *Marxism and the Interpretation of Culture*, London: Macmillan, 1988, pp. 271–313.

23   Berkhofer, 'The Challenge of Poetics', p. 148.

24   Jacques Derrida, *Of Grammatology*, trans. G. Chakravorty Spivak, Baltimore: John Hopkins University Press, 1976, p. 27.

25   Mark Cousins, 'The Practice of Historical Investigation' in Derek Attridge, Geoff Bennington and Robert Young, eds. *Poststructuralism and the Question of History*, Cambridge: Cambridge University Press, 1988, pp. 126–36.

26   Derek Attridge, 'Language as History/History as Language: Saussure and the Romance of Etymology' in Attridge et al., eds. *Poststructuralism and the Question of History*, pp. 183–212.

27   Keith Jenkins, 'Introduction: On Being Open About Our Closures' in Jenkins, ed. *The Postmodern History Reader*, p. 12.

28   See Gyan Pandey, 'In Defense of the Fragment: Writing about Hindu-Muslim Riots in India Today', *Representations*, 37, 1992, pp. 27–55.

29   Ibid., 40–1.

30   Chakrabarty, *Provincializing Europe*, p. 71.

31   Pandey, p. 50.

32   Cited in Suzanne Keen, *Romances of the Archive in Contemporary British Fiction*, Toronto: University of Toronto Press, 2001, p. 226.

33   Thomas Richards, *The Imperial Archive: Knowledge and the Fantasy of Empire*, London: Verso, 1993, p. 6.

34   Interview with Neluka Silva and Alex Tickell, *Kunapipi*, 19:3, 1997, p. 176.

35   See Robert Young, *White Mythologies: Writing History and the West*, London: Routledge, 1990, pp. 81–3, and Michel Foucault, *Language, Counter-Memory, Practice: Selected Essays and Interviews* ed. Donald F. Bouchard, trans. Donald F. Bouchard and Sherry Simon, Ithaca: Cornell University Press, 1977.

36   Chakrabarty, *Provincializing Europe*, p. 89.

37   Ibid.

38   Bishnupriya Ghosh, 'On Grafting the Vernacular: The Consequences of Postcolonial Spectrology', *boundary 2*, 31:2, 2004, p. 205.

39   Javed Majeed, 'Amitav Ghosh's *In an Antique Land*: The Ethnographer-Historian and the Limits of Irony', *Journal of Commonwealth Literature*, 30:2, 1995, p. 49.

40   Chakrabarty, *Provincializing Europe*, p. 243.

41   Sigmund Freud, 'The Uncanny' in *The Penguin Freud Library, Vol. 14: Art and Literature*, London: Penguin, 1985, pp. 335–76.

42   Chakrabarty, *Provincializing Europe*, p. 86, my emphasis.

43   Berkhofer, 'The Challenge of Poetics', p. 149.

44   Ermarth, *Sequel to History*, p. 27.

45   Shirley Chew, 'Texts and Worlds in Amitav Ghosh's *In an Antique Land*' in Maureen Bell, Shirley Chew, Simon Eliot, Lynette Hunter, and James L.W. West III, eds. *Reconstructing the Book: Literary Texts in Transmission*, Aldershot: Ashgate, 2001, p. 199. It is delightful that this comment is itself a footnote in Chew's text.

46   Chakrabarty, p. 86.

47   Salman Rushdie, *Haroun and the Sea of Stories*, London: Granta, 1990, p. 20.

48   Georg Lukács, *The Historical Novel*, London: Merlin Press, 1989, p. 19.

49   Ibid., 34.

50   Ibid., 36.

51   Ibid., 39; 45.

52   Ibid., 44.

53   Ibid., 65; 86.

54   Ibid., 38.

55   Ibid., 35.

56   Attridge, 'Language as History', p. 188.

57   Ibid., 190.

Chapter 5

1   *The Circle of Reason* won the *Prix Medicis Entrangère* (Paris) in 1990; *The Shadow Lines* won the annual prize of the Sahitya Akademi (Indian Academy of Literature) in 1990, and the *Ananda Puraskar* (Calcutta) also in 1990; *The Calcutta Chromosome* won the Arthur C. Clarke award for Science Fiction in 1996; *The Glass Palace* won the Grand Prize for Fiction at the Frankfurt eBook award, and it was also awarded the Commonwealth Writers Prize, which Ghosh subsequently declined. His reasons for doing so are posted on his website www.amitavghosh.com ; *The Hungry Tide* was recently awarded the *Hutch Crossword Book Award*, 2004.

2   The other monograph, by John C. Hawley, was published in the summer of 2005 as this book was being completed. See John C. Hawley, *Amitav Ghosh*, New Delhi: Foundation Books, 2005.

3   Another – again, published too recently to be considered here – is Nyla Ali Khan's *The Fiction of Nationality in an Era of Transnationalism*, London: Routledge, 2005.

4   Nagesh Rao, 'Cosmopolitanism, Class and Gender in *The Shadow Lines*', *South Asian Review*, 24:1, 2003, pp. 95–115. Suchitra Mathur's essay 'Caught Between the Goddess and the Cyborg: Third World Women and the Politics of Science in Three Works of Indian Science Fiction', *Journal of Commonwealth Literature*, 39:3, 2004, pp. 119–38, was published in a Western journal by an critic based at the Indian Institute of Technology, Kanpur.

5   Rajeswari Sunder Rajan, 'The Division of Experience in *The Shadow Lines*' in *The Shadow Lines*, New Delhi: Oxford University Press, 1995, p. 298.

6   See Anshuman A. Mondal, 'The Emblematics of Gender and Sexuality in Indian Nationalist Discourse', *Modern Asian Studies*, 36:4, 2002, pp. 913–36.

7   Jon Mee, '"The Burthen of the Mystery": Imagination and Difference in *The Shadow Lines*' in Tabish Khair, ed. *Amitav Ghosh: A Critical Companion*, Delhi: Permanent Black, 2003, p. 100.

8   Suvir Kaul, 'Separation Anxiety: Growing Up Inter/National in

Amitav Ghosh's *The Shadow Lines'*, *Oxford Literary Review*, 16, 1994, p. 131.

9   James Clifford, 'The transit lounge of culture' *Times Literary Supplement*, 3 May 1991, p. 8.

10 Suchitra Mathur, 'Caught Between the Goddess and the Cyborg,' p. 131.

11 A.N. Kaul, 'A Reading of *The Shadow Lines'* in *The Shadow Lines*, New Delhi: Oxford University Press, 1995, p. 299.

12 Ibid., 299; 307.

13 Ibid., 303.

14 Mee, '"Burthen"', p. 100.

15 Kaul, 'A Reading', p. 301.

16 Ibid., 305.

17 Ibid., 301.

18 Gauri Viswanathan, 'Beyond Orientalism: syncretism and the politics of knowledge' *Stanford Electronic Humanities Review*, 5:1, 1995 www.stanford.edu/group/SHR/5–l/text/viswanathan.html.

19 Ibid.

20 Ibid.

21 Robert Dixon, '"Travelling in the West": The Writing of Amitav Ghosh' in Khair, ed. *Amitav Ghosh*, p. 21; see also p. 10.

22 Ibid., 27.

23 The phrase is Martin Heidegger's and is cited by Dipesh Chakrabarty in his correspondence with Ghosh, 22 December 2000. www.amitavghosh.com.

Bibliography

Works by Amitav Ghosh

NOVELS

The Circle of Reason, London: Hamish Hamilton, 1986.
The Shadow Lines, London: Bloomsbury, 1988.
In an Antique Land, London: Granta, 1992.
The Calcutta Chromosome, London: Picador, 1996.
The Glass Palace, London: Harper Collins, 2000.
The Hungry Tide, London: Harper Collins, 2004.

(All of the above were published in India by Ravi Dayal Publishers, Delhi.)

NON-FICTION BOOKS

'Kinship in Relation to the Economic and Social Organization of an Egyptian Village Community', unpublished doctoral dissertation, Oxford: Bodleian Library, MS D.Phil, c. 4127, 1981.
Dancing in Cambodia, At Large in Burma Delhi: Ravi Dayal, 1998.
Countdown Delhi: Ravi Dayal, 1999.
The Imam and the Indian: Prose Pieces Delhi: Ravi Dayal and Permanent Black, 2002.
Incendiary Circumstances: A Chronicle of the Turmoil of Our Times, New York: Houghton Mifflin, 2005

ARTICLES, ESSAYS AND SHORT STORIES

'The Relations of Envy', *Ethnology*, Pittsburgh: University of Pittsburgh Press, 1984.
'The Imam and the Indian', *Granta: In Trouble Again*, 20, Winter 1986, pp. 135–46.
'Categories of Labour and the Orientation of the Fellah Economy', in

Peter Lienhardt Festschrift, ed. Ahmed al-Shahi, Oxford, 1988.

'Tibetan Dinner', *Granta: Murder*, 25, Autumn 1988, pp. 250–4.

'Four Corners', *Granta: Travel*, 26, Spring 1989, pp. 191–6.

'Pharoahs and Phantoms' (Review of *Egypt, Islam and the Arabs: The Search for Egyptian Nationhood 1900–1930* by Israel Gershoni and James Janowski), *The New Republic*, 5 June 1989, pp. 33–7.

'The Diaspora in Indian Culture', *Public Culture*, 2:1, 1989, pp. 73–8.

'The Human Comedy in Cairo: A Review of the Work of Naguib Mahfouz', *The New Republic*, 202, 7 May 1990, pp. 32–6.

'An Egyptian in Baghdad', *Granta: Death of a Harvard Man*, 34, Autumn 1990, pp. 173–93.

'In India, Death and Democracy', *New York Times*, 26 November 1990, A19.

'Petrofiction: The Oil Encounter and the Novel', *The New Republic*, 206, 2 March 1992, pp. 29–34.

'The Slave of MS. H.6', in *Subaltern Studies: Writing on Asian History and Society: VII*, eds. Partha Chatterjee and Gyanendra Pandey, New Delhi: Oxford University Press, 1992, pp. 159–220.

'Holiday in Cambodia', *The New Republic*, 208, 28 June 1993, pp. 21–5.

'Dancing in Cambodia', *Granta: The Last Place on Earth*, 44, Summer 1993, pp. 125–69.

'The Global Reservation: Notes Toward an Ethnography of International Peacekeeping', *Cultural Anthropology*, 9:3, 1994, 412–22.

'The World of a Bengali-speaker in New York', *Observer Magazine* (London), September, 1993.

'Stories in Stone', *Observer Magazine* (London) December 1993.

'The Indian Story: Notes on Some Preliminaries', *Civil Lines* (New Delhi), 1, pp. 35–49.

'The Ghosts of Mrs Gandhi', *The New Yorker*, 71, 17 July 1995, pp. 35–41.

'The Fundamentalist Challenge', *Wilson Quarterly*, 19, 2 Spring 1995, pp. 19–31. (This article has also appeared in *The Writer and Religion*, eds. William H. Gass and Lorin Cuoco, Carbondale, IL: Southern Illinois University Press, 2000, pp. 86–110.)

'The Hunger of Stones' (a translation of Rabindranath Tagore's Bengali short story). *Civil Lines* (New Delhi), 2, 1995, pp. 152–68.

'Fortifications and the Synagogue: The Fortress of Babylon and the Ben Ezra Synagogue', *American Journal of Archaeology*, 100:4, October 1996, pp. 808–9.

'Burma', *The New Yorker*, August 12, 1996.

'Empire and Soul: A Review of *The Baburnama*', *The New Republic*, 6 and 13 January 1997.

'India's Untold War of Independence', *The New Yorker*, 73, 23 and 30 June 1997, pp. 104–21.

'The March of the Novel through History: The Testimony of my Grandfather's Bookcase', *Kunapipi*, 19:3, 1997, pp. 2–13. (This article has also been published in *The Kenyon Review*, 20:2, Spring 1998, pp. 13–24).

'Why Can't Every Country Have the Bomb?', *The New Yorker*, 26 October and 2 November 1998, pp. 186–97.

'Calcutta's Global Ambassador', *The New York Times*, 29 June 2000.

'54 University Ave Yangon—Aung San Suu Kyi', *Kenyon Review*, 23:2, Spring 2001, pp. 158–65.

'The Indian Novel: An Introduction', *Europe-Revue Litteraire Mensuelle*, 79, 864, April 2001, pp. 36–45.

'The Magic of Reading V.S. Naipaul: An Adolescent Memoir', *Europe-Revue Litteraire Mensuelle*, 80, 873–4, January–Febuary 2002, pp. 293–5.

'Imperial Temptation', *Nation*, 274, 20, 27 May 2002, p. 24.

'Satyajit Ray' in Tabish Khair, ed. *Amitav Ghosh: A Critical Companion*, Delhi: Permanent Black, 2003, pp. 11–18.

(Other articles can be found on Amitav Ghosh's website: www.amitavghosh.com.)

Criticism on Ghosh

No author, 'Amitav Ghosh 1956: Indian novelist, essayist, and nonfiction writer'. *Contemporary Literary Criticism*, 153, 2002, pp. 81–132.

Acton, S.M., Review of *The Calcutta Chromosome*, 1998, Internet address: www.silcom.com/-manatee/ghosh calcutta.html.

Advani, Rukun, 'Novelists in Residence', *Seminar*, 384, August 1991, pp. 15–18.

Agarwalla, Shyam S., 'Magic Realism in Amitav Ghosh's *The Circle of Reason*', in *Studies in Indian English Fiction*, ed. Amar Nath Prasad, New Delhi: Sarup, 2001.

Bagchi, Nivedita, 'The Process of Validation in Relation to Materiality and Historical Reconstruction in Amitav Ghosh's *The Shadow Lines*', *Modern Fiction Studies*, 39:1, 1993, pp. 187–202.

Baker, Phil, 'Post-colonial Pox' (review of *The Calcutta Chromosome*), *Times Literary Supplement*, 1 August 1996, p. 23.

Banerji, Jaya, 'Bengali Braid' (review of *The Calcutta Chromosome*), *Indian Review of Books*, 5:9, 16 June–15 July 1996, pp. 22–3.

Barat, Urbashi, 'Time in the Novels of Amitav Ghosh and Arundhati Roy: Technique as Meaning' in *Indian Writing in English: A Critical Response*, ed. Syed Mashkoor Ali, New Delhi: Creative, 2001.

Basu, Ranjita, 'Amitav Ghosh's Action: Turning the Full Circle' in

Indian-English Fiction 1980–1990: An Assessment, eds. Nilufer E. Bharucha and Vrinda Sarang, New Delhi: B.R. Publishing, 1994, pp. 151–60.

Batra, K., 'Geographical and Generic Traversings in the Writings of Amitav Ghosh', *Thamyris: Intersecting Place, Sex, and Race,* 8, 2001, pp. 211–20.

Basu, R., 'The Novels of Amitav Ghosh', *London Magazine,* 37:3&4, August–September 1997, pp. 159–61.

Beliappa, K.C., 'Amitav Ghosh's *In an Antique Land*: An Excursion into Time Past and Time Present', in *The Postmodern Indian Novel: Interrogating the 1980s and 1990s,* ed. Viney Kirpal, Bombay: Allied Publishers, 1996, pp. 59–66.

Bharia, Meetu, 'Amitav Ghosh: Transfiguration of Memory in *The Shadow Lines*' in *Indian Writing in English: The Last Decade,* ed. Rajul Bhargava, New Delhi: Rawat, 2002.

Bhatt, Indira and Indira Nityanandam, eds. *The Fiction of Amitav Ghosh,* New Delhi: Creative, 2001.

——, eds. *Interpretations: Amitav Ghosh's* The Shadow Lines, New Delhi: Creative Books, 2000.

Chambers, Claire, 'The Relationship Between Knowledge and Power in the Work of Amitav Ghosh'. Unpublished PhD dissertation, University of Leeds, 2003.

——, 'Historicizing Scientific Reason in Amitav Ghosh's *The Circle of Reason*' in Tabish Khair, ed., *Amitav Ghosh: A Critical Companion,* pp. 36–55.

——, 'Postcolonial Science Fiction: Amitav Ghosh's *The Calcutta Chromosome*', *Journal of Commonwealth Literature,* 38:1, 2003, 57–72.

Chew, Shirley, 'Texts and Worlds in Amitav Ghosh's *In an Antique Land*', in *Re-Constructing the Book: Literary Texts in Transmission,* eds. Maureen Bell. Shirley Chew, Simon Eliot, Lynette Hunter and J.L.W. West III, Aldershot: Ashgate, 2001, pp. 197–209.

——, 'The Story Bug' (review of *The Calcutta Chromosome*), *New Statesman,* 6 September 1996, p. 47.

Chowdhary, Arvind, ed. *Amitav Ghosh's* The Shadow Lines: *Critical Essays,* New Delhi: Atlantic, 2002.

Clifford, James, 'Looking for Bomma', *London Review of Books,* 24 March 1994, pp. 26–7.

——'The Transit Lounge of Culture', *Times Literary Supplement,* 3 May 1991, pp. 77–8.

Clute, John, 'Excessive Candour: A Tale Decent Folk Can Buy' (Review of *The Calcutta Chromosome*), 1997. Internet address: www. amitavghosh.com/scifi.htm.

Couto, Maria, 'Threads and Shards' (review of *The Shadow Lines*),

Times Literary Supplement, 28 October–3 November 1988, p. 1212.

Dayal, Samir, 'The Emergence of the Fragile Subject: Amitav Ghosh's *In an Antique Land*', in *Hybridity and Postcolonialism: Twentieth-Century Indian Literature,* ed. Monika Fludernik, Tubingen (Germany): Stauffenburg, 1998, pp. 103–33.

Dhawan, R.K., ed., *The Novels of Amitav Ghosh,* New Delhi: Prestige Books, 1999.

Dixon, Robert, '"Travelling in the West": The Writing of Amitav Ghosh' in Tabish Khair, ed., *Amitav Ghosh: A Critical Companion,* pp. 9–35. (First published in *Journal of Commonwealth Literature,* 31:1, 1996, pp. 3–24.)

Docker, John, 'His Slave, My Tattoo: Romancing a Lost World', in *Unfinished Journeys: India File from Canberra,* eds. Debjani Ganguly and Kavita Nandan. Adelaide (Australia): CRNLE, 1998, pp. 181–200.

Dubbe, P.D., 'Postcolonial Discourse in the Novel of Amitav Ghosh's *The Shadow Lines*', *Indian English Literature: Vol. I,* ed. Basavaraj Naikar, New Delhi: Atlantic, 2002.

Elukin, Jim, '*In an Antique Land*: An Infidel in Egypt', *American Scholar,* 63:1, 1994, pp. 137–40.

Gandhi, Leela, '"A Choice of Histories": Ghosh vs. Hegel in *In an Antique Land*' in Tabish Khair, *Amitav Ghosh: A Critical Companion,* pp. 56–72.

Ganguly, Keya, 'Something Like a Snake: Pedagogy and Postcolonial Literature', *College Literature,* West Chester, PA, 19–20, 3:1 (Double issue), October 1992–Feburary 1993, pp. 185–90.

Geertz, Clifford, 'Review of Amitav Ghosh's *In an Antique Land*', *The Australian,* 25 August 1993, p. 30.

——, 'Amitav Ghosh's *In An Antique Land*', *New Republic,* 209, 8–9, 23 August 1993, p. 38.

Gera, Anjali, 'Desh Kothay? Amitav Ghosh Tells Old Wives Tales' in Tabish Khair, ed. *Amitav Ghosh: A Critical Companion,* pp. 109–27.

Ghosh, Bishnupriya, 'On Grafting the Vernacular: The Consequences of Postcolonial Spectrology', *boundary 2,* 31:2, 2004, pp. 197–218.

Ghosh-Schellhorn, Marrina, 'Chromosome der Utopie: Utopische Entwürfe in der anglophonen Literatur Indiens' in *Utopie und Dystopie in den neuen englischen Literaturen,* eds. Hans-Ulrich Seeber and Ralf Pordzik, Heidelberg: Carl Winter, 2002, pp. 275–87.

Gupta, Santosh, 'Looking into History: Amitav Ghosh's *The Glass Palace,*' in *Indian Writing in English: The Last Decade,* ed. Rajul Bhargava, New Delhi: Rawat, 2002.

Hawley, John C., *Amitav Ghosh*, New Delhi: Foundation Books, 2005.

Hemmadi, Usha, 'Amitav Ghosh: A Most Distinctive Voice', in *Mapping Cultural Spaces: Postcolonial Indian Literature in English: Essays in Honour of Nissim Ezekiel*, eds. Nilufer E. Bharucha and Vrinda Nabar, New Delhi: Vision, 1998.

Hiatt, Shobha, 'Review of *The Calcutta Chromosome*', 1998, Internet address: www.indolink.com/Book/calcutta.html.

Hulse, Michael, 'Review of *The Calcutta Chromosome*', *Spectator*, 277, 8771, 1996, p. 25.

Hussain, Shawkat, 'Post-Colonial Angst in Amitav Ghosh's *The Shadows Lines*', in *Colonial and Post-Colonial Encounters*, eds. Niaz Zaman, Firdous Azim and Shawkat Hussain, Dhaka: Manohar Publications, 1999.

Iyer, Pico, 'Review of *The Glass Palace*', *New York Review of Books*, 48:4, 2001, pp. 28–30.

James, Louis and Jan Shepherd, 'Shadow Lines: Cross-Cultural Perspectives in the Fiction of Amitav Ghosh', *Commonwealth Essays and Studies* (Dijon, France), 14:1, Autumn 1991, pp. 28–32.

Kamath, Rekha, 'Memory and Discourse: On Amitav Ghosh's *In an Antique Land*' in *The Poetics of Memory* ed. Thomas Wagenbaur, Tübingen (Germany): Stauffenburg, 1998, pp. 205–13.

Kapadia, Novy, 'Imagination and Politics in Amitav Ghosh's *The Shadow Lines*', in *The New Indian Novel in English: A Study of the 1980s*, ed. Viney Kirpal, New Delhi: Allied Publishers, 1990, pp. 201–12.

——, ed. *Amitav Ghosh's* The Shadow Lines*: Critical Perspectives*, New Delhi: Prestige, 2001.

Karpe, Anjali, 'The Concept of Freedom in *The Shadow Lines*: A Novel by Amitav Ghosh', in *Mapping Cultural Spaces: Postcolonial Indian Literature in English: Essays in Honour of Nissim Ezekiel*, eds. Nilufer E. Bharucha and Vrinda Nabar, New Delhi, Vision, 1998.

Kaul, A.N., 'The Shadow Lines', *Indian Literature*, 33:4, 1990, pp. 88–95.

——, 'A Reading of The *Shadow Lines*', in *The Shadow Lines*, New Delhi: Oxford University Press, 1995, pp. 299–309.

Kaul, Suvir, 'Separation Anxiety, Growing up Inter/National in Amitav Ghosh's *The Shadow Lines*', *Oxford Literary Review*, 16:1–2, 1994, pp. 125–45. (This paper has also appeared in *The Shadow Lines*, New Delhi: Oxford University Press, 1995, pp. 268–86).

Suzanne Keen, *Romances of the Archive in Contemporary British Fiction*, Toronto: University of Toronto Press, 2001. (Includes a chapter on Ghosh)

Khair, Tabish, 'The Example of Amitav Ghosh: (Re)Establishing Connections', in *Babu Fictions: Alienation in Contemporary Indian*

English Novels, New Delhi: Oxford University Press, 2001, pp. 302–32.

——, ed. Amitav Ghosh: A Critical Companion, Delhi: Permanent Black, 2003.

Khan, Amil, 'Book Review: In an Antique Land by Amitav Ghosh', 2000. Internet address: www.metimes.com/2K/issue2000–49/cultent/bookreview.htm.

Khan, Nyla Ali, The Fiction of Nationality in an Era of Transnationalism, London: Routledge, 2005. (Looks at Ghosh amongst other writers)

Kich, Martin, 'Mosquito Bites and Computer Bytes: Amitav Ghosh's The Calcutta Chromosome', Notes on Contemporary Literature (Carrollton, GA), 30:4, September 2000, pp. 99–12.

King, Bruce, 'In an Antique Land', World Literature Today, 68:2, 1994, p. 430.

Kiteley, Brian, 'Trapped by Language: On Amitav Ghosh's In an Antique Land', 2000. Internet address: www.du.edu/~bkiteley/ghoshtalk.html.

Kumar, Amitava, 'Rushdie's Children' (review of The Calcutta Chromosome) The Nation, 29 September 1997.

Kumar, Gajendra, 'The Calcutta Chromosome: A Strange Odyssey of Time and Mystery', in Indian Writings in English, Vol. IX, eds. Manmohan K. Bhatnagar and M. Rajeshwar, Delhi: Atlantic, 2000.

Lal, Vinay, 'A Meditation on History: Review Article on Amitav Ghosh's In an Antique Land', 1993. Internet address: www.sscnet.ucla.edu/southasia/History/British/Amitav_Ghosh.html.

Leer, Martin, 'Odologia Indica: The Significance of Railways in Anglo-Indian and Indian Fiction in English', Angles: On the English-Speaking World: Volume 1: UnhingingHinglish: The Language and Politics of Fiction in English from the Indian Subcontinent, eds. Nanette Hale and Tabish Khair, Copenhagen: University of Copenhagen Press, 2001, pp. 41–61.

Lutwick, Larry I., 'Review of The Calcutta Chromosome', in Infections in Medicine, 15:3, 1998, p. 173.

Majeed, Javed, 'Amitav Ghosh's In an Antique Land: The Ethnographer-Historian and the Limits of Irony', Journal of Commonwealth Literature, 30:2, 1995, pp. 45–55.

Mani, K. Ratna Sheila, 'Of Lines and Borders: A Reading of Amitav Ghosh's The Shadow Lines', in Perspectives on Indian English Fiction, ed. Jaydipsingh Dodiya, New Delhi: Dominant, 2002.

Martin, D., 'Amitav Ghosh', Magazine Litteraire, 362, 1998, pp. 82–4.

Mathur, O.P., 'The Indian Ambience of Amitav Ghosh's The Shadow Lines', in New Critical Approaches to Indian English Fiction, New Delhi: Sarup, 2001.

Mathur, Suchitra, 'Caught between the Goddess and the Cyborg: Third-World Women and the Politics of Science in Three Works of Indian Science Fiction', *Journal of Commonwealth Literature*, 39:3, 2004, pp. 119–38.

Mee, Jon, '"The Burthen of the Mystery": Imagination and Difference in *The Shadow Lines*' in Khair, ed. *Amitav Ghosh: A Critical Companion*, pp. 90–108.

Mhatre, L., '*The Shadow Lines*', *Confrontation*, 44–5, 1990, pp. 414–38.

Mishra, Pankaj, 'Review of *The Glass Palace*', *New York Times Book Review*, 106:6, 2001, p. 7.

Mongia, Padmini, 'Postcolonial Identity and Gender Boundaries in Amitav Ghosh's *The Shadow Lines*', *College Literature*, 20:1, 1993, pp. 225–8.

——, 'Medieval Travel in Postcolonial Times: Amitav Ghosh's *In an Antique Land*' in Tabish Khair, ed. *Amitav Ghosh: A Critical Companion*, pp. 73–89.

Mukherjee, Meenakshi, 'Maps and Mirrors: Coordinates of Meaning in *The Shadow Lines*', in *The Shadow Lines*, New Delhi: Oxford University Press, 1995, pp. 255–67. (Republished with the same title in Meenakshi Mukherjec's *The Perishable Empire: Essays on Indian Writing in English*, Delhi: Oxford University Press, 2000, pp. 134–48.)

——, 'In Antique Lands', *Indian Review of Books*, 7:10, 16 July–15 August 1998, pp. 66–8.

——, 'Dancing in Cambodia, At Large in Burma', *IndiaStar Review of Books*, 1998. Internet address: www.indiastar.com/mukherjeel.html.

Nair, Rukmini Bhaya, 'The Road from Mandalay: Reflections on Amitav Ghosh's *The Glass Palace*' in Tabish Khair, ed. *Amitav Ghosh: A Critical Companion*, pp. 162–74.

Nelson, Diane M., 'A Social Science Fiction of Fevers, Delirium and Discovery: *The Calcutta Chromosome*, the Colonial Laboratory, and the Postcolonial New Human', *Science Fiction Studies*, 30, 2003, pp. 246–66.

Prasad, Amar Nath, 'Amitav Ghosh's Countdown: A Portrayal of the Dance of Death', in *Indian Writings in English, Vol. IX*, eds. Manmohan K. Bhatnagar and M. Rajeshwar, Delhi: Atlantic, 2000.

Prasad, G.J.V., 'The Unfolding of a Raga: Narrative Structure in *The Circle of Reason*', in *The New Indian Novel in English: A Study of the 1980s*, ed. Viney Kirpal, New Delhi: Allied Publishers, 1990, pp. 101–8.

——, 'Really Imagined', *Seminar*, 384, August 1991, pp. 23–5.

Rajan, Rajeswari Sunder, 'The Division of Experience in *The Shadow Lines*', in *The Shadow Lines*, New Delhi: Oxford University Press, 1995, pp. 287–98.

Rao, Nagesh, 'Cosmopolitanism, Class and Gender in *The Shadow Lines*', *South Asian Review*, 24:1, 2003, pp. 95–115.

Ravi, P.S., *Modern Indian Fiction: History, Politics and Individual in the Novels of Salman Rushdie, Amitav Ghosh and Upamanyu Chatterjee*, New Delhi: Prestige, 2003.

Roy, Anjali Gera, 'Microstoria: Indian Nationalism's "Little Stories" in Amitav Ghosh's *The Shadow Lines*', *Journal of Commonwealth Literature*, 35:2, 2000, pp. 35–49.

Schulze-Engler, Frank, 'Literature in the Global Ecumene of Modernity: Amitav Ghosh's *The Circle of Reason* and *In an Antique Land*', in *English Literatures in International Contexts*, eds. HeinzAntor and Klaus Stiersrorfer, Heidelberg (Germany): Carl Winter Universitatsverlag, 2000, pp. 373–96.

Schumacher, Lyn, 'Review of *The Calcutta Chromosome*', *Foundation*, 71, 1997, pp. 120–2.

Sen, Asha, 'Crossing Boundaries in Amitav Ghosh's *The Shadow Lines*', *Journal of Commonwealth and Postcolonial Studies* (Statesboro, GA), 5:1, Autumn 1997, pp. 46–58.

Sen, Sudeep, '*The Calcutta Chromosome*', *World Literature Today*, 71, 1997, pp. 221–2.

Shack, Neville, 'Rational Capers' (review of *The Circle of Reason*), *Times Literary Supplement*, 11 April 1986, p. 382.

Shammas, Anton, 'The Once and Future Egypt' (review of *In an Antique Land*), *New York Times Book Review*, 1 August 1993. Sec VII, 26:1.

Shohat, Ella, 'Taboo Memories and Diasporic Visions: Columbus, Palestine, and Arab-Jews' in *Performing Hybridity*, eds. May Joseph and Jennifer Natalya Fink, Minneapolis: University of Minnesota Press, 1999, pp. 131–56. (On *In an Antique Land*)

Siddiqi, Y., 'Police and Postcolonial Rationality in Amitav Ghosh's *The Circle of Reason*', *Cultural Critique*, 50, Winter 2002, pp. 175–211.

Simon, Sherry, 'Frontières de la memoire: La Partition de 1'Inde dans *The Shadow Lines* d'Amitav Ghosh', *Etudes Françaises*, 34:1, 1998, pp. 29–43.

Singh, Sujala, 'Inventing London in Amitav Ghosh's *The Shadow Lines*', *Kunapipi*, 21:2, 1999, pp. 15–22.

Singh, Sushila, 'Double Self in Amitav Ghosh's *The Shadow Lines*', *Language Forum: A Half-Yearly journal of Language and Literature* (New Delhi), 18:1–2, 1992 January–December, pp. 135–42.

Sircar, Ajanta, 'Individualizing History: The 'Real' Self in *The Shadow*

Lines', *Social Scientist*, 19:12, 1991, pp. 33–46.

Sircar, Arjya, 'The Stranger Within: Amitav Ghosh's Quest for Identity', *Language Forum: A Half-Yearly Journal of Language and Literature* (New Delhi), 18:1–2 1992 January–December, pp. 143–7.

Soueif, Ahdaf, 'Review of *In an Antique Land*', *Times Literary Supplement*, 15 January 1993, p. 7.

Srivastava, Neelam, 'Amitav Ghosh's Ethnographic Fictions: Intertextual Links between *In an Antique Land* and his Doctoral Thesis', *Journal of Commonwealth Literature*, 36:2, September 2001, pp. 45–64.

Sudrann, Jean, 'Goings and Comings' (review of *The Shadow Lines*), *Yale Review*, 79:3 1990, pp. 414–38.

Tadie, A., 'Amitav Ghosh: The Nuances of History', *Esprit* (Paris), 1, 2002, pp. 62–73.

Thieme, John, 'Passages to England', in *Liminal Postmodernisms: The Postmodern, the (Post-) Colonial, and the (Post-) Feminist*, eds. Theo D'haen and Hans Bertens, Amsterdam: Rodopi, 1994, pp. 55–78.

——, 'The Discover-Discovered: Amitav Ghosh's *The Calcutta Chromosome*' in Tabish Khair, ed. *Amitav Ghosh: A Critical Companion*, Delhi: Permanent Black, 2003, pp. 128–41.

Viswanathan, Gauri, 'Beyond Orientalism: Syncretism and the Politics of Knowledge', *Stanford Humanities Review*, 5:1, 1995. Internet address: www.stanford.edu/group/SHR/5–l/text/viswanathan.html.

Wassef, Hind, 'Beyond the Divide: History and National Boundaries in the Work of Amitav Ghosh', *Alif: Journal of Comparative Poetics* (Cairo), 18, 1998, pp. 75–95 (English section); 212–13 (Arabic section).

Weisbord, Merrily, 'Amitav Ghosh', *College English Review*, 1:4, July–August 1997, pp. 4–5.

Zaman, Niaz, 'Nostalgic shadows: the partition in Sunil Gangopadhyay, Amitav Ghosh, and Taslima Nasreen', in *A Divided Legacy: The Partition in Selected Novels of India, Pakistan and Bangladesh*, Dhaka: Manohar Publications, 1999.

Index

adda(s) 4, 138–9, 193n.18
allochrony 79
    see also coevalness
Althusser, Louis 98
Anderson, Benedict 87, 127, 169
anthropology 21, 41, 75–82
    see also ethnography
Arabs 12
Arnold, David 45
Attridge, Derek 160
Aung San 123
Aung San Suu-Kyi 158

Babur 134–5
Bangladesh 3, 7, 18, 87, 97
    see also East Pakistan
battle for cultural parity 5, 31, 33
Battle of Diu (1509) 135
Bengal
    cultural imagination 4, 31
    literary tradition 30, 34, 37
    modern vernacular culture 4,
        34, 139
Bengal Renaissance 31–4, 36–7,
    184n.11
Berkhofer, Robert 130, 141, 154
Bhabha, Homi 115, 120
    'Of Mimicry and Man' 116
bhadralok 3, 32, 34, 36, 37, 47, 57
Black Atlantic 125, 126
Bose, J.C. 56, 57

Bose, Satyen 56
Bose, Subhas Chandra 1, 16
Brahmo Samaj 184n.11
Burgess, Anthony 7
Burma 15, 16, 28, 112, 123–4,
    125, 126, 128, 133

Calcutta 2–6, 18, 34, 46, 56, 87,
    97, 126, 143, 151, 175
    University 47
Carter, Paul 124
Cervantes, Miguel de 134
Chakrabarty, Dipesh 93, 122, 127,
    131, 136, 144, 150, 152–4,
    157, 162, 174
    Provincializing Europe 135,
    137–9
Chambers, Claire 61, 73, 102,
    164
Chaudhuri, K.N. 124, 134
Chew, Shirley 156
civilising mission 13, 44, 65, 68,
    82, 119, 120
Clifford, James 61, 79, 168
coevalness 76, 77, 82
    denial of 76, 79
colonialism 5, 12, 13, 16, 30, 39,
    48, 54, 60, 68, 107, 112,
    113, 116, 119, 120
communalism 24, 25, 99, 100–3,
    165, 174, 189n.17

communal riots 9, 10, 99, 103,
    132, 143, 144
Connor, Steven 21
cosmopolitanism 4, 12, 79, 92,
    106, 139, 166, 167
counter-science 58, 59, 60, 62,
    168
criminology 49, 50, 51

Dayal, Samir 78
Derrida, Jacques 58, 73, 141, 157
Descartes 83
Development
    ladder of 65
    technological 64, 65, 68
diaspora 15, 126, 127, 128
Dickens, Charles 60
Dixon, Robert 170–2
double 109, 153

East Pakistan 3, 87, 88
    see also Bangladesh
ecology 175, 176
Egypt 11, 68, 80, 83, 85, 103, 108,
    125, 161
Einstein, Albert 138
empiricism 33, 43, 46, 58, 62, 81
encounter 82–4
Enlightenment 21, 25, 26, 29, 31,
    33, 36, 45, 53, 70, 73, 130
environmentalism 18, 19, 176
epistemic violence 12, 74, 173
ethnography 21, 75–82
    ethnographic present 76
    fictive ethnography 80
    fieldwork account 78
    see also anthropology
Eurocentrism 2, 12, 75, 131, 133,
    135, 137

Fabian, Johannes 75, 76, 79, 81
Fanon, Frantz
    Black Skins/White Masks 16,
        122

The Wretched of the Earth
    123
Foucault, Michel 73, 149
    governmentality 26, 65, 67,
        69, 71, 72, 73
    colonial 66, 68, 70
    post-colonial 66, 70, 133,
        176
    The Order of Things 67
Freud, Sigmund 92
    'The Uncanny' 153

Gandhi, Indira 9, 24, 99
Gandhi, Leela 81
Gandhi, M.K. (Mahatma) 16, 36,
    113
Gellner, Ernest 169
gender 165–9
Geniza 11, 110, 149, 155
Ghosh, Amitav
    The Calcutta Chromosome
        5, 13–14, 34, 37, 39, 46,
        54–64, 68, 69, 72–4, 81, 83,
        122, 132, 133, 142, 146–50,
        154, 157, 160, 164, 165,
        168
    The Circle of Reason 2, 7–9,
        12, 17, 36, 39, 46–55, 56,
        66, 68, 72, 74, 83, 125, 132,
        133, 140, 150, 154, 164, 165
    Countdown 32, 101
    Dancing in Cambodia, At
        Large in Burma 20, 28,
        74–5, 123, 129
    'Empire and Soul' 134
    'The Ghosts of Mrs. Gandhi'
        9, 30, 36
    The Glass Palace 2, 14–16, 20,
        30, 38, 39, 84, 112–24, 128,
        133, 151, 154, 158–60, 165,
        168
    'The Global Reservation' 110,
        128–9
    The Hungry Tide 16–19, 39,

66, 133, 149, 151, 152, 154,
    160, 168, 174
'The Imam and the Indian'
    20, 41, 168
In an Antique Land 9, 11–15,
    17, 20, 27, 30, 36, 39,
    41–2, 46, 65, 66, 68, 74,
    77–83, 85–7, 103–12, 124,
    128, 132–6, 142, 149, 151,
    154–7, 160–1, 164, 165,
    168, 170–1
'India's Untold War of Inde-
    pendence' 20
'The March of the Novel' 5
The Shadow Lines 2, 3, 9–13,
    30, 36, 83, 86–103, 104,
    105, 106, 127, 129, 132,
    139, 142–6, 149, 151, 153,
    154, 160, 163, 165–70,
    174–5
'Slave of MS. H.6' 11, 27, 80,
    136
Ghosh, Bishnupriya 150
ghost 150–3
    see also phantom
ghost stories 60–1, 73
Gilroy, Paul 105, 125, 126
Gnosticism 59
    gnosis 60
Goitein, S.D. 155

Heaney, Seamus 38, 125
Hegel 47
Heidegger, Martin 83
Hindu 103
    Hindu College 47
    Hinduism 57, 135
    Hindu majoritarianism 24
History 14, 21, 39, 47, 75, 76, 81,
    108, 109, 112, 130–5, 138,
    141–4, 147, 149, 155, 157,
    160, 161
    Eurocentric narratives of 12
    historicism 33, 131, 137, 139,

141, 149, 158, 159, 160, 173
historiography 19, 21, 27, 32, 39,
    132, 140–1, 144, 153, 154
Howe, Stephen 124
humanism 29, 31, 36, 37, 81–2,
    92, 93, 102, 170, 171
    Bengali 32
hybridity 83
hypertextuality 73

imperialism 43, 117, 161, 170
India 1, 11, 12, 16, 80, 83, 86, 97,
    100, 101, 104, 108, 110,
    128, 164
    Constitution 23
    Indian Army 16, 25, 120
    Indian National Army 16,
        120, 123, 127, 133, 192n.6
    Indian National Congress 112
    Indian Ocean 15, 124, 125,
        132, 134, 135
    post-colonial state 23, 25, 26,
        28
    Quit India movement (1942)
        112
Internet 73
    see also World Wide Web
irony 22, 50, 53–4, 72, 97, 167,
    174
Islam 78, 103, 104, 107
Israel 85

Jenkins, Keith 142
Jews 12
    of Cairo 11
Judaism 86

Karenni 28, 123
Kaul, A.N. 169–70, 171, 172
Kaul, Suvir 168
Khair, Tabish 164
Khilnani, Sunil 11, 111
Kipling, Rudyard
    Kim 71

Lacan, Jacques 90–2, 98–9
Leer, Martin 70
liberalism 33, 111
Lukács, Georg 157–8
    The Historical Novel 158

Macaulay (Lord) Thomas
    Babington 44, 118
Macherey, Pierre 98
Mahabharata 119
Majeed, Javed 105
malaria 54, 55, 148
Malaya 114, 125, 127, 133
Malinowski, Bronislaw
    Argonauts of the Western
        Pacific 78
Marxism 26, 158
Mathur, Suchitra 168
medicine 54
    colonial 64
    tropical 48, 49
Mee, Jon 93, 167, 169
memory 143–6, 160
mesmerism 45
mimicry 115–16, 119, 120
modernism 36, 123
Morichjhãpi 17, 18, 133, 176
Mukherjee, Meenakshi 3
multiculturalism 111

Naipaul, V.S. 30
narcissism 92, 101
nation 87, 88, 97, 127, 143
    nationalism 86, 87, 92–6, 107,
        112, 122–8, 159, 164, 166,
        167, 170, 173
        English 93, 95, 96
        ethnic 110
        Hindu 25, 28, 135
        Indian 25, 26, 28, 31, 38,
            95, 100–3, 109, 136
        Nehruvian 29, 35
    nationhood 15, 88, 92, 95, 99
    nation-state(s) 4, 9, 85, 86, 87,

98, 111, 128–9, 132, 143
        post-colonial 27, 28, 129
national allegory 15
Nehru, Jawaharlal 16, 23, 25, 29,
    35, 110–11, 129, 170
    The Discovery of India 111
New Yorker 1, 16
Nora, Pierre 146

Pakistan 1, 11, 12, 86, 95, 97, 101,
    104
palimpsest 71, 95, 107, 132, 133,
    149–50, 151
Pandey, Gyan 100, 144
paradox 50–3, 56, 59, 74, 140,
    162, 174
Partition (1947) 2, 10, 12, 23, 86,
    88, 89, 99, 111, 189n.17
Pasteur, Louis, 47–9
    Life of Pasteur 47–8, 55
phantom 150–3
    see also ghost
phrenology 7, 49, 50, 51
police fiction 72
    see also thriller
politics of ambivalence 173, 178
positivism 33, 43, 46
postcolonialism 2, 22, 132, 163,
    164
    postcolonial studies 26, 40
postmodernism 20–3, 26, 27, 29,
    31, 35, 93, 106, 112, 163,
    171, 173
post-structuralism 22, 58, 171
power/knowledge 5, 8, 13
Pratt, Mary Louise 78
Progress 13, 21, 26, 33, 47, 49, 52,
    119, 130
pseudo-science 45, 50, 54, 164

racism 70, 120, 170
Radcliffe, Cyril 88
Raman, C.V. 56
Rao, Nagesh 165

rationalism 33, 74, 130
    scientific 60
Ray, Satyajit 34, 36–7
realism 153–4
Reason 7–8, 33, 43, 44, 46–54, 59,
    65, 72, 131, 140
Renu, Paneshwarnath 60
Richards, Thomas 146
Ross, Ronald (Sir) 54–7, 59–61,
    63, 71, 146, 147
    Memoirs 54, 55, 56, 61, 146,
    147
    Nobel Prize 54
Rushdie, Salman 1, 26, 29, 157,
    163, 164
    *Haroun and the Sea of
    Stories* 157
    Midnight's Children 1, 9, 26

Said, Edward 6
science 14, 42–8, 54, 59, 61, 63,
    64, 82, 164
    applied 49, 57
    colonial 45
    ideology of science 43, 48, 49,
    62
        colonial 49, 57
    scientific epistemology 13
    technology and 43, 49, 64, 65
science fiction 61, 73, 164
Second World War 93, 114, 133
secularism 25, 29, 100, 101, 143,
    173
    non-secular knowledge 61
    secular knowledge 61, 137
slavery 105
Spivak, Gayatri Chakravorty 140,
    171
Sri Lanka 3
state 69, 72
    colonial 66, 68
    post-colonial 66, 68
subaltern 8, 18, 20, 27, 56, 69, 70,
    77, 136–7, 139, 140, 142,
    148, 152, 159, 168, 173
    agency 70
    epistemology 57, 58
    historiography 28, 150
    history 139–40, 150, 154, 155,
    156, 161
    knowledge 55, 58, 59, 81
    narrative 57
    subaltern pasts 16, 138, 140,
    143, 146, 147, 152, 153,
    156, 159
    text 56
subalternity 59, 136, 138–40, 147
Subaltern Studies 26, 27, 136–7,
    171
Sundarbans 17, 176, 177
Sunder Rajan, Rajeswari 166, 167
syncretism 103, 111, 170

Tagore, Rabindranath 34–6, 129
    The Hungry Stones 34, 60,
    70, 122
    Nobel Prize 32
    nationalism and 35, 110–11
Tharoor, Shashi
    The Great Indian Novel 26
Third World 65, 83
thriller 72, 73
    see also police fiction
transnationalism 126
travelogues (travel writing) 79

UN *see* United Nations
uncanny 73, 109, 150–3
United Nations 128–9
universalism 44, 57, 70, 77, 79,
    83

visualism 81
Viswanathan, Gauri 170, 171, 172

World Wide Web 73, 74
    see also Internet